The Ted Nicholas SMALL BUSINESS COURSE

A Step-By-Step Guide to Starting & Running Your Own Business

by Ted Nicholas, author of the bestseller
How to Form Your Own Corporation Without a Lawyer for Under $75

Enterprise • Dearborn
a division of Dearborn Publishing Group, Inc.

While a great deal of care has been taken to provide accurate and current information, the ideas, suggestions, general principles and conclusions presented in this text are subject to local, state and federal laws and regulations, court cases and any revisions of same. The reader is thus urged to consult legal counsel regarding any points of law—this publication should not be used as a substitute for competent legal advice.

Publisher: Kathleen A. Welton
Acquisitions Editor: Patrick J. Hogan
Associate Editor: Karen A. Christensen
Senior Project Editor: Jack L. Kiburz
Interior Design: Lucy Jenkins
Cover Design: Taccone Art & Design

Published by Enterprise • Dearborn,
a division of Dearborn Publishing Group, Inc.

Printed in the United States of America

94 95 96 10 9 8 7 6 5 4 3 2 1

Library of Congress Cataloging-in-Publication Data

Nicholas, Ted, 1934-
Small business course / by Ted Nicholas.
p. cm.
ISBN 0-7931-0725-3
1. Small business—Management. 2. New business enterprises.
I. Title.
HD62.7.N534 1993
658.02'2—dc20 93-32057
CIP

DEDICATION

To The Independent Spirit of the Entrepreneur

The entrepreneur is the most important person in a free society—the creator of all jobs and wealth, the individual upon whom all others depend for their very existence. At the same time, the role of the entrepreneur is perhaps the most misunderstood of any member of a free enterprise–oriented economy. It is the author's desire that this work play a part in clarifying the role and importance of the entrepreneur to every free person.

BOOKS BY TED NICHOLAS

The Complete Book of Corporate Forms

The Complete Guide to Business Agreements

The Complete Guide to Consulting Success (coauthor, Howard Shenson)

The Complete Guide to Nonprofit Corporations

The Complete Guide to "S" Corporations

The Executive's Business Letter Book

43 Proven Ways To Raise Capital for Your Small Business

The Golden Mailbox: How To Get Rich Direct Marketing Your Product

How To Form Your Own Corporation Without a Lawyer for Under $75

How To Get a Top Job in Tough Times (coauthor, Bethany Waller)

How To Get Your Own Trademark

How To Publish a Book and Sell a Million Copies

Secrets of Entrepreneurial Leadership: Building Top Performance Through Trust and Teamwork

The Ted Nicholas Small Business Course

TABLE OF CONTENTS

PREFACE

There is one (and only one) weapon with which to fight the massive economic and social problems ahead of us. This weapon is the unleashing of the miraculous powers of the human spirit through the practice of free enterprise.

On the one hand, we have a vast array of problems to be solved, ranging from unemployment and unbridled government spending to crises in the cities and civil unrest, as evidenced in the growing number of strikes by both private industry and government workers. On the other hand, we have an army of unemployed and underemployed people available to do the job of averting these problems. The underemployed people, especially, are those who are wasting their time and talents in jobs utilizing only a fraction of their abilities. Great numbers of these people have tremendous ability and could help themselves and humanity by starting their own businesses.

Owning and managing your own business is one of the most exciting, challenging and worthwhile occupations known. It not only provides you with a source of income you generate yourself, but it also solves others' problems and creates jobs.

What is it, then, that keeps underemployed people from striking out on their own? There are several reasons. The major one is that they often lack the self-confidence and know-how to get started.

This course will supply some of the missing ingredients. In my own life, I have started 22 new businesses. In most of them, I had huge gaps in my knowledge at the beginning, but I filled those gaps, facing the day-to-day problems as they arose. Not all of my businesses were great successes, and two of them were failures. When I did fail, however, I thought of it as a setback and *not* a disaster. I probably learned more from the two failures than I did from the many successes.

Utilizing these experiences, then, I will show you the way to make your road to success that much shorter. My many years of actual experience in starting and building successful businesses is something that I did the hard way. *The Ted Nicholas Small Business Course* is a shortcut for you.

The first barrier faced by the individual considering the creation of his or her own business is the important one of overcoming fear. This usually concerns the "fear of failure." My view on this subject is a simple one. Periodic failure and setbacks are a normal part of living and should be accepted as such. People are not failures because they get knocked down. They are considered failures only when they fail to get back up again or refuse to learn from the experience.

The problem of fear and the attendant self-doubt is so crucial in the determination of success or failure that the entire first section is devoted to the subject.

The second barrier that prevents many individuals from developing a successful enterprise is the feeling that business is difficult to enter and requires a business degree, access to capital and "contacts." The successful entrepreneur is creative and finds solutions to problems that may stop others. The only difficulty in starting a small business is that it is sure to demand hard work. This book is designed as a self-study course to provide the general business information you need and encourage you to ask the right questions. If you have a good idea, understand the needs of the market and are determined to work hard to achieve your goals, you are sure to overcome initial difficulties in getting started.

The next barrier to overcome is that of making the wrong decision regarding which business to enter. The viewpoint of this course is that *businesses exist to solve customers' problems.* Every human problem represents a potential business opportunity, and the more difficult the solution to a given problem, the more attractive the opportunity.

The best way to discover opportunities for profitable new enterprises is to listen to the gripes, complaints and problems of the people around you. Many examples in this book are companies that succeeded by devoting themselves to solving the problems of the average individual, of special groups of people and of other businesses.

The intent is not merely to impress you with the success of the companies that are used as illustrations of this principle. They are presented in order to demonstrate the many ways this basic idea of solving others' problems can grow into a business that benefits others and rewards its creators. Most of the examples used are now well-known companies, but there are plenty of opportunities to duplicate their success by applying similar formulas. Similar principles can be applied to a different geographical area, for instance, or to a different product. You might be able to vary the formula somewhat, or combine two or more of them in your own company. Also included in this book is a discussion of what the future might hold to help you generate ideas that profit from these trends.

This course also covers the problems of getting started. You learn to analyze the characteristics of a desirable company, taking into consideration your own particular abilities and stressing which businesses are most appropriate for a small business enterprise. Emphasis is placed upon the importance of clearly defining the goals, the purposes and the intended image of your business. Legal creation of the company is discussed, including its various forms and the advantages and disadvantages of each. Methods of getting started are reviewed, including starting on a part-time basis, franchising and the purchase of an existing business. Sources of financing are discussed in detail.

Also covered are sources of information on specific businesses, and on business in general, that should help you in making decisions about which fields to enter.

Once your business is started, it is essential to maintain control and to know if it is profitable, what areas are the most profitable and which the least. This course presents a wealth of revenue-increasing and cost-cutting ideas. Many businesses that have failed would have succeeded if their owners had understood the concepts presented in this course.

Once you understand the basic ingredients in making a profit, you can be introduced to the world of big-time success. There are ways to magnify your time and abilities, your capital, your knowledge and your income many times over by understanding and using the principles of leverage. In the field of finance, this is often referred to as OPM, or "other people's money." The concept applies not only to money, but to all other ingredients essential for success. Each of these is covered in detail, including discussions of ways to pyramid results. This can be achieved through strategic patents and copyrights and through starting your own franchises.

You will also learn about the important subjects of taxation, with special emphasis on techniques to accelerate accumulation of wealth and conservation of assets.

It brings me much pleasure to know that you have purchased this course so that you can share some of the success it has taken me 20 years to accomplish. I can see a continually growing trend for people of all ages and backgrounds to start their own businesses. They are refusing to be lost in the shuffle of faceless, big company bureaucrats. Entrepreneurship is perhaps the noblest of all professions, and it is gratifying to me that so many are opting for self-sufficiency and independence.

Welcome to the ranks of the self-employed!

Ted Nicholas

CHAPTER 1

What Constitutes Success?

There are many who have the intelligence and ambition to succeed in life but who fall far short of their capabilities and potential for a very simple reason. They have such a fear of failure that they pass up opportunities simply because a certain amount of risk is involved.

The successful individual, on the other hand, is willing to enter businesses that involve risk, provided that the reward is large relative to the amount of risk taken. I recommend the following multiple approach to conquering this fear of failure:

- Adopt the philosophy that accepts risk as the price of opportunity.
- Accept the necessity of making errors as a part of the learning process.
- Convert the fear of failure into a motivating device that improves your mental and physical capabilities.
- Evaluate individual fears objectively, eliminating imaginary or exaggerated fears.

ACCEPTING RISK OF FAILURE AS THE PRICE OF OPPORTUNITY

Risk is an inescapable part of life, especially if you are to enjoy life's opportunities. I know of one individual who had a phobia about driving a car because he was afraid of being killed in an accident. As a result, he passed up better-paying jobs that would have required commuting by car. Although intensely interested in furthering his education, he rejected the opportunity of attending evening classes at a local university because driving would have been involved. His recreational activities were restricted by his fear of travel. He was able to begin his road to recovery only after his wife bluntly stated, "Why are you afraid of dying? You're not really *living* now!"

The same observation could be made of individuals in their occupational lives. Some cling to dismal jobs with large organizations because they fear striking out on their own. A job may be restricting your mental growth; it may involve frustrations that could shorten your life; it may offer a pay level far below your earning potential. But the false sense of security may keep you trapped. I use the phrase "false sense of security" because I believe *the only true security is your own ability*.

Working for someone else produces an *illusion* of security rather than security itself. In most cases, there is not even that illusion, as many unemployed people could now testify. Older employees who have devoted their lives to a company have found themselves pushed out in order to make room for younger people moving up the ladder. Most of these older people have tremendous ability but are so overspecialized they cannot find equivalent positions in other companies (which may be having similar problems).

These unfortunate individuals run from one employment agency to another, living on their life savings during their futile and tragic search for security. Unemployed anthropologists (who are overspecialized) end up driving taxicabs, and college professors, unable to find teaching jobs, feel fortunate to find work in the industrial trades. Yet many of these same individuals could turn their personal financial problems into the greatest opportunities of their lives by starting their own business.

For each person who has been shoved into the unemployment lines, there are several who know they have reached the end of the line with their present employers. They have not actually been fired but have been made painfully aware that they can be replaced with little difficulty. They are the living dead, just waiting for the inevitable to happen. They are personally deteriorating as their self-confidence declines. In many ways, they would be better off being unemployed, as this would force them to face up to their problems. Some would find themselves much happier in businesses of their own.

There is a risk in doing *anything*, including doing nothing at all. The individuals mentioned above are not unfortunate simply because of the risk they may lose their jobs. Their real misfortune is that there is no offsetting opportunity that makes that risk worthwhile.

In investment circles, this is known as the risk/reward ratio, although it is actually a reward/risk ratio. If you have various investment opportunities, it is necessary to consider both upside potential and downside risk. One investment with a 10 percent risk may be unattractive if the potential is only 3 percent (assuming each probability is the same). On the other hand, an investment with a 20 percent downside risk may be desirable if the potential reward is 100 percent (again assuming equal probabilities of each).

The first has a reward/risk ratio of only 0.3 to 1, while the second has a 5 to 1 ratio. Figure 1.1 gives various examples of this idea.

There is a tendency for rate of return to rise as risk increases, but only up to a point. Once the possible rate of return reaches speculative levels, such as the case with gambling, the reward/risk ratio tends to decline.

Figure 1.1 assumes there is equal probability of success and failure. Where the probabilities are different for each, this must be taken into consideration by multiplying the reward (if successful) by the probability of success, and the loss (if a failure) by the probability of failure.

Assume that the $10,000 investment will yield $1,500 if successful, and the probability is three out of ten. If a failure, the loss would be $1,000, and the probability is two out of ten. If ten projects of this type were tried, the reward would be 8 × $1,500, or $12,000. On the two projects which fail, the loss would be 2 × $1,000, or $2,000. The reward/risk ratio is six to one, arrived at by dividing $12,000 by $2,000.

Many of the skills you now possess were developed over time, using a trial-and-error process. The errors served the important function of telling you what went wrong. With this information, you made adjustments and tried again. Gradually, over a period of time, the number of correct responses increased as the percentage of total number of tries rose. In some cases,

FIGURE 1.1 Table of Reward/Risk Ratios of $10,000 Investment Where Probability of Failure and Probability of Success Are Equal

	Return on Investment if Success	*Loss on Investment if Failure*	*Reward/Risk Ratio Col. 1 divided by Col. 2*
Project A	$ 500	$ 500	1 to 1
Project B	1,000	800	1.25 to 1
Project C	1,500	1,000	1.5 to 1
Project D	4,500	1,500	3.0 to 1
Project E	10,000	5,000	2.0 to 1

you never reach absolute perfection but must be satisfied with a high ratio of successes to errors.

Even the best baseball hitter in the major leagues gets a hit less than 40 percent of the time. Most of us are not aware that the player who struck out most in baseball history was a gentleman by the name of Babe Ruth. He is remembered for his home run production, not for the number of times he failed to hit the ball.

When looking at a person who is an expert in a particular field, we tend to underestimate the amount of trial and error that was necessary for that skill to develop. Ted Williams, perhaps the greatest baseball hitter of all time, resents people attributing his skill to "natural ability." He attributes his success to practice and more practice, to the point where his hands often blistered and bled. Unquestionably he had natural aptitude, but it was prolonged practice that made him great.

The same approach is applicable to many business skills. The salesperson who becomes discouraged each time he or she is turned down by a prospect is unlikely to survive long in that occupation. The successful salesperson understands the laws of probability. A certain percentage of the prospects will buy the product and a certain percentage won't buy it. The more calls or contacts that are made, the more turn-downs received. *But more sales are made, too.* Salespeople also understand that their percentage of successes will rise as their skill increases, and their skill is determined by the amount of practice they get.

The capability of accepting errors as part of the learning process becomes more important as the skill being learned becomes more complex. In swinging at a ball, you know immediately whether you have hit it or missed it. This is not so obvious in certain other skills.

In business, for example, decisions have to be made as to which customers are good credit risks and which are not. Some errors in judgment will occur, but the quicker the error is detected, the less damage will be done. Reluctance to admit mistakes causes the problem to compound upon itself. The ability to recognize errors and learn from them is a key element in achieving success.

CONVERT THE FEAR OF FAILURE INTO A POSITIVE FORCE TO IMPROVE PERFORMANCE

Contrary to what most people believe, fear is not an undesirable emotion in all circumstances. Without fear, the human race would have perished long ago. Fear of various dangers motivated our ancestors to develop the tools and techniques to deal with them. In order to survive, we developed many skills, including the ability to plan ahead. Had our ancestors not been frightened of wild animals attacking them, they would not have developed their mental and physical capabilities and their ability to progress to intelligent human beings.

Only when it is allowed uncontrolled rein can fear become a disadvantage. When facing physical dangers, a person may freeze, even though that is not an appropriate response. Similarly, in business situations, an individual may be faced with a serious problem that requires an immediate solution. Unlike physical danger (where the decision involves only whether to run, and in which direction), the business problem is complex. A number of possible actions can be taken, and each has a number of unknowns.

Faced with such uncertainty, it is tempting to procrastinate and make no decision at all. The procrastinator may concentrate on disguising the fear by use of various tranquilizers—narcotics, alcohol, overeating or frantic activity in some pastime or "busy work." Not only does the problem not get solved, but the person's ability to solve the problem diminishes.

In contrast, the healthier response to fear is action, directed toward the source of the fear. An army fearing attack could relieve the tension by building barricades, digging foxholes and checking the readiness of weapons and fortifications. All these activities are directed toward protecting themselves from the basis of their fear. If the same army, fearing the same attack, were to get drunk, play harmonicas, write letters home or shrink into a corner and hide, these actions would have little effect on dissipating their fears. Similarly, an individual contemplating a business venture can convert any pertinent fears into useful channels.

For instance, there may be trepidation about certain legal aspects of the business. This fear may be the quite useful motivation needed to learn the basics of business law. Many colleges offer courses in business law through evening divisions or by correspondence.

Lack of self-confidence in the ability to deal with the public, as another example, could be alleviated by taking courses in public speaking, joining social and service clubs, or by teaching your own courses. Once you're in business, fear of failure can give you the energy to work extra hours when necessary, and learn what you need to know to avoid failure.

It is not always easy to recognize or admit to having fears. The manager who cannot force himself to make a crucial decision may excuse inaction by waiting for more complete information. People may conceal a fear of travel from themselves by rationalizing that a good family man or woman always stays close to home. Honesty with yourself is the first step in dealing with fear.

For those who face up to fear and overcome it, the effect on self-confidence can be tremendous. It is intensely satisfying to become an expert in a subject or skill that you were once afraid to even try. Many outstanding public speakers, for example, have admitted to being terrified when making their first public appearance.

SOME COMMON BUT UNFOUNDED FEARS ABOUT PERSONAL FACTORS NEEDED FOR SUCCESS IN BUSINESS

We all have our own particular combination of concerns about starting a business. However, the following fears are so widely held and so unfounded that they deserve special mention:

- Will my age be a handicap?
- Do I have enough education to succeed?

- Do I have the right family background for success in business?
- Will my race or ethnic background interfere?
- Am I the right personality type for success in business?
- Does a woman have as much chance for success as a man?

Each of the above doubts appears to be reasonable on the surface. An investigation of the actual facts involved does not support these contentions, however.

THE QUESTION OF AGE

One of the most frequent reservations is expressed in the phrase, "I'm too old to start a new career now." This comment is not restricted to senior citizens exclusively, but is often expressed by people in their thirties and forties who feel old beyond their years. The frustration of doing narrowly specialized work for somebody else in a large bureaucratic organization can create such a feeling of being "over the hill." For those individuals who move out of such situations into businesses of their own, the effect can be one of rejuvenation. People can become years younger in mental attitude and appearance as they start to grow again and contribute to the welfare of their fellow citizens.

Age is certainly no barrier to success, although it may determine what type of business a person might try. Every age group has its own advantages. Youth, for instance, has faith, energy, boundless enthusiasm and the optimism that is essential for success in certain enterprises. A middle-aged business executive once reminisced about his first big success, achieved while he was still in his twenties: "If I knew then what I know now, I would never have even tried to make that deal—I would have known it was impossible. But, being stupid, I went ahead and it made our company a million dollars."

Middle age also has its advantages in many enterprises. By this time, a person has had a number of years to develop judgment. He or she may lack the energy of a 20-year-old but has learned to concentrate what energy there is on desired objectives rather than scattering it in many directions. Working many years for other people may have produced tremendous amounts of pent-up frustration, which has a great motivating effect. Skills in dealing with people have been developed, and the broad group of friends, acquaintances and associates that come with age can be invaluable.

Opportunity is still available in retirement years as well. People at 60 years of age today are not necessarily as worn out as their parents and grandparents might have been at the same age. A person may start off with a hobby, for instance, and before long develop it into a profitable part-time business. They may be doing what they wanted to do all their lives but were afraid to try during the period of maximum responsibilities.

THE QUESTION OF EDUCATIONAL BACKGROUND

In a famous short story, a janitor at a church had been doing a good job for years, but lost his position when a new personnel directive of the organization required that all employees be able to read and write, which he could not. Fortunately, he had saved some money and, encouraged by an intelligent and sympathetic friend, he opened a tobacco shop. Apparently he had the right combination of qualities that made for success in that field, because the business prospered. Over the years, he developed a chain of such stores. A business associate discovered that he could not read and write and was amazed that he could be so successful without such a necessary skill.

He asked, "I wonder what you would be if you were literate?" The ex-janitor replied, "That's easy to answer; I'd still be a janitor if I could read and write."

While this is fiction, there are many examples in business history of people who were successful in their own businesses without a great deal of formal education. This is particularly true of immigrants, who found the United States to be such a land of opportunity that their enthusiasm knew no bounds. Immigrants, too, it must be remembered, were in many cases operating without benefit of their native language.

In evaluating your educational background, consider your total education rather than your formal classroom experience exclusively.

One of my research associates tells the story of a young man he hired for a management-training program. He was impressed by the fact that the young man had actually started a business of his own at the age of 14 and had not only worked his way through college without outside help, but had come out with several thousand dollars in savings. Although most of the management trainees in this particular program were MBAs with high grades, this individual with a bachelor's degree and a C average was able to run circles around his colleagues.

He was usually able to complete a project while his more learned competition was still theorizing how it should be done. The executives of the firm quickly recognized that this young man was the one who could get things done. He had left the others far behind.

Even when a person's educational background has deficiencies, these can be corrected as conditions demand. In my own career, I have found that a business project, such as writing a book, tends to mushroom in many different directions. A basic law of learning is that the mind tends to retain what it can use and rejects what appears to be irrelevant.

Business requires such broad knowledge that learning is greatly stimulated. The more you know, the easier it is to learn something new, so that learning becomes a chain reaction, so to speak. When a particular problem needs to be solved, you will find it surprisingly easy to master a subject that you once might have avoided.

THE QUESTION OF FAMILY BACKGROUND

Successful businesspeople come from all backgrounds, but there is a somewhat higher probability of success for children of professional people and small business owners. Often the children of such parents get some experience at business during their early years. They also learn some of the practical aspects of business from their parents' experiences, which gives them a head start over the competition. Like the children of ambitious immigrants, many are highly motivated.

The children of *extremely* successful businesspeople often do not follow in the footsteps of their parents. While they may have a number of the qualities needed for success in the field, they often lack motivation. Their ambitions may lie in politics or the arts. Some are not really interested in *any* occupation. There are, of course, many successful children of successful parents, but the results are lower than one might expect, considering the advantages of such offspring.

It is interesting to note some of the reasons certain children of highly successful businesspeople follow in the footsteps of their parents. In one case, a son was never given an allowance by his parents but was instead given money to invest in some chickens. His "allowance" was then earned through selling eggs to people in the vicinity. The experience was a valuable one in teaching salesmanship, not to mention the areas of credit and collection. Eventually, the egg route was sold to younger members of the family, providing the youngster with experience in finance and investments.

THE QUESTION OF RACE OR ETHNIC BACKGROUND

One of the most successful business owners of our time is Kim Woo-Choong. He began as a penniless paperboy in Korea and went on to found the Daewoo Group with sales of more than $25 billion. Daewoo is larger than Xerox, Eastman Kodak or RJR Nabisco. Choong's Horatio Alger story epitomizes the entrepreneurial spirit: he created a world-class industrial group in an impossibly short period of time against formidable challenges.

The discrimination faced by minorities causes in some individuals a tremendous determination to overcome barriers. This attitude is a powerful motivating force and no doubt accounts for part of the unusual success of minority groups in sports, arts and intellectual pursuits. The same force has also been working in the business world, and its effects should increase further in the future. While there may be some resentment against members of minority groups who are permanently on welfare, there is a very strong feeling in favor of enterprising minority group members who are working for success.

The best place for minority groups to seek success is in their own companies. This statement is made with the full realization that outstanding members of minority groups are vigorously sought after by large companies who need to fill their "quotas" to meet government regulations. Many of these companies are sincere and attempt to give challenging assignments to the minority recruits. It will be easy to achieve a certain amount of organizational success, and as long as a person isn't a complete failure (and doesn't rock the boat too much), the opportunity to move part of the way up the ladder will be there.

But the path is too easy, simply because it has been facilitated and accommodated to the needs of the individual to too great an extent. These people will not develop the skills, the courage to make controversial decisions and stand behind them, and the ability to lead. All of these characteristics will be required for real (not token) success. The small business route is much more challenging.

One special road to success for the minority group person should be stressed. Capitalize on ethnic markets. Many products have been developed specifically for the tastes of the Anglo-Saxon market; there are numerous opportunities to bring out corresponding products tailored to the ethnic markets. It is likely that some of these would also obtain success in the total consumer market, not just the original market for which they were intended.

It is certainly difficult to think of pizza or chili or spaghetti as non-American products, yet they were brought out specifically for ethnic groups' consumption.

THE QUESTION OF GENDER

Women have a paradoxical position in the field of business. They own a little less than half of all businesses directly, while they control (or will control) well over 50 percent of all businesses indirectly. This is because they generally outlive their husbands. While the above may seem to be an unfair or biased statement, there is a large offsetting factor involved.

For years, many businesses have actually been run by women, but they were not the owners. They were the wives and/or secretaries of the owners. The men involved were little more than glorified salesmen (and often not very good ones) or "idea men," while the women behind them were the ones who kept the businesses going, handling all the essential nuts-and-bolts operations. Without these capable and talented women, few of these businesses would have succeeded.

Things appear to be changing. The National Association of Women Business Owners estimates that there are six million women-owned businesses. According to the U.S. Bureau of

Labor Statistics, companies owned by women employ 11 million people, more than all the Fortune 500 companies put together.

Because women have traditionally been such capable members of the business community, and because the women's movement has encouraged so many to seek challenging careers, women are no longer willing to be relegated to clerical and secretarial work in which there is no future. This is evidenced by the growing shortage of applicants for secretarial positions. Women of talent and ambition now want complete control of their careers, and a growing number of them are electing entrepreneurship.

It is pleasing to see women of ability coming into their own, and I strongly recommend that their gender should not stand in their way. In many respects, they have the same strong motivation as the minority group that has been set free to compete on equal terms with the majority.

THE QUESTION OF PERSONALITY TYPE

Generally, classifying people as to personality "type" does more harm than good. An excellent illustration of the problems that can be caused is the case of Paul J. Meyer, founder of Success Motivation Institute.

Mr. Meyer had a drive to be a great salesman, but he was turned down repeatedly as being unsuited for sales work when he applied for jobs at insurance companies. According to aptitude tests given him, he was "introverted, shy and lacking in sales aptitude." He was also considered slightly defective in his speech. At 20 years of age, he was being classified as a failure—*before he could even get started in life!*

But seven years after flunking their sales aptitude tests, he became a millionaire, having made his fortune in the insurance field. Mr. Meyer is an excellent example of how misleading personality tests can be. Many of the best salespeople were shy when they were young. During this period, they developed an intense desire to become good conversationalists. They also became good listeners, developing a keen sensitivity to the moods and responses of others. All they really needed to become good conversationalists was practice. When they were exposed to the opportunity and overcame their initial shyness, they reached a much higher level of excellence. Often their ability was greater than that of the person who never had a "shyness problem."

There are no specific personality types that appear more successful than others in independent business, for several reasons. First, there are an infinite number of business opportunities, and you can choose those that best suit your personality. Second, personality characteristics are not fixed. When you take a new job, it is similar to buying an overcoat that is too large; you must grow into it. A person should never take a job for which he or she is already fully qualified; this would be passing up the opportunity to grow. There are businesses particularly suited to gregarious, outgoing types, and companies that are more appropriate for thinkers and those who prefer to remain behind the scenes.

Also, businesses do not have to be formed by one individual alone. Often the most successful businesses are those formed by teams of people who complement each other. To oversimplify, one partner may be more of a "thinker" and one a "doer." Or one is a "front-office" type, while the other is strictly "back-office." Or one is a salesperson and a colleague is a financial expert.

In reviewing literature on successful people and combining this with my own personal observations, the following characteristics seem to occur most frequently:

- A hard worker, putting in more hours and working more intensely than associates or colleagues
- Motivated by more than money alone; enjoys building a successful business and doesn't anticipate the wealth at the end of the journey as the sole reward
- Practical and results-oriented; doesn't work hard merely for the sake of working hard but wants to accomplish something
- Enjoys taking responsibility and is willing to make unpopular decisions that many others would avoid.
- Able to concentrate attention on a desired objective.

SUMMARY

When looking at people who are successful in their fields, there is a tendency to overestimate how much natural ability contributed to their success. By comparison, we may downgrade our potential. But we are looking at the finished product of a successful person. Just as Ted Williams did not become a "natural hitter" until after thousands of hours of batting practice, so the professional business manager did not become an expert decision-maker or organizational-developer overnight. Plenty of mistakes have undoubtedly been made, but these served as teachers to the successful person. Fears and feelings of inadequacy were definitely experienced, but they functioned as motivating forces rather than as excuses for not trying. Setbacks that occurred were the price that had to be paid for striving after opportunity. One of my favorite quotes, and one that is probably a favorite among all entrepreneurs, is: "The deepest regrets come not from races we have run and lost, but from thinking about those contests in life we failed to enter."

None of the attributes that lead to success in business are due to heredity. Many of the necessary skills cannot be taught in school but are learned only through hands-on experience. The fear of failure is the biggest obstacle that can keep you from getting that experience. It is a difficult challenge, but be assured that the freedom of opportunity available to you makes it worthwhile if you can challenge that fear successfully.

The following questions are for your use in reviewing what you've learned in this section. Check the answer which appears to be most correct. You will find the answers at the end of this section.

SELF-TEST QUESTIONS

Multiple Choice

1. You would like to enter a certain field of business but believe that you lack the skills to succeed in that business. You should do the following:
   a. Team up with a partner who has those skills you lack.
   b. Take practical training that will enable you to overcome these deficiencies.
   c. Assume that you can develop some of the missing skills after you have entered the business.
   d. All of the above

2. As a member of a minority group, your best chances for personal development would be to
   a. enter government service, where you are protected from discrimination by your voting power.
   b. enter big business, where you can sue if you feel you've been discriminated against.
   c. develop a business that serves only your own minority group, which will discriminate in your favor rather than against you.
   d. None of the above

3. The most important factor for success in business is
   a. formal education.
   b. attractive appearance and the "gift of gab."
   c. motivation to succeed.
   d. charm and wit.

4. Successful businesspeople tend to work long hours because
   a. they are one-sided, having few other interests.
   b. they are money-crazy.
   c. they enjoy making their businesses grow.
   d. All of the above

5. Many types of people succeed in business, proving
   a. business is simple, so anyone should succeed.
   b. there is a wide variety of opportunities in business.
   c. no special training is required for business.
   d. success in business depends on who you know, not what you know.

6. Children of parents who run small businesses have above-average prospects of success in business because
   a. they respect the free enterprise system.
   b. they get a chance to work in business at an early age.
   c. they develop good work habits.
   d. All of the above

7. Failure in one business does not mean you would fail in another venture if
   a. you learned from your previous failure.
   b. you pick a new venture where your background is more appropriate.
   c. you have more time.
   d. All of the above

8. Many people have better prospects for running their own businesses in their later years than when they were younger, because
   a. they become more conservative as they mature.
   b. they become more careful and avoid risks.
   c. they learn what they want to accomplish and concentrate their energies in that direction.
   d. None of the above

True or False

9. It takes a certain type of person to be a success in business.

   True ☐ False ☐

10. You should never start a business until you know everything there is to know about it.

    True ☐ False ☐

11. If you've tried your own business once and failed, this is proof that you should think about doing something else.

    True ☐ False ☐

12. It is easier to be a business success if you come from a wealthy background than if you come from a middle-class background.

    True ☐ False ☐

13. Age should not be a deterrent in keeping you out of business, but it is a factor in determining the best business for you.

    True ☐ False ☐

14. A person who likes to work just for the sake of work is likely to be more successful than the person who is interested in getting the job done as efficiently as possible.

    True ☐ False ☐

15. Physical or personal handicaps can be tremendous sources of motivation.

    True ☐ False ☐

16. People who work hard tend to age rapidly.

    True ☐ False ☐

17. Successful people enjoy facing seemingly insurmountable problems.

    True ☐ False ☐

18. A person who has been a successful employee in a large organization should find it easy to succeed in a small business of his or her own.

    True ☐ False ☐

19. Some of the world's best salespeople were shy at one time.

    True ☐ False ☐

20. Women should restrict themselves to businesses catering to the female market.

    True ☐ False ☐

Answers

1.d, 2.d, 3.c, 4.c, 5.b, 6.d, 7.d, 8.c 9.F, 10.F, 11.F, 12.F, 13.T, 14.F, 15.T, 16.F, 17.T, 17.F, 19.T, 20.F

CHAPTER 2

Is Business an Attractive Career?

I am surprised by the number of people I have come across who could have had successful business careers but failed to do so. In some cases it seems as if they avoided the field of business altogether, while in others they took jobs with companies but demonstrated such a lack of enthusiasm that they practically guaranteed their own failures.

These people "served their time" in order to get a periodic paycheck. There was a great deal of creative energy wasted in anticipating the nonworking hours of their lives, as they were hardly able to wait until they could walk out the door and be "free." To my way of thinking, this is a tragedy. Over half our waking hours are spent in some form of occupation or in pursuit of "making a living," and this time should be as enjoyable and satisfying as nonworking time. It is a mistake to think of one's job as a necessary evil and a means to support free-time activities. To "put in time" is tantamount to spending time in prison. I've heard it said many times that the highest salary in the world couldn't make up for the misery of a boring or stifling job.

In contrast, the people who have impressed me as pursuing successful careers (in any field) seem to have one thing in common. They strongly believe that their life's work is extremely important in and of itself. They are interested in making money, of course, because of the need for income and their desire to be rewarded for their efforts. But if they should suddenly inherit such a huge sum that they would be comfortable for the rest of their lives, these people would undoubtedly continue to work. What makes them successful is their devotion to working longer and harder than others, their interest in learning and expanding their skills, and their belief that each hour is ultimately important and must be used intensely and effectively. Waste of time, to these people, is one of the most heinous crimes. People who are simply trying to get by or keep from losing their jobs do not feel this way.

The individual contemplating a business career must develop a dedicated and enthusiastic attitude toward business in order to succeed. During our formative years, most of us have been exposed to constant negative thinking about the business world, which must be overcome. Seldom has any economic system benefitted humanity more than the free enterprise system. But since "capitalism" has become somewhat of a dirty word in many households, the free enterprise system has taken a great deal of criticism of late.

There are five myths about business that have been the biggest contributors to discouraging people from entering the business world. These are:

Myth 1: Business is difficult to enter.
Myth 2: Business is not creative, nor is it intellectually stimulating.
Myth 3: Business is selfish and not humanitarian.
Myth 4: Small business cannot compete in today's world of big business giants.
Myth 5: Having your own business is much riskier than the usual ways of earning a living.

MYTH 1: BUSINESS IS DIFFICULT TO ENTER

It is easy to assume that business requires having a background that includes a business degree, access to capital and contacts. But the fact is that companies are started every day without these ingredients. Other factors—such as having a good business idea, understanding the needs of your market and being willing to work hard—are probably more important. In some ways starting a business is hard. But generally you can find nontraditional ways to control the factors that seem to limit you. To the extent you say circumstances are out of your control, you don't have what it takes to be a small business owner.

Stuart Bewley began California Cooler simply with a good recipe for a wine and fruit juice beverage. He then made a "to do" list of items that needed to be accomplished before he could begin selling. Then Bewley and his partner started taking care of those issues; each one he solved in his own way. Instead of needing consultants to tell him how to proceed, Bewley offered cooler samples on college campuses to students who then filled out a survey. The survey asked if the student would purchase the cooler product, if he or she felt it should be sold in four-packs or six-packs and what a good name would be.

Licenses needed to be acquired to start producing the product, and accounts had to be set up with grocery and liquor stores. Bewley needed to be paid by the retail outlets before bills came from his suppliers. But he had a unique product and was able to negotiate favorable terms. Bewley then began putting in long days in which he would bottle coolers, load them on the delivery trucks and handle recordkeeping and other matters later. After getting his business established, he was able to sell it to a national distillery.

Although there are points in the life of a business when access to capital or trained managers is important, their absence does not necessarily mean someone cannot start his or her own firm. Creativity allows an entrepreneur to accomplish what needs to be done in spite of what someone else might consider a problem or limitation. By their very nature, small businesses break the rules followed by more-established firms. They find unmet needs and discover ways to satisfy them. New methods, materials and technologies are sometimes used in this process. But the most important attribute is an eagerness to find out what works best.

A small business shouldn't be started without an assessment of its strengths and weaknesses. In fact, it's important to have backup plans when things don't go according to schedule. Yet if you give too much thought to the potential problems, you will probably never even try to make your dream of business ownership come true.

MYTH 2: BUSINESS IS NEITHER CREATIVE NOR INTELLECTUALLY STIMULATING

It is amazing that people who live in our modern, miracle world of jet planes, television, home appliances, automobiles, lifesaving drugs, *ad infinitum,* can say that business is not creative. The business world *created* all these products that we so often take for granted. Business critics prefer to give the credit for new discoveries to the scientists. Scientific discoveries, however, could remain merely interesting laboratory curiosities if there was not the entrepreneur to convert them into useful products.

The greatest inventor of ancient times was Hero of Alexandria, who was many centuries ahead of his time. Using principles common in present-day machinery, he invented a mill driven by steam, a vending machine that released holy water when a coin was inserted, fountains, a fire engine and automatic temple doors triggered by compressed air. The inventions were considered merely amusing toys by his friends and acquaintances. His writings on the use of cogs, gears, cranks and camshafts, however, contained the basic concepts of the machinery that revolutionized industry in the nineteenth century. It was not until the emergence of business and industry that inventions of this nature were readily changed into useful products for consumers.

It can be argued that businesspeople get many of their ideas for useful products from the nonbusiness world. This reminds me of the comment by an old river boat pilot who was a contemporary of Mark Twain. He could not understand why Twain was such a celebrity, since he knew as many stories as Twain did. The only difference, according to this man, was that Twain had written them down. But what a difference!

Even that is not the whole story, however. There are thousands of well-written books on a variety of valuable subjects that are gathering dust in warehouses because of inadequate sales efforts. To me, this is incomplete creation. Having an idea for a product is only the beginning. Making a model or test sample of the product is an important second step. The business enterpriser finishes the act of creation by finding ways to make and distribute the product to potential customers at prices they are able and willing to pay. The business person who is not creative will not survive in our competitive world.

Business is intellectually stimulating and challenging as well as creative. Some bright college students who found jobs in the business world, after none had materialized in their own academic specialties, have found that business requires as much intelligence as any other field. The main difference would be that business requires a broader, more general intelligence than specialized professions. A real-world approach to problems is required, rather than an intellectual approach.

One highly educated individual with a Ph.D. in nuclear physics was employed in a government-related research firm. Although still quite young, he had been successful enough to be singled out as a future management candidate at the firm. Not knowing anything about management, he began a program of reading business books, since most of the management literature readily available to him was found in business books. He became intrigued.

His wife was a part-time distributor of toiletry and cosmetic products, and he thought it would be an interesting experiment to apply his scientific approach and his increasing knowledge of business to her operation. Within four months (and working only on a part-time basis), he earned as much in this business as he would have in his full-time position at the "think tank" in a full year. More important, he found it to be a much more challenging job and decided to devote his full time to it.

In your own business, the intellectual challenge is endless. To use but one example from my own companies, I decided several years ago that my knowledge of incorporating a business (learned from actual experience) could be useful to many small business people. After writing a book on the subject, I found that this was only about 10 percent of the task. The other 90 percent was to get the book into the hands of potential customers. Conventional publishers were not encouraging.

It was essential to become knowledgeable in the field of publishing to get the book onto the market. This required learning about printing, cost accounting and advertising. Each of these subjects led to others. For example, advertising is basically applied psychology, and my interest in this new field was stimulated. To get free advertising exposure, I managed to get several guest spots on television programs. This, too, was extremely educational. Talks to groups of high school and college students about careers in business stimulated an interest in education. Each activity set up a chain reaction, stimulating both sales and new ideas.

Businesspeople live in the real world, and they cannot rely on a knowledge of their own specialized business alone. They must keep up with changes taking place in the political arena, the economy and the society in which they live and work. Staying on top of what is happening keeps you active intellectually.

MYTH 3: BUSINESS IS SELFISH AND NOT HUMANITARIAN

According to some business critics, business owners work for their own profit, whereas people in the "really worthy" professions work for the benefit of humanity. This view can be challenged on two counts:

1. Is the motivation of the business owner or manager really different from that of people in any other profession?
2. Should not people be judged on their actual contribution to humanity, which can be observed and even measured to an extent, rather than by their motives (which can never really be known)?

In regard to differences in motivation between people in the business world and those in the nonbusiness world, any difference that might have once existed is now vanishing. At one time, teachers were not expected to work for pay, because this would have been undignified. In contrast, this group is now active in unionizing and striking for higher wages and benefits. The humanitarian medical profession is now well compensated in monetary terms. Doctors may be the highest-paid profession in history. Even police and firefighters have joined in striking for better wages. I would not question that these people still have nonmonetary reasons for practicing their professions, but the financial considerations are certainly apparent.

On the other hand, the nonmonetary motives of businesspeople are greatly underrated. These individuals assume civic responsibilities and are active in many public and charitable organizations. It is ironic that criticism and charges of negative selfishness about the business world come from certain universities, which came into existence and are currently supported by funds from successful businesses.

The real test of business's contribution to humanity is not a vague measurement of motivation but results that have been achieved. These results have been remarkable. Business has multiplied the wealth and standard of living of the population manyfold. Some critics have questioned whether this material progress represents human progress, but it is difficult to separate the two.

Until people satisfied their own basic needs for food, clothing and shelter, they had little time to worry about the finer things in life. One of the major differences between the human being and lower animals is that human childhood is prolonged for many years, during which a child can learn the arts of life. This was not possible until the child's parents were able to provide not only for themselves but for their dependent children.

Another step upward in civilization occurred when the first business owners (the farmers) could not only provide for their own families but produce a surplus that could be used by others. This permitted the division of labor, which has greatly increased productivity by enabling us to benefit from the skills of others as well as our own.

The division of labor permitted some people to specialize in other skills besides food production. Some became specialists in tool-making, and they earned their keep by making farmers more productive through simple tools. Specialists developed to transport and trade goods between differing geographical areas and between groups with different areas of expertise. Progress in production of goods permitted the growth of specialists in such fields as engineering, and they in turn earned their keep by increasing the productivity of their supporters. Cultural progress paralleled this material progress, as the increased productivity of the economy permitted a limited number of people to devote themselves to teaching, art, philosophy, religion and cultural activities.

The Industrial Revolution accelerated growth in the output of goods by increasing the productivity of an individual, directly providing him or her with tools and equipment to increase output. In its early stages, the Industrial Revolution contributed little to the standard of living of humanity, as the worker essentially traded a life of rural poverty for one of urban poverty. As the Industrial Revolution progressed, however, the fruits of productivity have benefitted the entire industrialized world. Per capita income has risen substantially, while the number of hours worked and the amount of physical effort required have been greatly reduced. Leisure time activities now represent some of our most rapidly growing industries, as time and money for leisure is no longer confined to the elite few.

In spite of the contributions already made by business, the challenges that lie ahead are just as exciting. There will be need for new products and services made possible by technological advances. In addition, it will be necessary to produce more products for a greater number of people, with less damage to the environment and with a dwindling natural resource base.

An equally important challenge is to use working members of the population productively in meaningful jobs to produce the needed goods and services. Business is in an excellent position to alleviate pressing social problems, as unemployment and underemployment are at the heart of these ills. Unlike welfare, which merely transfers purchasing power from the employed to the unemployed, business creates goods and services simultaneously with the creation of purchasing power for the employee. It is not necessary to tax Peter in order to provide welfare for Paul. The employee of a growing, profitable business does not have the limited future of the welfare recipient. The business owner can create excellent growth opportunities for employees. Successful employees are likely to become stable elements in the community, and their children are less likely to be community problems. Perhaps the most humanitarian act one individual can do for another is to create a job. This deed is possible only for the entrepreneur.

MYTH 4: SMALL BUSINESS CANNOT COMPETE IN TODAY'S WORLD OF BIG BUSINESS

To debunk this myth, merely look about at flourishing businesses that did not exist 20 or even 10 years ago. Some have been so successful that they can no longer be considered small businesses. But they were certainly not as large many years ago. Two observations can be made regarding this myth:

1. While small businesses may not be able to compete effectively against big business in certain industries, they can run circles around big business in other areas of the economy. The areas in which they compete best are those subject to rapid change, requiring close customer contact and demanding great flexibility. The most interesting areas of the economy are the ones likely to be the most rewarding.
2. Small business and big business are highly dependent on each other for success. While they compete in certain areas, they are more often cooperative. Many small businesses come into being to meet the needs of a large business. In turn, small businesses must depend on big business to supply certain materials or services that would be difficult for small business to produce. Businesses compete with each other, but they are also suppliers and customers of each other. There is plenty of room for both.

In regard to the first point, no two industries have the same ideal size, and the same industry does not have the same ideal-size company during its life cycle. The smaller company usually has an advantage when a new product is first developed. At this stage, production is limited and production techniques are still being developed, so that specialized equipment is not practical. Nor can the business benefit from large-scale purchasing of materials and services, which would be the case if it were larger. Once the product succeeds and becomes standardized, however, it becomes economical to install specialized equipment, and the minimum size of the business grows. Eventually, industry output is so great that it may be essential to guarantee access to certain strategic raw materials. The steel company may have to invest in iron ore reserves, for example, and the auto company may have to acquire steel mills.

When great size has become an important advantage, an individual should not start a new business that competes directly with the well-established mass-production and mass-distribution companies. But these giant companies never have provided (and never will provide) consumers with all their needs. A small business may be able to make substantial profits on a product with a sales volume of $1 million, whereas a large company in the industry might need a sales volume of $5 million just to break even on that product.

To illustrate the point, one large conglomerate company acquired a small specialty company that had been quite profitable. A year later, the parent company wrote a critical letter to the president of the acquired company, pointing out that the profitability had plummeted since it had been overtaken. The president of the acquired company replied that profitability was exactly the same except for one new factor: they were now being charged a substantial amount by the parent company to cover their "share" of the overhead.

Many illustrations exist that demonstrate the ways in which small businesses can find and profitably fill niches in the market left vacant by the large companies. This is not meant to imply that the small business must stay small to avoid competition with larger companies. The areas chosen should have rapid growth potential and above-average profitability so that the business should have great competitive advantages by the time it is large enough to attract the attention of big competitors.

An illuminating example of this is the case of Polaroid, which marketed its first instant camera in 1948 but did not encounter direct competition with Eastman Kodak (the giant of the industry) until the mid-1970s. This protected position has been attributed to the ability of Dr. Edwin Land, inventor of the camera and founder of the company, to keep well ahead of the technology in the field. Polaroid has more than 1,000 patents in the field of instant photography. It must be remembered, however, that Eastman Kodak is not merely a giant company but is ranked as one of the great technological companies of all time.

In addition to its technological abilities, the success of Polaroid has been attributed by some analysts to the following reasons:

- The market size for instant photography did not warrant Eastman Kodak's making the necessary research and development expenditures to catch up to Polaroid until about 1965, when Polaroid's film sales surpassed the $100 million mark.
- Kodak indirectly participated in Polaroid's revenue by selling Polaroid about $50 million worth of film per year.
- Management of Kodak feared endangering its own conventional camera sales.

The aforementioned is a common pattern that is often seen in business. The ballpoint pen was not developed and sold by an established pen company, because this would have involved destroying its established fountain pen business. As a result, several conventional pen companies found themselves put out of business by an outsider through their refusal to adapt to change.

The stainless steel blade was not introduced by Gillette, the king of the safety razor field, but by a smaller competitor, the Wilkinson Sword Company. Fortunately for Gillette, its management adapted to the new challenge and beat off the threat before too much damage was done.

Today, in the computer business, International Business Machines (IBM) is suffering. They became dependent on the large-frame and minicomputer markets, while their competitors sold "clones" at bargain prices through the mail. Now companies like Compaq, Gateway and Dell are household names.

MYTH 5: HAVING ONE'S OWN BUSINESS IS RISKIER THAN BEING EMPLOYED BY SOMEONE ELSE

Many (if not most) myths have an element of truth to them. This one is no exception. It is a fact that many new companies survive less than five years. Nevertheless, the above statement is a myth for two basic reasons:

1. A company can go out of business and still not have been a failure.
2. The risk of having your own business can be greatly reduced with proper preparation. Indeed, a major purpose of this course is to help provide that preparation.

Many small companies are operated as individual proprietorships or partnerships. Individuals who sell their businesses to someone else technically go out of business, but the enterprises may have provided an excellent living while owned and made substantial profits when sold. In the case of a partnership, addition or withdrawal of a partner terminates the existing company. Many small companies are also set up as temporary situations.

A builder may set up a separate corporation to handle each of the projects in which the company is engaged so that financial problems in one would not affect the others. When a project is completed, the separate corporation is dissolved. While this would be included in the statistics of companies going out of existence, the particular project may have been a success. Many other businesses are discontinued when owners retire or move to other areas of the country. Statistics on small business failures are thus distorted by the inclusion of the above-mentioned types of situations.

The other factor that distorts the mortality figures on new small businesses is the complete lack of preparation by many people starting their own firms.

Many tradespeople start their own businesses not realizing the need for accurate bookkeeping records. It is not surprising that inadequate management is a common contributor to small business failure. Some people enter businesses for which they are not suited by either background or personality. Others enter businesses that are already overcrowded rather than searching for less-saturated markets.

Considering how easy it is to enter the business field, it is not surprising that the failure rate is high. I am convinced that the failure rate can be reduced to modest levels for readers who follow the basic concepts incorporated in this course.

This myth also fails to recognize the risk of working for others. Regardless of your contributions to an organization for which you work, your future is largely beyond your control. The company may be merged into a larger organization, resulting in some duplicate positions. Jobs may also be lost as companies eliminate products or divisions operating at a loss. Other company operations may be transferred to geographical areas to which you might not wish to relocate.

SUMMARY

Business is an attractive field to enter. It incorporates many of the enjoyable and challenging aspects of other professions, including creativity, intellectual stimulation and challenge, humanitarianism, healthy competition and personal security.

SELF-TEST QUESTIONS

Multiple Choice

1. Most small businesses fail in the first five years. This proves that
   a. small business is being crowded out by big business.
   b. small business is too risky as a career.
   c. most people enter the small business field without adequate knowledge of how to succeed in the field.
   d. there are no longer any opportunities in America.

2. Division of labor is
   a. a technique to prevent labor unions from forming.
   b. a negative factor that has retarded growth of the economy.
   c. a weakness of capitalism.
   d. specialization of skills, which has increased productivity growth.

3. Businesspeople contribute best to the solution of social problems by
   a. providing good employment opportunities.
   b. developing new products and services to meet people's needs.
   c. reducing inflation by adapting new methods, systems and technology, which improves productivity.
   d. All of the above

4. Elimination of profits would reduce or eliminate the following:
   a. Long-term inflationary trends
   b. Long-term growth of the economy
   c. Unemployment
   d. Social problems

6. High profits in a business indicate that
   a. workers are being underpaid.
   b. customers are being overcharged.
   c. competition is being restricted.
   d. the company is able to produce a product or service with a value to its customers well in excess of its costs to produce it.

6. The primary purpose of business is to
   a. serve the needs of our government.
   b. solve the problems of customers.
   c. serve as a scapegoat when things go wrong in the economy.
   d. provide employment.

7. The relation of small business to big business is as follows:
   a. They compete with each other.
   b. They are customers of each other.
   c. Small businesses may grow into big businesses.
   d. All of the above

True or False

8. The best career is one that will permit you to retire the fastest so that you can enjoy life.

   True ☐ False ☐

9. Progress in supplying the material needs of life goes hand in hand with advancement in culture, education and civilization in general.

   True ☐ False ☐

10. The private sector of our economy has had a faster growth rate in productivity than the economy as a whole.

    True ☐ False ☐

11. The possibility of failure stimulates business to try to do a better job.

    True ☐ False ☐

12. A large business can usually make a profit on a smaller volume of sales of a product than can the small business.

    True ☐ False ☐

13. Small companies tend to be more successful than large companies where service, personal contact and flexibility are essential.

    True ☐ False ☐

14. If businesses were not heavily regulated, customers would have no protection from unscrupulous businesspeople.

    True ☐ False ☐

15. The successful businessperson is likely to be one who enjoys work.

    True ☐ False ☐

16. The businessperson's intelligence is likely to be more general and practical than that of his academic critics.

    True ☐ False ☐

17. The ideal size of a company in an industry changes over a period of time.

    True ☐ False ☐

18. Perhaps the most humanitarian act possible is to create jobs through starting your own business.
True ☐ False ☐

Answers
1.c, 2.d, 3.d, 4.b, 5.d, 6.b, 7.d, 8.F, 9.T, 10.T, 11.T, 12.F, 13.T, 14.F 15.T 16.T, 17.T, 18.T

CHAPTER 3

Succeeding in Consumer Markets

Today a company needs more than a good product or service to reach customers. It must encourage workers to constantly meet customer expectations by doing the out-of-the-ordinary. Repeat business results as much from service levels as from product benefits.

Young firms also must develop strategies to survive during all economic cycles. In this chapter, we'll look at how a business owner can adapt—and perhaps even gain market share—when the economy is slow. We'll also describe tax-planning techniques that help you to actually benefit if you have a loss.

Innovation is a key for consumer-oriented firms, and this chapter contains profiles of two companies that attribute their growth mainly to new techniques. You'll not only see that it's helpful to use new technologies to provide benefits to your customers, but also that new ideas can make your workers happier, as well as more productive and committed.

EMPOWERING WORKERS

When customers call to ask a question about their latest invoice, usually the calls will be routed to an accounts receivable clerk. But if customers also want to know if their most recent order has been shipped, can your billing clerk tell them that? If not, consider empowering your workers to do more tasks. You'll give better customer service and have a more efficient operation.

Customers get annoyed when they must talk with several people to get a basic question answered. In addition, it ties up your phone lines and gets several people on your staff involved. But a good computer system can put all the information your customer service representatives need at their fingertips.

Retail companies can implement this business tactic by making every worker who deals with the public capable of handling any transaction and able to answer all questions. Training is necessary to bring workers to this level. But empowered employees—in contrast to those who do the same task over and over—tend to be more efficient and happier.

Training shouldn't be devoted just to product features and company policies. Also show your workers how to relate to clients. Make sure they understand your customers' needs and concerns, and teach them how to handle an unhappy customer.

Because the employees who work with customers help form their opinion of your firm, it makes a difference to have workers in those roles who are capable of taking care of anything that comes up.

ADAPTING TO TODAY'S ECONOMY

Change causes concern. No one likes having his or her comfort level jostled—especially if it could mean fewer sales. But opportunities—and risks—actually increase when the economy is volatile. Here's why: companies that are less flexible and hard-working will not be able to cope. Some of them will even go out of business. If the pie becomes a little smaller, there will be fewer firms trying to get a piece of it. In fact, it is possible to increase your market share and sales in tough times.

Doing so won't be easy. New strategies are necessary to keep sales up during slow times. However, there are some constructive actions you can take.

Concentrate on cementing relationships with past clients and referral sources rather than on developing new sources of business. As your competition sees their sales falling off, they will hold on to their best accounts for all they're worth. They will start pricing more competitively so as not to lose a single deal. Taking that business away will be very difficult.

Although you will gain new accounts as competitors leave the marketplace, your first goal is to hang on to your best customers without having to cut your margins. One way to do so is by adding products and services that will make working with you more important to them than ever.

Other people need help in a slow market. What unique benefits are you bringing to them? By offering new services, you'll stand out in your customers' minds. Whatever your market specialty is, you need to have some concrete benefits that you consistently bring to the table.

Market effectively; not all prospects are created equal. You know that, but it can be difficult to put into practice. Nevertheless, doing so is essential during slower times. Here's why: you'll need to be contacting more prospects to get the same amount of business, so you must be more efficient.

Find ways to qualify prospects quickly, and don't waste time on those who aren't likely to buy from you. Consider developing a list of questions to ask your prospects to uncover their needs. Professionals such as doctors or lawyers ask their clients questions up front to find out if they can assist them. If your customers regard you as a professional, then you should act similarly.

It's not necessary to be cold toward others. You can still be warm, because you will be focused on discovering the needs of the other person. If the prospect has no current need for your services, you won't be rude. Instead, you'll be happy that you quickly found out what the situation was, and you then can graciously excuse yourself to find a better prospect.

Practice your presentation skills. You might have gotten a little rusty at asking for the order and countering objections when times were easier. But now every meeting must be purposeful and to the point. Again, there's no need to be harsh. But learn how to communicate the benefits of what you offer.

Everyone's time and energy are at a premium—including yours. Make the most of every opportunity. But don't be in a rush to tell about your product or service. Find out first what it is customers need, and see if you can help them.

Don't be overly concerned if your pricing isn't the lowest. When you or I need something and it is reasonably priced, we will buy it. Whether the store makes 5 or 50 percent won't concern us if we want that particular item from that store, and if we think it's fairly priced. But we might buy less junk food if we knew how much of our money was lining someone else's pocket. When something is both overpriced and unnecessary, knowing the markup could be enough to make us put it back on the shelf. It's not how much you charge, it's how much value you offer that matters to your customers.

You can often realize savings by simplifying your procedures and allowing workers to take early retirement or move to part-time status. However, don't cut costs in ways that will reduce your efficiency. Cutting wages is tempting, but output almost certainly will fall.

Some capital investments may be justified expenses even if demand is falling. Old, unreliable equipment should be replaced, for instance. You might be able to get good deals on what you need if demand is low.

Providing incentives also can help productivity. One manufacturer rewards worker teams for increasing their overall output. Management has found that less supervision is required, because underachievers are disciplined by their peers. And in order to increase their overall performance bonus, workers often ask that workers who leave not be replaced.

By shepherding resources and keeping your company healthy, you will be in a better position to expand when times improve. The best time to market more aggressively and obtain greater market share is when people are in a position to buy your goods and services.

Your accountant should help you plan tax strategies as the economy changes. For instance, a recession can create an unexpected loss in companies that have grown profitably up to that point. Because they have never been in that situation, many firms remain unaware of tax strategies that might allow them to recover all the taxes they've paid over the prior three years.

Corporations are allowed to "carryback" current losses. In other words, a firm can rework its taxes so the loss effectively reduces previous profits.

Companies considering this strategy should take as many expenses as possible in the current tax year while delaying as much income as possible until the following year.

Of course, doing so makes your financial statement look weaker, so discuss this strategy with your financial advisers before implementing it.

NEW PROCESS HELPS ALL AMERICA TERMITE GROW

Using new methods to deliver a traditional service has allowed All America Termite and Pest Control, Inc., in Orlando, Florida, to grow to $64 million in sales in 1992 from its start in 1977. Founder Charles P. Steinmetz expects sales to reach $100 million by 1995. Previously Steinmetz had spent 17 years with two national extermination companies.

"I realized that I was very limited in terms of my future position and earnings," Steinmetz says. "I was very unhappy with my upward potential."

His employer actually encouraged Steinmetz to open his own firm and offered to lend him money. Steinmetz bought Middleton Pest Control in Orlando to get started, and instituted three steps:

1. "A different level of quality for customers." Steinmetz uses a new technique that relies on placing insect traps instead of spraying chemicals. Homeowners don't have to breathe the same substances used to kill their roaches and termites.

   Steinmetz adds that these techniques are well-known, but to adopt them the national extermination companies would have to totally change their operations—which they are unwilling to do.
2. "Let workers make two times the industry average." Since traps last for a full year, whereas sprays must be repeated monthly, fewer visits to homes are required. Workers thus are more productive and can earn more money. Entry-level wages at All America Termite have gone from the industry-standard $1,000 per month to three times that amount. All America charges "a little bit less" than more traditional exterminators do, adds Steinmetz.
3. "Generate a basic business model that could be duplicated." Steinmetz wanted his business to grow, so he needed something that could easily expand. In 1981 he got his opportunity to expand when Sears Pest Control had problems, and All America got the license.

With the Sears name behind it—and with access to their customer lists—All America has now moved into

> eight states. In addition, the company is growing without borrowing. Steinmetz isn't franchising All America, and he doesn't want to go public; yet he has 1,200 employees and 75 locations.

Three-quarters of All America's ad budget goes to television commercials. Steinmetz has used TV ads since All America's first year in business. In addition, he does "a lot of direct mail to neighbors of past customers." He also mails offers to households with demographic characteristics similar to his customers.

A schedule of working from 7:45 AM to 5 PM five days a week keeps Steinmetz full of energy and vigor on the job. "I never, never work on weekends," he explains. "I like to play racquetball." Keeping to a regimen allows him to "come in fresh" every morning.

"I'm a pretty good delegator," adds Steinmetz, who has an administrative staff of 50. He notes that as a company gets larger it becomes easier to manage, because specialists can be hired to handle such issues as training, purchasing and fleet administration. But, he adds, "You have to reconfigure how the business works when you go from 20,000 to 200,000 accounts."

Generally, one person does both selling and servicing in an area. In larger regions, renewal business and new sales are handled separately. Leads often come when people call a Sears store and are referred to a local All America office. "It's been an outstanding relationship with Sears," Steinmetz says. He adds that it would have been difficult to introduce the novel idea of once-a-year pest control without having the trust that goes along with being recommended by Sears.

Half of All America's customers renew after their year of service is up. But a year later, 80 percent of those original customers renew, because by then bugs are coming back.

Steinmetz says his job "is to decide where we're going; to delegate to others how to get there; and to protect our ethical standards." Sticking to a superior business strategy has allowed his company to grow quickly without taking on debt. It is possible for a business that is dominated by large national companies, and that is not seen as a big growth industry, to become a wonderful opportunity for an entrepreneur.

PATAGONIA SCALES NEW PEAKS

Patagonia, Inc., is a company that doesn't want to grow too fast. Founder Yvon Chouinard is dedicated to keeping quality high, and thus put the brakes on growth projections several years back. In addition, Chouinard didn't like the idea of not knowing all his workers by name.

After all, it wasn't long ago that he was working out of a tin shed. He picked the Southern California coastline to start his business because he could surf half the year and go rock climbing the rest of the time. He and a friend rented the tin building behind the Hobson Meat Packing plant in Ventura, California, in 1964. A blacksmith's forge was set up there, and they began making their own climbing tools, which they sold to climbing buddies from their car.

His rock-climbing passion actually grew out of an interest in falconry, which requires climbing to nests. Chouinard had started making climbing equipment for himself about ten years earlier, when he was just out of high school. He purchased an anvil, a forge to set up in his parents' backyard and a book on blacksmithing. A piton made out of hard steel, dubbed the "Lost Arrow," was his first product. Up until then, pitons, which are metal spikes driven into rock faces to help secure climbers, had come from Europe and been made out of soft metal.

Ten years later he was still inventing new tools, along with novel climbing techniques to use with them. Chouinard pioneered "clean climbing," which discourages the use of pitons, which damage the natural rock face. But he then developed "chocks," which wedge into rock cracks and leave no evidence that they've been there. Chouinard's design rule for his first piton still guides the company: "Any number of shapes will work, but there must be one shape that will ultimately work best; by best, I mean it is the most functional, with the least material, with the smoothest lines, with strength and lasting qualities."

Soon he began making cotton canvas shorts that were tough enough for rock climbing. Previously, rock climbers would have to discard normal clothes after one climb. Chouinard also imported rugby shirts because of their durability. Today the clothing line has been expanded to accommodate outdoor needs ranging from those of fly fishermen to cross-country skiers.

Durability and functionality are important criteria in designing clothes for mountain climbers, kayakers and cyclists.

New fabrics have been pioneered by Patagonia, including Capilene polyester—often used for long underwear because it draws perspiration from the skin—and quick-drying Synchilla pile, which makes warm clothes. Bright colors are also a Patagonia innovation. Instead of the traditional khakis and forest greens for outdoor clothing, items now come in Burnt Chili or Saffron.

Prototypes of new clothes are sent to adventure sport professionals for their feedback. However, Patagonia doesn't believe in paying anyone to wear its clothes as an endorsement. Sportswear and children's clothing also are in the Patagonia line, and all come with a lifetime guarantee.

Patagonia stores are found in the United States, France, Japan, Germany and Ireland. In addition, 1,400 stores carry Patagonia goods, and catalogs that contain material of interest to environmentalists come out several times a year.

Although the tin shed that once housed Chouinard's blacksmith shop still stands, Patagonia now occupies a set of buildings that contain heavy wooden desks and no private offices. Creativity, teamwork and ensuring plenty of input into decisions are reasons for keeping everyone out in the open.

In many ways, Patagonia has a unique working environment. Flex-time is available, which means that surfers can take a two- or three-hour lunch if they work late and it's okay with the rest of their department.

On-site child care is offered, and parents often eat meals with their children in the company cafeteria. Some mothers have their babies sleeping in cribs next to their desks. School-age childen are picked up by a van after class is over and brought to the day-care center for the rest of the afternoon. Eight weeks of paid maternity and paternity leave are provided, and then two more months of unpaid leave is available if desired. Elder care leave and a 401(k) plan plus vision, dental and medical insurance all are included in the benefits package.

Such benefits are important to many workers today. Rather than seeing them as extra costs, some companies feel they can't afford not to provide what workers need to be happy and productive. A survey conducted by The Gallup Organization, Inc. for the Employee Benefit Research Institute (EBRI) found that two-thirds of the respondees thought employers should play a role in providing child-care assistance to workers.

Over one-third said child care should be offered even if that meant reducing wages and benefits for all employees.

If offered identical jobs with and without child care, survey respondees said the position without child care would have to pay an average of $3,151 more before they would accept it.

Just 30 percent of those surveyed had children at home under age 13. In addition, only 3 percent of the participants said that an employer's child-care policy had been the reason for their accepting, quitting or changing a job.

Almost four out of five respondees said employers should be required to provide unpaid leaves of absence to workers after the birth or adoption of a child. An average leave period of 60 days was requested by survey participants.

Over 70 percent of respondees also said employers should be mandated to give unpaid leaves to employees whose child, spouse or parent was ill. Although granting a leave of absence takes a person off the payroll, when the leave is over the employer is required to have a job available for that person.

Job sharing and cross-training are offered at Patagonia, and any worker can take a six-week leave of absence with pay to work for a nonprofit group. Every six months workers enjoy two classes on the environment, such as visiting tidepools or oil derricks. People at Patagonia are encouraged to consider how their life is affecting the world.

Patagonia wants to both produce quality outdoor clothes and also serve as a model for social change. Many of the employees do volunteer work, and the company gives 1 percent of its annual sales to groups working to preserve and restore the environment.

Patagonia hopes to enjoy a profit of 3–4 percent from its good work environment and high-quality products. By holding profits as only one of several goals, Chouinard and his coworkers can stay true to their beliefs about how a business should be run.

SELF-TEST QUESTIONS

Multiple Choice

1. Empowering your employees means
   a. giving them free snacks.
   b. providing more electrical outlets for computers.
   c. letting them set policies based on what seems right to them.
   d. giving them the tools to respond immediately to customer needs.

2. A tax carryback means
   a. you have to pay back taxes.
   b. the IRS made a mistake and they give you a refund.
   c. a current loss allows you to rework your last three business returns, reducing any profits on them.
   d. you get a tax credit for any loss incurred last year that can be deducted from the year's profit.

3. All America Termite's case shows that new technology —
   a. is too expensive.
   b. can be used to win market share.
   c. doesn't help most businesses.
   d. requires special training of workers.

4. Patagonia's unique corporate features include
   a. interest in preserving the environment.
   b. providing extensive child daycare facilities.
   c. offering flex time.
   d. All of the above

5. During an economic slowdown, you should strongly consider
   a. cutting wages.
   b. basing compensation on productivity.
   c. not investing in new equipment.
   d. making no changes at all.

6. Workers moving to a new job that doesn't offer child care would expect it to pay this much more than a job with child-care benefits
   a. Under $1,000
   b. $1,000 to $2,000
   c. $2,000 to $3,000
   d. $3,000 to $4,000

True or False

7. During slow economic times, it's best to try to take business from your competition.

   True ☐ False ☐

8. If a customer feels your product or service is valuable, price becomes a secondary issue.

   True ☐ False ☐

9. Using new fabrics has been instrumental in Patagonia's growth.

   True ☐ False ☐

10. Training is important in order to empower your employees.

    True ☐ False ☐

11. Some companies will prosper, even if their industry is having hard times.

    True ☐ False ☐

12. Supplying products or services to a large company provides an opportunity for growth.

    True ☐ False ☐

Answers

1.d, 2.c, 3.b, 4.d, 5.b, 6.d, 7.F, 8.T, 9.T, 10.T, 11.T, 12.T

CHAPTER 4

Listening for Today's Opportunities

Almost all of us are poor listeners. We don't really hear what our families, employees or customers are saying. We miscommunicate with our banker, accountant and suppliers. In the process, we lose opportunities to make our life more enjoyable and rewarding.

Listening to what those around you need, as well as to your own thoughts, can help you put together a company that works in today's nontraditional environment. One firm, MMS Institute, is profiled here as helping other companies "design their own future," even in the wake of restructurings and layoffs. It has found that delivering better customer service is possible while also helping managers and workers to handle the stress of change.

Seeing possibilities where others see problems can be a small business owner's key to success. In this chapter we'll meet Edith Gorter, who took over her brother's trucking company after his death. Although she had little business experience, was leading a severely weakened firm in a male-dominated industry and couldn't get credit to buy equipment, Gorter found the resources within herself to be successful.

LEARNING TO LISTEN

When meeting with customers or prospects, a business owner usually wants to start telling them about his or her firm. Yet that may not be the best approach for building a lasting relationship.

Spend more time listening than speaking when you first meet someone. Get others talking about their needs, and discover whether or not you can satisfy them.

You'll find that some people like to spend time chatting about their families or what's happening in the community before moving onto business matters. But others want to get to the point as quickly as possible.

A good listener is aware of these differences in people and adjusts his or her communication style to put them at ease. Making someone comfortable is a big step toward getting them to open up.

To make sure the topic eventually comes around to business, you might say something like "Mr. Prospect, I appreciate meeting with you today. I wanted to take a few minutes to find out what your company's needs are concerning (your product or service)."

Once they see you are genuinely interested in their needs rather than in simply selling them something, you'll be amazed at the information they will provide.

A person who was cool toward you at the start of the meeting will warm up as he or she begins talking about the firm. Often they will answer questions you wouldn't have ventured to ask before, such as "What is your budget for this project?"

Your goal is to isolate your prospect's most important need. If you can find that out, you've gone a long way toward getting an order. Afterward you can go back to your office and put together a proposal detailing how your company could work with them. Having listened to them, you'll then have something important to say.

APPEALING TO DIFFERENT CUSTOMERS

One of the first things anyone going into business learns is the "80/20 rule." This states that 80 percent of your business will come from 20 percent of your customers. What the 80/20 rule implies is that if you spend equal amounts of time and money on all your prospects, you are hurting yourself. Identifying and pursuing those who are willing to work with you repeatedly is essential to success.

No one would argue with that. But who wants to stop at 80 percent of their sales? No business is willing to give that up. The other side of the 80/20 rule is, to get that last 20 percent, there is no alternative to hard work.

It's easy to say, "We're going to skim the cream." But looking more closely at the issues involved shows that's not as easy as one might think. For instance, you can talk about giving the best service in your business, but do you back that up with action? To do so might mean more staff, increased levels of training and more phone lines. A business willing to talk about the importance of service without taking the necessary steps to provide it probably won't achieve the success it envisions.

How do you encourage more business from your best customers while also handling the 20 percent who buy infrequently? Different strategies are demanded by these two markets. Your ongoing customers should respond to offers that encourage repeat business. Marketing will need to identify those customers and deliver those sales messages.

Marketing messages work best when they emphasize specific products and benefits. You should avoid the tendency to try to be all things to all people.

If your primary and secondary customers are worlds apart, your position in the marketplace will be confusing. Although it's certainly possible to provide goods and services to a wide variety of people, you won't be able to have a consistent marketing message if you are trying to appeal to vastly different groups. A luxury-car dealership that also sells used clunkers isn't going to be totally trusted by either of its target groups.

Often the best restaurants have the most limited menus. Simplicity is important if a business is to be consistent in its products and services. However, companies often change as they grow. With expansion, new markets can be reached and some older markets are no longer as important. Obviously, it's best to grow without losing any markets at all. For instance, you might start with one product or service, only to find that once you grow, a different market has other needs. Try to establish a new division to reach the new market rather than moving your whole company in that direction.

For this reason, it's especially hard for an entrepreneur to manage a new firm. He or she is always coming up with new ideas. But a young company can't develop itself in its chosen markets while simultaneously trying to explore new ventures. If you're such a person, then rely on professional managers while you pursue other dreams.

Focus is almost always necessary for success. If you are trying to give great service to both your repeat and one-time customers, you soon will find yourself stretched thin. In order to grow, you'll need to start delegating some aspect of what you used to do, whether it's marketing, management or operations. You might put someone else in charge of one group of customers. Giving attention to all parts of a business while making sure it works as a whole is a key to success as an entrepreneur. Having a business with one weak area is like having a tire with one leak. Eventually, it will stop rolling.

What is most important is not your idea or plan but your implementation. Is your team skillful and flexible enough to do well when your original plan is proven faulty? When the unexpected happens, can your company recover? Resilience, health, technical expertise, capital, ongoing marketing and luck are some of the ingredients generally needed to make an idea into a viable business.

When the ability to adapt is present, other factors can be absent. There is no right or wrong time to start a company. Instead of relying on other things being right, make your own future. "The harder I work," says trainer Tommy Hopkins, "the luckier I get."

Every new business needs two things: some initial customers who can supply cash flow until the company gets established, and a means of marketing that is both sustainable and will bring in good leads. Without these elements, your business is in trouble. About the only way to get around this equation is by having lots of capital for marketing in order to build a customer base.

MMS INSTITUTE DESIGNS THE FUTURE

Challenges are facing companies that for decades have been among the most powerful in their industries. AT&T, IBM and General Motors are among the firms that have found that "business as usual" is not possible now. Leading companies in industries ranging from computers to steel manufacturing have restructured and redirected themselves over the past decade. More of the same is to be expected in the future.

But what happens to managers and workers, who often have given decades to a company in the hope of a secure retirement, when they learn that the rules have changed and many of them will have to go—or else adjust to a changed company? Cherie Carter-Scott started MMS Institute to help companies deal with these issues. Often she begins by helping managers talk out the situation. Although they think they're confused, they'll usually discover that they actually have a clear idea of what outcome they'd like to occur. Further questioning clarifies this vision. MMS then helps the managers build a team that is devoted to helping the company realize its goal, whether it's reducing absenteeism or remolding the entire firm.

Workers are often more skeptical, and they also have to express their feelings if they feel disillusioned or taken advantage of during a time of change. Soon afterward they can begin "possibility thinking"—seeing that they actually can design their own future. What started as an abrupt, painful process can then be seen as a time to seize control of necessary change.

MMS Institute teaches managers specific skills needed in such environments, including

- how to listen well,
- conflict management and dealing with difficult employees,
- goal setting,
- running successful meetings,
- interviewing,
- presentation skills,
- stress management,
- telephone courtesy, and
- time management.

One client in the telephone industry reports higher motivation levels, fewer conflicts and a sales increase of more than 140 percent after working with the MMS Institute. Another MMS client, an insurance agency, says that "the consultative sales approach has really opened my eyes to the entire sales process. Instead of facing the painful tasks of prospecting, data gathering and trying to close deals, we are now building relationships, asking questions and listening. The process of closing the sale has changed from being a stressful confrontation to a natural step in the relationship."

Carter-Scott has found that her background in theater and education, along with "enthusiasm and desire to support people and help them get their blocks out of the way," makes her an ideal consultant. Instead of talking people into something, she listens and helps them find their own solution. MMS today offers both personal growth seminars for individuals and business management consulting. "Anybody who hangs up their shingle can be a consultant," she notes. But Carter-Scott adds, "We're coaches. We don't take over the company." A common problem is that most executives "are taught how to manage, but they're reluctant leaders."

Implementing a concept of change is difficult for most companies, she adds. "A worker will say, 'I've been taking orders for 20 years. Now you want me to think?' " Carter-Scott starts by asking open-ended questions in a safe environment. For instance, she might start by simply wanting to know "What's working?" Carter-Scott says, "It's best to be a generalist. If you 'know,' then you're part of the existing paradigm." She prefers "asking questions that need to be asked, such as, 'How come we don't talk to each other?' or 'Why do we sabotage each other?' " Often MMS helps different groups within a company learn to work together.

All the information will be synthesized and put into a document diagnosing the health and climate of the business. Then she will work with managers to brainstorm behaviors, attitudes and cultural changes in the business, and help them design and put their plan into action. Additionally, she'll follow managers around during the day and give them feedback on things they might not be aware of. For example, Carter-Scott and her associates will point out when the manager did something effective—or when behavior caused a negative reaction from a coworker.

The only clear direction for change is inner direction, says Carter-Scott. "Leaders have to go inside themselves and find out what they want to accomplish. If you look outside for direction, such as at the economy, you'll get more confused." She compares the process to putting a man on the moon. Having a vision brought creativity and energy to the project. It then could be broken down into smaller missions that accomplished necessary steps in the process.

UPSCALE NICHE FOR GORTER MOTOR EXPRESS

Edith Gorter took over the presidency of Thomas C. Gorter Motor Express, Inc., in Grand Rapids, Michigan, when her brother died after a long illness in 1973. Gorter Motor Express then "had nothing left—there was only one employee," she recalls. "But if you want it badly enough, you can do it."

Yet, Gorter notes, "You can't say, 'This is the way to do it.' It's constantly changing! There are no formulas for being successful—so many variables are present." Proving that you can cope with today's needs is the challenge faced by entrepreneurs, says Gorter. "All college can teach you is history."

Not surprisingly, "Everyone said I couldn't do it," Gorter recalls. After all, she was a woman in a traditionally male business, trying to coax an ailing company to health. In addition, Gorter had limited business experience: previously she had managed a fabric shop. But she explains that "all of us downplay ourselves. Often you have the knowledge and don't even know it."

Much of her management has been done almost intuitively. When making decisions, "I would think about all the things that could happen that were bad. If I could live with them, I went ahead and did it." Gorter adds that she "made very few mistakes—none that were serious." When Gorter's banker wanted to know how expenses were kept so stable, "I don't know," was the reply. "It's almost instinctive." Her sense of where the company was financially also frustrated her accountant. Gorter could tell him where the bookkeeping was wrong, even though he was keeping the books. "I could sense something was off." But she also keeps her own set of financials—"the pulse of the business. It soothes me to know immediately how we are spending money."

Noting around 1989 that "the economy feels funny," she renegotiated the rent on her truck trailers, cutting it in half. "You wouldn't want to negotiate with me," Gorter adds. She had used the trailers for five years, and reminded the owner that they had added many more miles over that time. He agreed, although she knew they were in good shape due to the maintenance she performs. But once she got the rent reduced by half, she didn't go for the last possible dollar. "Everybody has to make money," she said, not wanting to hurt the trailer owner.

When Gorter was first rebuilding the business, two sympathetic suppliers helped her. One dealer let her use a tractor for

16,000 miles before she paid a penny on it. "I couldn't get a loan from a bank," she notes.

Fuel and insurance used to be two of the smallest expenses for trucking firms. But now they rank right after payroll as a percentage of total outlay. Another change in the business—deregulation of the trucking industry—"was great for me," adds Gorter. Before deregulation it was almost impossible to get a license to operate in other states, she adds. By law, a firm wishing to start delivering in those areas had to prove a need — and other companies could challenge an application. Big trucking firms with large legal staffs could "keep you in litigation for years," says Gorter, which kept smaller truckers from even trying to get a license.

But deregulation cut out the right to challenge an application. In addition, the government was looking for minority- and female-owned firms. "I didn't even use an attorney while getting authority to run in 48 states," Gorter says.

Her firm specializes in delivering furniture. Gorter Motor Express delivered seats from the factory to the University of Iowa's athletic stadium and to the Detroit Pistons' arena. Office furniture in buildings from St. Louis to Boston have arrived on her trucks. In addition, Gorter has a five-year project going with the Chrysler Building, which is "so big you can drive trucks inside it," she says. "Only the Pentagon is larger."

Gorter's 16 drivers are known for being on time with their deliveries. Most of them have been with the company 15 to 20 years, and their average age is 41. "All are married with children," Gorter adds. "They don't fit the stereotype of a trucker."

Because there's nothing they can do about the cost of fuel, some firms, in an effort to cut costs, are lowering trucker salaries. But for Gorter, keeping her drivers is important. "It's very difficult to get good drivers," she says. Her drivers take pride in their reputation for arriving on time, as well as in their rusty-red Kenworth tractors and white trailers. "Gorter Motor Express" is hand-painted on the doors with gold lettering.

She talks with each driver at least once a week and doesn't reduce wages when a truck gets dented, as other firms do. A mechanic is on duty, and a tire man comes by twice a week. An oil and filter supplier also stops by regularly to check on the trucks. Having suppliers help keep the trucks maintained works well for Gorter. "I pay a little more for oil," she says, "but I don't have breakdowns."

Most of her time is spent with people, Gorter says, ranging from customers to bankers. "I sell myself better than anybody else can." She'll ask customers if Gorter Express can do more for them and if their prices are satisfactory. "Competition today is very rough," she adds, citing "predatory rates" by firms running their trucks under cost just to keep from losing an account. Although she prices competitively, "there is a point beyond which I cannot go. If you play that way, somebody can always undercut you."

Gorter's clients get first-class service. "We deliver anytime the customer wants it." Most of her business comes from regular accounts, who initially heard of Gorter Express through its reputation. Since Gorter has been president, the firm has run only one ad—"and that just attracted salespeople."

She plans on staying with the furniture accounts. "Stay with what you do best," Gorter notes. "You can't be everything to everybody." But she would like to put up a warehouse to store freight. Gorter wants to grow more, although she recalls the year she got two new accounts at the same time. "We grew 122 percent overnight," she says. "I felt like a train was chasing me" as she scrambled to handle the extra expenses associated with that business before receiving the income from it. Gorter had to borrow money for cash-flow purposes that year.

But she remarks that Gorter Motor Express has been profitable every year except for two since she's been there. "That's very good for the trucking business," Gorter explains. "You do something, and it works out—it gives you confidence." Although she has concerns for the future, Gorter simply says, "We'll adjust."

SELF-TEST QUESTIONS

Multiple Choice

1. When talking with someone, you should
   a. try to find their most important business needs.
   b. tell them about your company.
   c. ask about their family and interests.
   d. describe what you know about their competition.

2. When you come up with a good business idea,
   a. implement it yourself.
   b. put someone else in your company in charge of it.
   c. set up a new division to handle it.
   d. forget it.

3. A new company often can get by on little capital if it has
   a. a customer base.
   b. an effective marketing plan.
   c. disciplined management.
   d. All of the above

4. A company's direction should come from
   a. analyzing the economy.
   b. management's dreams.
   c. watching the competition.
   d. hiring a consultant.

5. Which of the following is essential for business success?
   a. Experience in the industry
   b. A college degree
   c. Financing
   d. None of the above

True or False

6. Listening is difficult for most entrepreneurs.

   True ☐ False ☐

7. The "80/20 rule" implies we have to market to two sets of customers.

   True ☐ False ☐

8. Change is something we can't control at all in business.

   True ☐ False ☐

9. Often the best questions are simple.

   True ☐ False ☐

10. It's best to promise a lot in your marketing.

    True ☐ False ☐

11. Suppliers often are willing to help your company expand.

    True ☐ False ☐

12. In a competitive industry, price is always more important than service.

    True ☐ False ☐

Answers
1.a, 2.c, 3.d, 4.b, 5.d, 6.T, 7.T, 8.F, 9.T, 10.F, 11.T, 12.F

CHAPTER 5

Finding a Profitable Niche

What causes a company to rise from the middle of the pack to dominate its industry? In this chapter, let's start by considering Countrywide Funding, which has become the nation's number-one provider of home loans by using techniques that can help any business. Not every entrepreneur finds the path so well-lit. My own experience encompassed many different businesses before I found the field I most enjoy.

Once you've discovered your preferred business niche, you'll need tools to help you make the most of it. To discover some of them, let's explore the benefits of strategic planning, ways to reduce overhead and using financial ratios to judge your company's health.

BANKING ON THE HOME

Home loans are big business. In an average year, about $550 billion in home mortgages are funded, although cyclical peaks can reach around $800 billion in annual lending. Banks, savings and loans, credit unions and mortgage banking firms provide mortgages.

For years, it was uncommon for a single lender to have even 1 percent of the national market. Mortgage lending was basically a regional business. A few companies that sought to become national in scope met with failure along the way. Lomas & Nettleton was the nation's largest mortgage banker in the late 1980s but went bankrupt in 1991. Just two months before filing Chapter 11, its debts were considered investment grade.

Citicorp Mortgage—a subsidiary of what was then the nation's largest bank—tried to make the home loan process simpler and quicker with a program called "MortgagePower." By not thoroughly reviewing a borrower's income and credit, this program did save time. Citicorp officials thought they could compensate for any additional risk incurred from quick processing by requiring a higher-than-normal down payment on the loan. In the words of one executive, Citicorp was "willing to bet our balance sheet" that the higher down payment would keep people from missing loan payments.

But soon after MortgagePower began, real estate values started dropping in various parts of the country. Citicorp Mortgage then found itself sitting on a massive pile of delinquent loans and foreclosures. Eventually the entire mortgage subsidiary—which at one time led the nation in production—was disbanded by the parent bank.

In addition to the risk of nonpayment by borrowers, originating mortgages—the process of going from application to loan closing—is expensive. In fact, loans often are originated at a loss. Lenders make most of their profits gradually, by collecting a small fee off each monthly payment. However, if loans are not paid off, either because the house is sold or refinanced or through delinquency, then the origination loss will not be recouped.

Is it possible to be an aggressive growth company while simultaneously managing a lending business prudently? One wrong policy can translate into billions of dollars in subpar loans, as the savings and loan industry discovered late in the eighties. Into this market vacuum the mortgage bankers stepped. Foremost among them is Countrywide Funding, of Pasadena, California. Founded in 1969 by Bronx-born Angelo Mozilo and his partner David Loeb, the company had performed steadily and was one of the nation's leaders.

As other competitors are retreating, Countrywide is quickly emerging as the nation's preeminent lender. In the space of a few years, its share of the national market has shot up to almost 4 percent—an unheard-of performance a few years ago. Yet Countrywide is talking about gaining a 10 percent market share. And it seems to be doing so through innovation rather than by taking on more credit risk. By playing smart and hard, Countrywide is rewriting the rules of mortgage lending.

Listed below are some of the tools Countrywide is using to make itself the top lender. None are revolutionary by themselves, but when combined, they allow Countrywide to offer mortgages at a better rate than much of its competition does. By offering a small price advantage, more often than not the firm is chosen as the lender when someone wants to buy or refinance a home.

Countrywide Funding's Tools for Increasing Market Share

Unorthodox Methods. Early in the company's history, Loeb told Mozilo that the high commissions being paid to loan officers were keeping Countrywide from showing a profit. Commissioned salespeople are a standard in mortgage lending, as they are in many businesses. So it was with a heavy heart that Mozilo disbanded the sales force and went back to one branch.

In this office he put salaried workers with technical backgrounds rather than salespeople. Besides requiring less compensation, workers with loan underwriting and processing backgrounds are more likely to accept only good loans than are most salespeople, who are eager to earn commissions. As a result, costs went down while loan quality rose.

Unique Marketing. But how did the business come in if there were no salespeople? Traditionally, loan officers rely heavily on developing good personal relationships with a number of real estate agents, who, in turn, refer their buyers to that loan officer.

Countrywide changed this formula by using mailings and special events to build REALTOR® loyalty to the company, instead of paying loan officers to do so one-on-one. In this way, Countrywide is able to originate loans profitably, whereas most lenders lose money in the process.

Multiple Avenues of Business Generation. Over the years, Countrywide has opened new divisions that bring in loans from other sources. Today the company buys mortgages from banks, savings and loans, credit unions, mortgage brokers and directly from consumers, as well as getting referrals from real estate agents. With a number of tributaries, its stream of loans can build more quickly.

Effective Research and Information Systems. Before opening a branch, Countrywide looks at a variety of information about housing, jobs and competition from other lenders in that area. Only after determining that its chances of success are good does the firm proceed with the expense of a new branch. In addition, smaller satellite branches—which cover a nearby area with fewer staff and less office space—are established off the main ones until a new territory has proven itself.

In addition, Countrywide executives enjoy the benefits of a computer system that updates them every half hour as to what is happening in every branch. A manager can look at the whole company's production, then at a region, an office—even at individual production within an office. Potential problems thus are spotted and dealt with before they can get out of hand.

Technology. Countrywide is in the forefront of a number of new advances that promise to both speed up the loan process and save money. Computers with "artificial intelligence" are now being implemented for approving loan applications, with the expectation that eventually they will handle 70 percent of the volume. Human underwriters will be reserved to work on the more difficult cases.

Document imaging also will enable loan files—which are several inches thick—to be stored electronically for quick access by workers, instead of in filing cabinets or on microfilm.

Decentralized Decision Making. Because workers in branches are in the local market, they are best able to make certain decisions. And requiring them to do so increases their professionalism.

Capital. Money is necessary to assemble a branch network and fill it with technology. Countrywide was one of the first mortgage banking firms to be publicly traded. Its shares are offered on the New York Stock Exchange. Although other mortgage institutions have issued stock, Countrywide has the longest track record and thus receives the most capital.

Subsidiaries. Subsidiary companies—most of which require little capital—expose the Countrywide name to niche opportunities within the mortgage lending business. For instance, one

Countrywide subsidiary sells mortgage-backed securities to regional stockbrokers.

A Strong Management Team. Good managers coordinate the efforts of the company. And having the founders of the firm still working in it daily keeps everyone sharp.

At the end of the most recent quarter, Countrywide led its nearest national competitor by 30 percent in originations, and its market share was 4 percent and growing. Less than three years ago, Countrywide was ranked tenth in the nation and had just 1 percent of the market.

NICHOLAS DIRECT FINDS "GOLDEN MAILBOX"

My business background started with Peterson's House of Fudge, a candy and ice cream manufacturing and retail firm I purchased at the age of 21. A unique marketing touch—a 75-foot-long, moving billboard showing a big chef stirring a bowl—helped get customers off the highway and into my store.

In all, I've owned more than 20 businesses. And it was my frustration with the process of incorporating that led me to start my most successful endeavor. The incorporation form in Delaware, where I lived at that time, was a simple one-page document. But whenever I wanted to start a business, I had to hire an attorney, who charged several hundred dollars just to have a secretary fill out and mail this form.

Upset at this expense, I wrote my own handbook on how to incorporate by yourself. I knew I would have used one, had something like it been available when I was forming my companies. Then I sent the manuscript to various publishers. Books of forms were not in fashion then, and I was turned down by numerous companies. Still believing in my book, I typeset it with the title *How To Form Your Own Corporation Without a Lawyer for Under $75*—and took out a small ad in *The Wall Street Journal's* eastern edition.

The exciting thing about direct mail is that you quickly find out, through sales, what customers think of your product and marketing. My first ad cost $90, and the books were at the printer when it ran. If that ad paid off, I would have the money to pay the printer, ship books and buy another ad—maybe even a larger one. Little capital was required—and the sky was the limit!

My first ad brought in $360 in orders. Within a few months, I was taking out full-page ads in national publications such as *Business Week* and *TIME*. I was spending $50,000 a month on advertising—and running the entire business out of a corner of my recreation room. Today more than 900,000 copies of *How To Form Your Own Corporation Without a Lawyer for Under $75* are in print. As far as I know, it's the best-selling business book ever marketed by direct mail. From the sale of that first book in March 1973, my venture grew into a small business-publishing firm with $10 million in annual sales. In 1991 I sold my company, Enterprise Publishing, to Dearborn Financial Publishing, Inc.

One of the interesting things I've learned in business is how to "fail forward." Many things can turn against an entrepreneur, and even in the best of times he or she already is trying to manage half a dozen concerns at once. For instance, when a new highway took much of the traffic from the road where my fudge billboard was, it was almost impossible to keep profits up to the levels I wanted, and so I sold the business.

Similarly, a direct mail writer soon finds that only a handful of attempts really do well. Of the 50 full-page ads I wrote for my first book, 15 to 20 of them were profitable. Yet one of them—"The Ultimate Tax Shelter"—has sold over 200,000 copies. Making the most of both our successes and our failures keeps small business owners moving ahead.

Today I work as a mail order consultant. I'm happy to see that many other small publishers, and other types of companies, are profitably using direct mail to sell to specialized audiences. I enjoy helping them increase those profits.

PLANNING HELPS AVOID MISTAKES

A printing firm can get excited thinking about the expensive four-color print jobs it could do if it had a larger press. Similarly, an insurance brokerage might forecast additional sales if it offered more financial products.

But implementation is not always easy. Managers need to consider if their employees have the expertise to handle new tasks. And can the company also afford to pay for equipment, training and marketing before a new venture shows a return? It often helps to talk ideas through with your accountant or another outside business adviser who can help spot the risks as well as identify business opportunities.

Mistakes can be avoided when businesses expand under the discipline of a plan and a budget. Below are four suggested steps to follow:

1. Write out how you envision the opportunity, assessing both your company's strengths and weaknesses in terms of what needs to be done. Also list what competition is present, as well as any problems you foresee.
2. Map out all the actions that must be taken. Be specific; then decide who in your company will be responsible for taking those steps, and what resources they need.
3. Set up a timetable and a budget. Make sure that workers involved in this project can spare the time. Also set aside funds to cover the new expenses.
4. Choose points at which you will reassess before devoting any more resources to the project. Review what you've learned up to then to see if your assumptions about both the venture's potential and the costs for reaching your goal are realistic.

   If you see that your estimates of cost and time involved are incorrect, then the entire project should be reevaluated. Be cautious about putting money into equipment, leases, employees or a marketing campaign until you have received promising results.

Managers of young businesses who feel pressure to generate earnings often will think first of raising prices. However, that can lead to a drop in sales. Entrepreneurs shouldn't be afraid to increase prices to reflect inflation, but they also should recognize that some customers could decide to make purchases elsewhere.

It's best to raise prices when things are going well and you can afford to risk losing some volume. But when business is not going well, often the problem is in cash flow timing, not profit margins.

If bills from suppliers are due before enough merchandise is sold to pay them, a business will feel squeezed. Small firms should always try to negotiate terms with their suppliers that correspond to their ability to make the payments.

Many suppliers have the flexibility to provide specialized terms. If a company offers to increase its order or to use only that supplier, often a longer billing period can be negotiated.

By giving better terms, the supplier knows it is gaining a long-term customer relationship. But before entering into such a deal, it's also smart to have an agreement about how much the supplier can increase prices in the future.

INCREASING VARIABLE EXPENSES

After all, a company with high overhead must work hard to bring in enough business. It then might make deals it would rather not have just to build volume.

On the other hand, a firm with lower fixed costs is in the enviable position of not ever needing a deal but always wanting one. To accomplish this, it helps to have both low monthly expenses and a strong marketing presence. Without having lots of prospects, it becomes difficult to turn down any business.

One way to judge your firm's potential for profits is to look at its ratio of fixed to variable expenses. Large fixed expenses increase the amount of sales necessary to break even.

Fixed expenses are bills that stay the same whether or not the company makes any sales. Salaries, rents and other predetermined costs are examples of fixed expenses.

Variable costs tend to increase as sales rise. Bills for raw materials and advertising are examples of variable expenses. To handle your costs of doing business, it usually makes sense to link expenses to sales whenever possible.

Some companies aggressively seek to make more costs variable. For instance, tying employee compensation to sales ensures that personnel costs won't be out of line. Although you might think your employees won't go for anything but being paid a salary, you could be wrong.

Even if you don't change your payroll practices, just recognizing the importance of reducing fixed costs can change a business. A desire for fancy offices might give way to humbler quarters and a larger advertising budget. Doing so can help the business in several ways.

When an entrepreneur is focusing on his or her company's daily operations, it can be difficult to keep track of the firm's overall financial situation. For that reason, certain financial guidelines can serve as goals and red flags to point out the direction of important trends concerning your corporate health. Chapters 13, 14 and 15 contain valuable information on the financial issues that will determine your profitability and your success.

SELF-TEST QUESTIONS

Multiple Choice

1. Countrywide has done all of the following except
   a. work nontraditionally.
   b. take on excessive risk.
   c. use new technology.
   d. raise capital for growth.

2. They also reduced the cost of marketing by all means except
   a. relying completely on salespeople.
   b. advertising.
   c. mailings.
   d. conventions and special events.

3. To "fail forward" means
   a. to adopt a positive attitude if you ever make a mistake.
   b. to use your failures to better see what works, and then focus more effort there.
   c. it's time to get out of that venture.
   d. None of the above

4. When you get an idea for expanding your business,
   a. do it if it feels good.
   b. ask your banker's advice.
   c. lay out a plan of action to see if success seems reasonable.
   d. think about it on the weekends.

5. Reducing your overhead means
   a. you'll then need less business to break even.
   b. you'll have more freedom to make decisions.
   c. expenses and revenue should better match.
   d. All of the above

True or False

6. Companies that lead an industry never have problems.

   True ☐ False ☐

7. Misguided policies can affect a company's performance for years after they've been discontinued.

   True ☐ False ☐

8. Decentralizing decision-making won't work for a big company.

   True ☐ False ☐

9. A small firm can't afford to market itself uniquely.

   True ☐ False ☐

10. Ideas for new businesses are all around us.

    True ☐ False ☐

11. If your company is profitable, cash flow will never be a problem.

    True ☐ False ☐

12. Financial ratios can quickly show the health of a business.

    True ☐ False ☐

13. Entrepreneurs often get their business and personal finances intertwined.

    True ☐ False ☐

Answers

1.b, 2.a, 3.b, 4.c, 5.d, 6.F, 7.T, 8.F, 9.F, 10.T, 11.F, 12.T, 13.T

CHAPTER 6

Making the Most of Technology

Change is sweeping even the most basic of industries. Most of us acknowledge this fact, but only by working with change will we realize its potential. For instance, adopting new technologies from around the world to build steel "mini-mills" has helped Nucor become the country's largest *profitable* steel maker. Streamlined operating procedures are combined with new steel-making methods to produce positive cash flow. If you're also running a lean organization, in this chapter you'll find ways to control employee theft by being aware of how it occurs.

We'll go from steel mills to cutting-edge "artificial intelligence" computer technology, and observe how defining a niche has helped CYBERTEK-COGENSYS establish itself as a leader. New approaches also have benefitted Ace Mailing, whose founder started from a background in social work. By adding services to help meet customer needs, the firm has grown. Yet no amount of technology or innovation can help if workers are demoralized, so we'll consider some techniques to keep your people excited and working as a team.

BASIC CHANGES

Whereas U.S. Steel and Bethlehem Steel require three to four man-hours of work per ton of steel produced, Nucor Corporation is doing so with just 0.8 man-hour per ton. Based in Charlotte, North Carolina, Nucor is the sixth-largest steel maker in America, having produced 4.3 million tons last year.

Not only is it one of the largest, but Nucor is also the only profitable large steel maker in the U.S., says chairman and CEO Ken Iverson. "We've had no losses since 1965," he adds. That was three years before Nucor built its first steel mill. It was losing $400,000 annually then and had defaulted on two loans. The president resigned—and since Iverson headed the only division making money, he became Nucor's new president.

At that time, Nucor was concentrating on steel fabricating. Because the cost of steel was half of their expense, management decided to build their own steel mills. To be competitive, Nucor relied on untested technology and designed mills costing hundreds of millions of dollars even as they built them. And they've been successful. Iverson points out that Nucor stock prices have gone up 7,000 percent over the last 20 years, and dividends also have increased every one of those years.

Just 21 people are in the corporate offices. "We push responsibility down to lower levels," Iverson says. "Most day-to-day decisions are made by the divisions." Marketing usually is handled by each mill or steel fabrication plant, rather than by corporate headquarters. In that way, the sales force can stay close to customers. "Steel is usually sold within 400 to 500 miles of a mill," Iverson explains.

Another unusual quality is that many of Nucor's workers start with no previous experience. Nucor typically builds mills in farming areas of states such as South Carolina, Texas, Arkansas and Indiana. It trains local residents to work in the mills and saves money, because these are nonunion areas. However, Iverson is aware of his impact as the major employer in many regions. "We have not laid off a single employee for more than 20 years," he says. "We are almost always the largest employer in the region, so we have a social responsibility." Worker hours might get cut back, "but everybody still has a job. That would be difficult to do in a union environment, where there is seniority."

Nucor also provides $2,000 annually for each employee's child who is attending college. "We have 470 children of employees in 130 learning institutions," he says. "I don't know why more companies don't do it."

One of Nucor's biggest successes has come from using a new thin-slab process to make steel just two inches thick, as compared to the usual eight to ten inches. In addition, Nucor can produce the steel for $50 less per ton than its competitors. "In Crawfordsville, Indiana, 427 people produce one million tons a year," Iverson notes. Nucor uses scrap metal, not ore, as raw material in its steel mills. Old automobiles and other scrap is melted down and reworked.

Production incentive groups are a key for Nucor. Iverson says 25 to 35 people will work together on a specific task. A production standard is set, and they get paid extra for exceeding it. "There's no upper limit," adds Iverson. Most workers double their base pay with these incentives. He adds that the groups police themselves, by either teaching workers how to work fast or by encouraging them to leave. Iverson says his "average hourly worker earns over $40,000 annually."

People from both the central office and divisions travel around the world looking for new technologies. Often inventors from Japan, Germany and Sweden approach Nucor first, knowing they are more likely than other steel makers to try an unproven piece of machinery. A willingness to take some risks and to work hard is helping Nucor bring in good profits from the difficult steel business.

HOW TO KEEP EMPLOYEES HONEST

One concern of companies with a small ratio of administrative staff to hourly workers is the possibility of internal theft. In fact, in most firms the risk of pilferage is greater than the possibility of break-ins or shoplifting by persons outside the company. But you can reduce the chances that you will become a victim by setting up and monitoring policies that help keep workers honest.

Keeping employees from being in situations where they'll be tempted is a key. Unfortunately, such situations can occur in many places. Primary examples are the warehouse, bookkeeping and shipping.

Having one worker do part of a job and another one complete the task keeps them from manipulating accounts or inventory.

If one employee records sales but another updates customer accounts, it is less likely those amounts will be altered. At times workers have lowered customer balances and then stolen what was left after the correct invoice was paid.

Let one person approve invoices to be paid, but get someone else to write the checks. And have one person in your warehouse fill an order and then another one check it before it leaves.

Once you recognize that thievery is possible, you can avoid many incidents through preventive practices. For instance, policing workers helps keep illegal activity from starting. Set up a good inventory system, and also spot-check departing trucks for stolen items.

Make sure your invoices are paid only once. Finally, to lessen the chance that a system for stealing can be established, rotate employees working in areas where pilferage is possible.

NARROW FOCUS HELPS CYBERTEK-COGENSYS

Automation allows for more productivity by requiring fewer workers. Whether they're robots in factories or ATMs at banks, machines are helping businesses expand their operations at a lower cost than they could in the past. Today automation is taking some surprisingly large steps forward. One new technology, dubbed "artificial intelligence," is seen as a way to automate many mental tasks. Just as spreadsheets have taken the drudgery out of doing calculations and databases have made recordkeeping easier, artificial intelligence holds out the promise of revolutionizing some business tasks.

One company on the forefront of developing applications for artificial intelligence is CYBERTEK-COGENSYS in Dallas. Founded in 1986 as COGENSYS Corp. with the help of venture capital, the company has developed artificial intelligence software that allows desktop computers to emulate the human decision-making process.

Let's assume we'd like to be able to have a computer decide whether credit card applicants should be sent a card. First, thousands of previous applications will be fed into the computer, along with reasons for whether or not the applications were granted. CYBERTEK-COGENSYS' system will "learn" how the interplay of an applicant's salary level, job history, existing debts, credit report and other assets combine to make a decision. It is a complex situation in which there is no one formula or set of rules for making a decision.

On the other hand, the computer is not simply looking for a match with an existing file in order to make its decision. It actually comes to mimic the mindset of whoever is serving as the "mentor" of the project—generally the company's best underwriter or credit analyst.

"Quality of decisions, consistency and improved productivity" are reasons for the growth of artificial intelligence, says CYBERTEK-COGENSYS president and CEO Joseph Filoseta. He adds that "30 percent productivity gains are not uncommon" for artificial intelligence users. Because the computer can evaluate a file faster than a human can, more work can be accomplished with fewer people.

Usually, companies use artificial intelligence to accept typical applications, which make up the bulk of their business. No one will be turned down by the system. If the computer has doubts about an application, the reasons for not accepting it are noted and the file is forwarded to a human for the final decision.

Whenever the CYBERTEK-COGENSYS system makes a decision, it also provides a numeric rating showing how confident it is that its decision is correct. If the situation is markedly different from anything ever encountered before, its certainty will be relatively low.

Artificial intelligence software is costly, and it generally takes three to nine months to complete a sale, notes Filoseta. He adds that at first the company "tried to be all things to all people." Sales of the new technology weren't up to expectations, and in 1991 CYBERTEK was sold to COGENSYS Corporation and became CYBERTEK-COGENSYS Corporation.

Since then, CYBERTEK-COGENSYS has focused on the banking business and is emerging as a leader. Having a strong partner also makes potential customers more confident that CYBERTEK-COGENSYS will be available in the future to provide technical support.

Today, annual sales of the artificial intelligence software are about $3 million. A large part of the firm's marketing strategy is simply educating the lending community about artificial intelligence.

The company also is developing new varieties of the artificial intelligence system. Instead of teaching the software to make decisions according to the purchaser's criteria, preprogrammed modules are available for various lending and valuation situations. By defining its market and approaching it in several ways, CYBERTEK-COGENSYS is coming into its own.

ACE MAILING BECOMES "RECESSION-PROOF"

Gwen Kaplan was a social worker until government funding cutbacks caused her to be laid off. At that time, she decided to start her own company. "I didn't know a great deal about business," she recalls, "but we did a lot of market research." Kaplan spent several months in libraries and on the telephone, gathering information. "I knew I wanted a business-to-business firm. We didn't have much money and wanted something with growth potential." Eventually she settled on the mailing business and started Ace Mailing. Mail houses put out bulk mailings for companies, involving anything from surveys to product samples.

A good mailing service is quick and accurate. Often a large mailing will be broken into groups, with different parties receiving varying packages. Since every mailing is different, a lot of focus on detail is necessary. Each item must receive the right mailing label. Additionally, mailings must comply with all U.S. Postal Service regulations regarding size and weight. Mail houses can help their customers save on postage by sorting by ZIP Codes, and, in a sense, serve as a consultant to help them do effective mailings.

One of the reasons Kaplan chose the mailing business was because she "could rent a mailing machine for a few hundred dollars a month." She adds that those machines aren't leased very often now, and they cost $80,000 to buy.

Kaplan started her firm in 1976. After getting her first clients through phone and mail solicitations, she began vying for acceptance into San Francisco's Ft. Mason, which housed 55 nonprofit groups. When Ace Mailing was accepted as a supplier to the groups, "it was a dream come true."

Ft. Mason has lovely views, is close to Kaplan's home and also allowed Ace Mailing "to move into one of our major markets. It gave us a lot of credibility." Since that time, Ace Mailing has diversified its client base "to build a recession-proof business. It's easy to be the arm and leg of two or three big businesses, and then that changes and you're out," Kaplan notes.

"We never paid any attention to the competition—still don't. We're very different," she adds. "Nobody in our business came to it the way we did. It's a function of our personalities." Most owners of mailing houses are either "machine jockeys" or got into it simply as an adjunct to a printing business they already owned.

Customer service is the primary focus at Ace Mailing. "We return every phone call and respond to client needs," says Kaplan. "We don't promise anything we can't deliver." This can be easier said than done in such a detail-oriented business. "We hire very independent people," Kaplan adds. "I want people who can think for themselves, and question me and everyone else around. They should be asking, 'Are you sure that's right?' " Any foulup—whether it's not putting the proper insertions in a package or items being sent out late—can affect a mailing.

A mistake that isn't spotted can ruin a mailing. "One thing builds on another once a mistake is made," Kaplan explains. So Ace Mailing employees are known for watching for mistakes—even if they are the clients. For instance, jobs printed incorrectly—perhaps an expiration date on an offer is already outdated—are mentioned to clients.

Her 40 workers are drawn from a diverse neighborhood, and Kaplan is pleased that her business reflects many ethnic groups. "Because of my social work background, I can teach somebody anything," Kaplan says. "But I can't teach a work ethic. We look for people who are motivated," and for that reason often investigate community job programs when looking for new employees.

Kaplan has received a number of honors. She has been named California Small Business Advocate of the Year, and has received the San Francisco Chamber of Commerce's "Excellence in Business" award. Ace Mailing now is a leader in the Bay area. "The toughest thing for a small business is getting your name known," Kaplan says. She adds that her awards were unsought but have served to help publicize the firm. Kaplan works with a multitude of industries, and handles projects ranging from 500,000-unit mailings to fulfilling orders gained through television and radio advertising.

To stay up on the business, she teaches a ten-session course in direct marketing at the University of California at Berkeley. Besides teaching classes, Kaplan also is a local commissioner. She feels a need to be responsible to her community. Giving something back is important, she notes.

Today she is seeking growth for her company: "Not just growing to grow, but growth in the most profitable way." One means has been setting up different departments to serve client needs. Each one is almost a new business. For example, a client might ask, "Can you print this for me?" and Kaplan will respond, "Yes." She then would have to find out about printing. But now she can design a mailer, print it and maintain a client's mailing list, as well as send out the job. Today Kaplan's firm designs a third of its mailings and prints half of them. In terms of profitability, Kaplan says, "We try to make every department stand on its own."

MORALE BUILDERS

Most workers enjoy feeling as if they are contributing to a team effort. Managers use specific techniques to build that spirit and to keep employees excited. There are many ways you can increase the enthusiasm of your work force.

Have a party on a worker's first day. Generally, parties are given for associates who are leaving; but why not show the same spirit when someone comes on board?

Even if you don't have a party, make sure that you don't isolate employees on their first day. Too often a supervisor won't take the time to give a new worker something specific to accomplish from the time he or she starts.

Make goals important. Your business probably won't grow and become more profitable unless your workers increase their efficiency.

Every year, ask employees to list their major job functions. Have your workers then write down specific goals as to how much work they will do and what its quality will be.

For instance, a receptionist's goal might be to always answer calls before the third ring and to have a cheerful voice.

Don't be content with people saying they'll work hard; to build a team, everyone must do what is expected of them. That means you need to have specific, measurable goals.

If each team member in a manufacturing plant can rely on the others to do their job, they'll move together toward the larger goal of more output and better quality.

Measure both team and individual efforts. Keep a tally in a visible place showing how teams are advancing toward their goal; it will help build their excitement.

On some jobs you might even monitor production hourly. Compare current accomplishments to what a worker or team was doing last quarter and last year.

Reward on a team basis. If the team doesn't reach its goal, then no one should receive an incentive. In this way, you'll make all your workers team players.

You can take this idea a step further by rewarding only when companywide goals are met. In this way, your clerical, production and marketing departments will start working together.

Establish the right environment. Some managers have been able to double their output in just a few weeks by establishing these guidelines. But the commitment starts at the top. If managers are not bringing excitement, new ideas and a "can-do" attitude to the job, no one else will pick up the slack.

You might also need to provide training to ensure that your workers have the necessary skills to reach their goals. But if you start with a set of measurable tasks for each worker, it should be easy to tell whether they can accomplish their work.

Empower your workers. Given the proper environment, you'll find that individuals and teams are soon setting higher goals for themselves than the company would normally expect. In return, many employees will want to have a say in how they work.

For example, when a team is rushing to finish a project, let them decide if they should work into the evening, come in on Saturday or hire temporary help. Or if your workers say that offering flex-time would improve the productivity of some employees, then seriously consider making that a company policy.

Bring some fun to the job. Some managers give their workers mirrors to keep at their desks. If they are talking on the phone with a tough customer, the manager will remind them to "take out your mirror." Just looking at yourself usually is enough to make you smile. And when we smile, the person on the other end of the line can sense it.

When markets are competitive and margins are tight, finding ways to increase employee efficiency through smarter management is a key to profitability.

SELF-TEST QUESTIONS

Multiple Choice

1. Which of the following are important to Nucor's success?
   a. Nonunion workers
   b. New technology
   c. Production incentives
   d. All of the above

2. Companies most commonly face the risk of
   a. employee stealing.
   b. break-ins.
   c. shoplifting.
   d. fires.

3. Pilferage most commonly occurs
   a. in the warehouse.
   b. in bookkeeping.
   c. in shipping.
   d. All of the above

4. Ace Mailing has found it's important to
   a. have a background like others in the business.
   b. give back to the community.
   c. make sure workers follow company policies.

5. Good service includes the following:
   a. Returning all telephone calls
   b. Delivering on your promises
   c. Giving attention to detail
   d. All of the above

True or False

6. America's large steel companies are all losing money.
   True ☐ False ☐

7. Nucor has found that divisions can be responsible for most daily decisions.
   True ☐ False ☐

8. Splitting tasks into parts can help stop employee pilferage.
   True ☐ False ☐

9. Automation is making American business more productive.
   True ☐ False ☐

10. A good way to start a business is by leasing equipment.
    True ☐ False ☐

11. Relying on a couple of big clients is a good strategy.
    True ☐ False ☐

12. A business can grow by adding related services that meet customer needs.

    True ☐ False ☐

Answers
1.d, 2.a, 3.d, 4.b, 5.d, 6.F, 7.T, 8.T, 9.T, 10.T, 11.F, 12.T

CHAPTER 7

What the Future Holds

Planning for the future involves spotting trends and being nimble enough to align your company with them. In this chapter, we'll look at what small business owners should know about tomorrow's world. New technologies and customer needs will cause some industries to grow while others shrink. In addition, existing businesses will change due to new marketing methods, shifts in government policy and changing lifestyle patterns.

ON TARGET

Small companies are helping the U.S. economy. According to a study by Cognetics Inc., firms with fewer than 100 employees produced a net 5.86 million jobs between 1987 and 1992. Average or better wages were paid for 85 percent of those positions. In contrast, large companies lost a net 2.32 million jobs during that period—96 percent of which paid high salaries. Jobs were added in all types of businesses, the study added.

Almost anyone wanting to start a company will be affected by the stunning changes happening in our world. Just to give you an idea of how different the world will soon be, here are some predictions made by futurist Edith Weiner concerning the challenges which tomorrow's businesses will encounter.

- The mapping of the human genome and subsequent alterations of genetic material will affect the pension and life insurance industries. Agricultural genetics will change farming. New opportunities in marketing those doctored food products also will be created.
- The changing nature of households as the nation ages will affect construction, marketing and consumer goods. Later in this section, implications of the "graying of America" are discussed fully.
- As medical costs rise faster than inflation, more money from the government, insurance companies and the elderly will be needed. Among other things, expect to see a drop in savings rates and less consumer spending.
- Expanding gray and underground economies will affect the profits of normal businesses. Today the U.S. underground economy is estimated to be from 15 percent to 30 percent of the gross domestic product.
- Increasing countertrade within and between countries, including barter deals, will challenge traditional tax and accounting systems.
- Desktop publishing is making it possible to create professional-quality brochures, newsletters, ads and other communications with an investment of under $2,000.
- Rural, suburban and urban populations and environments are being melded, changing lifestyles and values. Urban problems are creeping into the suburbs, wealthy city dwellers are migrating to rural areas and many rural residents are leaving their home towns to look for work.
- Virtual-reality technology lets computer users interact with a simulated environment, such as a building that is being designed for construction.
- Ownership of intellectual property is more crucial—and murkier—as workers and technologies flow between companies and across geographic borders.

As the world continues to change rapidly, the structure and culture of companies also is changing. Owners of small companies need to recognize ways to build a firm that will attract the best talent. What we are seeing is more than just the coming and going of managerial fads. It used to be that the breadwinner needed a stable career, with predictable advancement and retirement at the end. Now working couples are finding that issues such as day care and flex-time are high on the list of job necessities.

Although there are plenty of potential employees, the number of those who are sufficiently skilled to handle rapidly-changing technical disciplines, whether in manufacturing or service businesses, is dwindling. Companies will be competing for the best workers, and pay often is not the deciding factor it once was. Allowing people to keep their lifestyle intact by offering a flexible culture and different benefits is important to many workers.

New management skills will be necessary to help employees adjust to the new workplace. Robots are already being run by humans, and computers are printing out daily tasks. Helping workers cope with these changes will soon be an important skill.

Companies are departing from traditional ways of running a business, since they no longer can find adequate numbers of workers who want a straight 9-to-5 job. Flex-time schedules, job sharing and working from home offices are already coming into practice. In fact, some startups have done well by hiring working mothers. By making sure day-care facilities are nearby and having a flexible attitude toward giving time off due to family needs, they are able to attract plenty of motivated women who have helped them to prosper.

The erosion of middle management means that companies will require workers to make more decisions. In order to both compete and attract quality workers, small businesses will need to be on the forefront of these changes.

HOT BUSINESS OPPORTUNITIES

Where there is a problem, there is also a business opportunity. Changing needs of companies means entrepreneurs can help supply solutions. For instance, corporate training budgets are growing as the skill levels of people coming out of schools is declining. Training also is ongoing in many businesses today, rather than just an entry-level exercise. Mature workers need to refine their skills and discover the latest industry trends.

It's also possible to mold your business to fit the future. Listed below are government predictions of the fastest-growing occupations from 1990 to 2005. Opportunities for businesses in these fields will rise as follows:

- Home health aides—92 percent growth from 1990 to 2005
- Systems analysts and computer scientists—79 percent
- Personal and home care aides—77 percent
- Medical assistants—74 percent
- Human services workers—71 percent
- Radiologic technologists/technicians—70 percent
- Medical secretaries—68 percent
- Psychologists—64 percent
- Travel agents—62 percent
- Corrections officers—61 percent
- Flight attendants—59 percent
- Computer programmers—56 percent
- Management analysts—52 percent
- Child-care workers—49 percent

You can also build a company of your own by supplying to these growth businesses. For example, from 1989 to the end of the century, the number of passengers traveling on U.S. airlines is expected to more than quadruple, to 2 billion persons. Although you probably don't want to start an airline, it is possible to find a way to support that industry.

Most new jobs being created are in the service sector, which includes financial services, transportation, communications, wholesale and retail trade, health care, education and business services. One estimate anticipates four out of five new jobs being in the service sector by the year 2000.

IMPORTANCE OF TECHNOLOGY

New technologies are driving the growth of many businesses, ranging from entertainment, fuels and marketing to biotechnology, medicine and communications. Whenever new technologies become available, there's an opportunity to remake a business. Here's a look at a few areas that technology will change.

Health care will be more in demand due to both new technology and the aging of our population. Cost control and availability also are becoming more important issues.

Hospitality and recreation offer opportunities to a nation that takes its diversions seriously.

Personal services includes many areas in which an entrepreneur can start small. Delivering food from restaurants, walking pets and shopping are examples of valued personal services. And new services are emerging, such as computer training.

Entertainment will change as technology offers new products, such as high-definition television.

Environmental concerns provide opportunities for traditional businesses to appeal to the ecologically-conscious by changing methods or materials. In addition, there are many ways to start a company that helps clean up the environment: working with recycling, pollution control and renewable energy are just a few examples.

Yet technology also provides challenges. Today's communications explosion—including fax, tv, radio and satellite disks—means that it will be hard to get the attention of your potential customers.

Be aware of trends that can help you build a business. For instance, some observers note that Asians are growing in both number and wealth and will be a potent consumer force in the future. Other businesses are fashioning jobs for groups known to be looking for work, including senior citizens and the disabled.

Awareness of the needs of disabled workers and customers is the intent of the Americans with Disabilities Act (ADA). Ever since July 26, 1992, employers with 25 or more workers have been subject to the requirements of the ADA. On July 26, 1994, firms with at least 15 employees also will be covered by the law.

ADA is a far-reaching statute that gives people the right to sue companies for back pay, reinstatement, seniority, front pay, attorney's fees, and both compensatory and punitive damages. Small businesses are affected mainly by provisions designed to protect persons with disabilities against employment discrimination and to remove physical barriers in workplaces and businesses open to the public.

Covered by the law are such physiological disorders as blindness or paralysis and mental or psychological disabilities, including retardation, mental illness and learning disabilities.

Companies must avoid discrimination against someone who is qualified and can perform a job as well as against a worker or applicant who has a past history of disabilities—whether back problems or tuberculosis. Employers are also required to make "reasonable accommodation" to allow people with disabilities to perform their jobs.

The Job Accommodation Network (JAN) recently studied 10,000 workers with disabilities and found that for 31 percent of them, the special training or equipment they needed to accomplish their jobs cost the employer nothing. JAN provides free phone consultations with businesses about the costs of hiring or retraining disabled persons at 1-800-526-7234.

However, 46 percent of those who filed ADA cases in 1992 claimed they lost their job because of a disability, whereas only 15 percent cite hiring discrimination, says Milt Wright, president of Milt Wright & Associates, Inc., in Chatsworth, California. Back injuries are the main complaint mentioned by ADA claim filers, Wright adds.

To avoid ADA problems, Wright recommends that companies do three things:

1. Talk to injured workers before they get an attorney involved.
2. Provide "reasonable accommodations" for people with disabilities. Installing a pulley can help someone lift boxes, for instance. Or a worker can be allowed to sit rather than having to stand.
3. Be objective when hiring. Know what abilities a person must have to do the job.

Wright adds that under the law, "undue hardship" can't be placed on companies to accommodate worker needs. Being willing to restructure jobs or work schedules, making sure facilities are accessible to an individual with a disability, and modifying equipment used on the job are common accommodation strategies.

People who are alcoholic are not protected by the law. While you cannot discriminate against individuals for being alcoholic, you can hold them to the same work standards as other employees and discipline them if those work standards are not met.

CHANGES REQUIRED IN FACILITIES

To provide access to workplaces and public buildings, the U.S. Architectural and Transportation Barriers Compliance Board has published very specific guidelines for new construction, additions and alterations to existing buildings. Construction standards cover everything from parking spaces to elevators, hallways to entrances and restrooms to countertops.

Businesses that are affected by these rules include restaurants, medical care facilities, public businesses, motels and retail stores. For a copy of the accessibility guidelines, contact the U.S. Architectural and Transportation Barriers Compliance Board at 202-272-5434.

MISSION STATEMENTS

When working with new technologies and marketing tools as well as a diverse work force, communicating a vision of your company is more important than ever. In a few minutes, a sour receptionist or unresponsive customer service representative can damage a customer relationship that was built through years of marketing efforts by your company. You can't always be there to remind your workers about the importance of giving attention to what they're doing. But managers who, along with their staff, have corporate mission statements tend to develop a more energized team. Some firms are writing mission statements and then giving them to workers on laminated cards that fit into wallets or purses.

Having mission statements commits everyone to the company's values. For instance, one section of your statement might be "We will answer every customer inquiry within 24 hours." Workers then feel a responsibility to uphold your firm's standards. Although you should start with a company mission statement, individual groups within your firm will also want to have their own. Once the idea catches on, each worker can have a personal action plan to help contribute to the company's goals. By participating in this process, each employee feels as though he or she is a part of the team's direction and responsible for its success.

How do you communicate this mission? Rather than preaching, tell stories showing the values at work. Describe how one of your employees went out of his or her way to help a customer, and read the "thank you" letter the customer wrote. Tying bonuses to meeting team goals helps get people working together. Letting workers know how they stand against one another and their own past performance also serves as incentive in some positions.

Reviewing staff performance by having department heads meet with each worker every quarter keeps the energy alive. By making your culture real, you will inspire workers to reach for new heights. To keep the team spirit alive, managers must stay enthusiastic. Spot problems quickly, but get people who are responsible for those areas to come up with solutions. You might be surprised at the resources your workers show you.

GRAYING OF AMERICA

Other changes involve America's aging population. During the Baby Boom—the 19 years from 1946 to 1964—76 million children were born. In the preceding 19 years, just 49 million came into the world, and in the 19 years after, another 66 million were born. As this group grows older, they have more political and consumer power. And they redefine the needed products and services, as well as the business opportunities in this country. For every retired person at the end of World War II, there were 32 workers. Now that ratio has shrunk to three to one, and government spending on the elderly is equal to the defense budget.

Because of their longevity, health and relative wealth, senior citizens now live differently from previous generations. Cruises, theme parks and living communities are springing up just for older people. Schools and tours are marketing to their needs. Some observers believe that the pattern of life may be changing from school, work and then retirement to cycles of work, education and play.

What is crucial for businesses to see is that within this large trend there are many subgroups. Just to stay active and have more funds, many people over 65 are choosing to keep working at least part-time. Others are full-time retirees. Obviously, these groups have different needs and lifestyles. If you are marketing recreation for the elderly, you'll be most effective if you can target your offering to those who are dedicated to leisure.

As people grow older, they naturally become more feeble. Health-related businesses thus are expected to grow quickly in the coming years. Additionally, the children of these elderly often have both jobs and children of their own. Services to help them cope with all the details in their lives—on the job, around the house, with their children and with their parents—also will be in demand. As noted earlier, companies that have programs to help their employees deal with these problems will be able to attract some of the best workers.

People 50 and over today own more than three-quarters of all financial assets and account for 40 percent of all consumer demand. This consolidation will continue, and it is a trend many businesses should include in their planning. Purchases made by the elderly emphasize quality; they tend to be savvy buyers who are less swayed by fads. Products need to be designed and tested specifically with older people in mind. And marketing messages need to be appealing to mature consumers, not insulting.

Don't assume anything. Restaurant managers should know, for instance, that an 80-year-old has just a little over a third the number of taste buds that a 30-year-old has. Test everything to ensure that what you think an older person will like is actually what he or she wants.

OTHER AGE GROUPS

If you don't see a way to align yourself with the aging of America, that's fine. A small business doesn't need a huge market to be successful. Although it's good to be aware of large trends in the economy, you might find less competition and more opportunity with another market niche. For instance, the teenage population will grow by 13 percent by the year 2000. And it should be a group of young people unlike any ever seen, for they've grown up with divorces, working mothers, computers, videos, school violence—a whole host of social changes and consumer paraphernalia that no other generation has encountered. Today's preteens watch an average of 24 hours of television each week, including 520 commercials. Some two-income parents want their children to "have everything," and thus will spend on designer clothes and other items that previously would have been considered luxuries.

MARKETING TOOLS

How often have you gone to purchase a product or service for either yourself or your business, and didn't buy because you couldn't find exactly what you wanted? Perhaps you thought you knew the best place to look, but what you found was a little too expensive, not sturdy enough or had a weak warranty. Is it possible to keep your customers from having similar experiences when they look at what you offer? With the proliferation of specialty stores and catalogs today, many buyers can find exactly what they want. You'll never be able to stock enough inventory to meet every prospect's desires. But you can turn many fence-sitters into buyers with "good-better-best" offers.

If one product or service is a staple for your firm, develop two other similar products to attract customers who aren't satisfied with your primary offering. A key to making this work is that each of the three offers must provide good value.

For instance, a store selling eyeglasses might respond to customer inquiries by making contact lenses available. But if they are not priced competitively, the store hasn't really expanded. It is still an eyeglass retailer, which sells a few contact lenses to people who aren't comparison shoppers. However, if you target three similar offers to different market segments, then you can grow.

A consultant can use this strategy by offering clients different levels of involvement. If his primary product is executive seminars, he can sell audiotapes from those conferences to people who can't afford to attend.

Or he can offer private consulting sessions for firms wanting more in-depth attention. Each offer fits a specific market need, and none should be priced inappropriately unless you want to discourage that business.

Finally, be sure to analyze the results of your good-better-best offers. They provide a growing company with a relatively risk-free means of trying out new products and new target markets. By looking at your sales figures, you might discover unmet needs you didn't know about.

SELF-TEST QUESTIONS

Multiple Choice

1. Firms with fewer than 100 employees
   a. added almost six million net jobs from 1987 to 1992.
   b. paid at least average wages for 85 percent of these jobs.
   c. created more jobs than did the Fortune 500 companies.
   d. All of the above

2. Aging baby boomers will affect
   a. government policies.
   b. consumer products and services.
   c. investment products.
   d. All of the above

3. Opportunities for the future will be found in
   a. corporate training.
   b. health care.
   c. computer technology.
   d. All of the above

4. Mission statements
   a. get employees involved with a company's vision.
   b. give workers leeway to make decisions.
   c. can be printed and carried at all times.
   d. All of the above

5. Today's senior citizens can find their own
   a. living communities.
   b. theme parks.
   c. cruises.
   d. All of the above

True or False

6. Skilled technical workers will be in short supply in the future.
   True ☐ False ☐

7. Tomorrow's managers will need to help workers cope with a changing world and workplace.
   True ☐ False ☐

8. The erosion of middle management means some workers will make more decisions.
   True ☐ False ☐

9. Manufacturing firms will add the most jobs in the future.
   True ☐ False ☐

10. In 1994, companies with 15 or more workers will have to comply with the Americans with Disabilities Act.

    True ☐ False ☐

11. Most disability discrimination suits are filed by workers who have been denied a job.

    True ☐ False ☐

12. Stories help communicate a company's culture.

    True ☐ False ☐

Answers

1.c, 2.d, 3.d, 4.d, 5.d, 6.T, 7.T, 8.T, 9.F, 10.T, 11.F, 12.T

CHAPTER 8

Eleven Factors To Be Considered in Selecting a Business

A review of a substantial number of books on starting a business reveals a curious omission. Very few identify the characteristics that make one business attractive and another business one to avoid. This section faces the problem squarely and lists the 11 most important factors to consider in selecting the business in which you should be involved.

No business can score perfectly in each of these factors, or everyone would select the same business. Nor should each business receive the same score from each person, as some factors may be much more important to one person than to another.

For example, a young, ambitious person may prefer a very competitive industry, provided it has strong growth potential and high profitability. A person approaching retirement, on the other hand, may prefer a business that has little competition, even though the growth prospects are modest and the profitability only average.

The factors that should be considered in any business prospect are:

- Is it seasonal?
- How much is the business affected by the national economy?

- How regulated is it?
- Is it heavily dependent on elements of uncertain supply or cost?
- Is the business expanding?
- How profitable is it?
- Are major changes taking place in the basic factors that influence the success of the business?
- Can it benefit from technological changes taking place?
- Is it insulated from competition to a reasonable degree?
- Does the business appeal to you personally?
- Is the business easy to enter?

The significance of each of these factors is covered below.

1. IS IT SEASONAL?

Most businesses have some seasonal pattern to their sales and profits. If the seasonal effect is extreme, it forces management to make major adjustments to offset the problem. A common technique is to have more than one business, each with different seasonal patterns. The manufacturer of storm windows and doors may add a line of awnings to offer during the summer months. The business specializing in heating products may also handle air-conditioning equipment.

A second adjustment that the business owner can make is to supplement a small permanent staff with temporary employees during peak seasons.

A third adjustment would be to produce evenly throughout the year and build substantial inventories during the peak months.

The above adjustments and others permit the owner to operate on a reasonably efficient basis. A higher degree of business expertise is required, however, and there is more risk involved in certain adjustments (such as building inventories). Therefore, a strong seasonal pattern must be considered a negative factor. Yet for certain individuals, the disadvantage might be negligible. The semiretired person who likes to spend winters vacationing in Florida might find a Dairy Queen stand in a northern state to be an excellent business. When volume declines during the cold months, the owner could close up shop and head south. A person with school-age children might also benefit from such a business, while providing employment for the children during summer vacations.

2. IS THE BUSINESS GREATLY AFFECTED BY THE ECONOMY?

With very few exceptions, most businesses are negatively affected by a downturn in the economy. Low-priced consumer necessities, however, seem to be the least affected. Some "trading down" may occur, with the high-priced brand of a particular product losing some share of the market to the lower-priced brand. There may even be substitutions among related products, such as more cereal for breakfast and less bacon and fewer eggs. Generally speaking, consumer nondurable necessities are stable during a downturn in the economy.

As items become more postponable, the economic cycle becomes a factor. Consumers who want to replace their automobiles may be able to postpone the purchase for a year or more. As a result, an automobile company may find itself operating at full capacity during a good year and 60 percent during a bad one. If the company needs to operate at 80 percent to break even, a substantial profit is made in one year and an equally substantial loss occurs in the other year. Failure to understand how a business is affected by the economy has been a major cause of troubles, if not of failures.

There are methods of softening the impact of economic downturns. The techniques to offset seasonal factors are applicable countermeasures with some modifications. An ideal solution in an expanding industry would be to time your expansion so that new facilities and personnel are added as the economy begins to recover. Another method of maintaining equilibrium is to plan your business so that it can operate efficiently and profitably at the bottom of the business cycle. In this way, you would add temporary expansion facilities to capitalize on surging demand when the economy turns upward. Or, if yours is a manufacturing business, buy your ingredients or finished products from other suppliers and resell them as your own.

3. HOW REGULATED IS THE INDUSTRY?

A learned judge once said that the power to tax is the power to destroy. If he were alive today, he might add that the power to regulate is also the power to destroy. Unfortunately, our unaware citizenry has allowed the noose of regulation to continually tighten around the neck of the free-enterprise system. Vote-hungry politicians, urged on by self-appointed consumer "protectionists" and some organized labor, may succeed in legislating our economy to a complete standstill.

In spite of the nation's pressing need to develop greater self-sufficiency in energy supplies, development of major new sources of supply have been delayed or, in the case of nuclear plants, forced to operate at uneconomical levels. In the case of the drug industry, the regulators have slowed down the flow of new drug products. While this has protected consumers from unanticipated negative side effects of new products, zealous overregulation has also "protected" consumers from drugs that might improve their health or even save lives.

Regulated industries are very vulnerable during inflationary times. One of the most impressive growth industries of this century, the electric utility industry, was brought to near-chaotic condition during periods of uncontrolled inflation. Essentially, the cost structure of the electric utility industry is dependent on the cost of the plant, the interest costs incurred to finance that plant and the cost of fuels that are converted into electricity. When these factors increased rapidly in price, the electric utilities were faced with the need to increase their own prices substantially.

Regulators could not adapt to the drastic changes in the electric company's circumstances. They knew they were responsible for preventing utilities from taking advantage of consumers with unjustified rate increases. But apparently most regulators were unaware that they were also responsible for keeping the industry in existence. Consequently, the industry was not permitted to earn a sufficiently high return to stay healthy in an inflationary environment. Accounting methods were permitted to change so that reported earnings appeared to be higher. The utilities also borrowed more money to make up for the shortfall in earnings. Rate increases were granted during this period, but they were always too little and too late to keep the industry healthy. As a result of the regulatory problem, the investment value of the electric-utility industry plunged during the period of spiraling inflation.

The electric-utility industry has been used to illustrate misguided regulation because the case is so clear and readily documented. Yet all areas of the economy are retarded by unenlightened regulation of one type or another, either directly or indirectly. Before going into any business, particular attention should be given to the various governmental regulations affecting the enterprise. Highest marks should go to the business with least regulation. You ought to attempt to avoid completely those businesses that are in the early stages of regulation. In such cases, you get caught in a game where the rules have yet to be made, keep changing, and are often retroactive.

The following is a list of the most highly regulated industries in the country today:

- Communications (including radio and television broadcasting)
- Drug manufacturing
- Cosmetics (anything that is put into or on the body)
- Food manufacturing
- Securities
- Insurance
- Alcoholic beverages

4. IS THE BUSINESS HEAVILY DEPENDENT ON ELEMENTS OF UNCERTAIN SUPPLY OR COST?

A regulated economy is likely to be one of shortages. In a free-enterprise economy, the price of a product approaching short supply is likely to increase in price, reducing the demand and encouraging producers to increase the supply. In a regulated economy, consumers are protected from the price increase, and suppliers are discouraged from increasing supply. This results in shortages that will not be alleviated. The price is likely to increase after the shortage forces a crisis, so consumer protection is largely a myth.

If a business is heavily dependent upon a raw material of which there will be an eventual shortage, its future is in grave jeopardy. Many smaller businesses have been unable to obtain sufficient oil or natural gas for fuel or raw materials in order to operate. This may become a more common problem in the coming years. When an essential material is not a major portion of the product's total cost, uncertain supply can be partially guarded against by building large inventories of that particular item. Some commodities can be hedged in the futures markets (at least, hedged against price volatility), and some protection can be gained by long-term contracts.

Long-term contracts offer only limited protection, however, as they are valid only if the supplier is able to perform. Consequently, a business in which raw material shortages could lead to unsatisfactory profits is one to avoid.

One factor favoring service companies is that services are relatively free of dependence on basic materials. Raw materials, however, are not the only vital factor.

Businesses that are heavily dependent upon low-cost labor may find themselves with an unsatisfactory supply during boom periods, as other companies may outbid them for the best workers. A company that depends on a key employee for sales contracts or technical expertise could be critically threatened by that employee's departure.

In all of these cases, some safeguards can be instituted. Key-employee insurance protects against the untimely death of a vitally important person. Stock options, profit-sharing or other fringe benefits may keep valuable employees from changing jobs. Nevertheless, unusual risk from lack of control over strategic factors must be considered a negative when evaluating a potential business.

5. IS THE BUSINESS EXPANDING?

This factor is of crucial importance to many entrepreneurs who greatly value opportunity over security. Even if growth were not desirable for its own sake, it would still be a desirable characteristic in a business.

A stagnant company is likely to experience profit difficulties. As a business grows in size, it is often able to adopt more productive techniques or equipment. This permits better cost control, a key factor in our inflationary economy. Growth is also essential if high-quality employees are to be retained. In brief, a business either grows or it stagnates; there is seldom a middle ground.

In evaluating the growth of a business, sales volume in terms of dollars is not an adequate measurement. An increase in dollar sales can be achieved by growth in physical volume, an increase in prices or a combination of both. A business that relies solely upon price increases for growth in sales and profits runs the risk of pricing itself out of the market if its rate of price increases exceeds the inflation of the overall economy.

The stock of U.S. Steel was a favorite investment at one time because of the company's ability to raise prices as needed to maintain profitability. However, rapid increases in the price of steel severely undermined the industry's competitive position. Domestic steel lost ground to foreign steel, and steel lost ground to many other materials, such as plastics.

A word of caution is advisable when looking for growth businesses. Industries in early growth stages may provide exceptionally high growth prospects for those companies in the industry that survive. But the rate of survival may be extremely low. In the post–World War II period, the television industry experienced phenomenal growth. At least 100 companies, many of them large ones, entered the field. After less than a decade, only a handful had retained their competitive positions. The vast majority had left the arena with large losses, or maintained insignificant positions in the industry. The same pattern has been repeated elsewhere.

So the average businessperson should avoid industries that are in this early, exciting stage of growth. Even if a new company enjoys rapid growth, fast expansion also creates problems of financing and keeping control of an enterprise.

It is possible to have a rapidly growing company even in a slow-growth industry, provided the company is small relative to the size of the overall industry, and provided the company has an advantage over its competitors.

6. HOW PROFITABLE IS THE BUSINESS?

Profitability is the ultimate measure of business success. The great successes in history have one major characteristic in common: they had above-average profitability. This permitted high rates of growth. A company with a 6 percent rate of return can double its money in 12 years. A 20 percent rate of return would result in a ninefold increase in the same period.

A high rate of profit has its defensive purposes as well. A company with above average profitability in its industry is better able to finance itself with less debt. This reduces its vulnerability during economic downturns. The more profitable company can introduce cost-cutting equipment. In case of a severe economic period for the industry, the financially stronger companies within it can gain an additional share of the available market from the businesses that go under. This increase in share-of-market reduces the decline in profit that would otherwise occur.

Profit is considered by some critics to result from failure to pay labor its fair price. It is difficult to see how an intelligent business critic can reconcile the fact that most profitable companies also pay the highest wages to their employees.

Individuals tend to act in their own self interest. Profit is a return on investment, just as the interest rate that the saver receives from the bank is a rate of return. The business owner does not get a guaranteed rate of return, and therefore deserves the highest rate achievable to justify the higher risk. Were this not so, few new businesses would be started.

The other factor affecting the rate of profitability is innovation. The company introducing a better and more profitable way of producing goods or services can earn above-average profits until competitors adopt the new methods. Profit is a necessary ingredient in economic progress. This relationship of profit to risk-taking and innovation is somewhat obscured during inflationary periods. In selecting a business, a person ought to choose the combination of high profit justified by a superior product or service relative to the competition. Too many people are attracted to businesses with high profitability but also dangerously high risk.

7. ARE MAJOR CHANGES TAKING PLACE IN THE BASIC FACTORS THAT INFLUENCE THE SUCCESS OF THE BUSINESS?

In selecting a business, it is the future that counts in determining success. The future cannot actually be forecast with any great success, so past trends must be projected to estimate future results. Successful business operators learn the fundamental factors affecting their company's sales and profits. Some of those factors may continue into the future along the same trend lines as the past. Other factors will change, and some of those changes are highly unpredictable.

Changes in the age structure of our population, for example, can be projected many years into the future. That is, they can be estimated barring national disasters, changes in attitudes among people of childbearing age, new advances in birth control (or government cancellation of available methods), and legislation affecting abortion and sterilization. This change in population mix is one of the most important factors in the viability of many of our businesses, and it has contributed to the rise and fall of their prosperity.

One industry that misread the trends, having based its projections on past behavior, was the automobile industry. Planners decided that by the 1980s almost every family would own at least three cars. This was because they believed that the number of teen-age children would increase right along with per capita income. Because the baby-boom generation decided to have fewer (if any) children, and at a later time than did their parents, the predominance of the three-car family did not emerge. The auto industry was caught in the middle, having planned on more production, cheaper-to-produce cars and bigger cars. The small foreign imports stole the market, leaving the U.S. auto industry in shock, scrambling to catch up.

There are many other examples of industries caught by an unforeseen shift from trends based on the past. The growth in sales of a new durable product, such as a color television, must slow down after most people have purchased one. A company that has tripled its share of the market from 10 percent to 30 percent is likely to find it more difficult to triple its current 30 percent share to 90 percent.

8. CAN THE BUSINESS BENEFIT FROM TECHNOLOGICAL CHANGE NOW TAKING PLACE?

Many of the most attractive business opportunities result from technological change. Technical innovations, as opposed to demographic or even political change, produce relatively sudden opportunities. When they occur, it seems that everyone is trying to get into the act. A flurry of publicity, advertising and product display gets prospective customers caught up in the excitement. Their interest, in turn, feeds the action among suppliers. Some of the suppliers emerge as winners; others drop out. And some never get started.

There can be good reason for a new company or an individual not to join the rush to something new. It may be entirely alien to one's best interest or capability. It might require too heavy an investment. It might be considered a "flash in the pan," or simply too crowded a race. Timing can be critical. Enter too soon and you might miss important modifications that steal the market. Enter too late and you may get left behind. If you are not confident about your timing and competitive capabilities, you are better off staying away from it.

Besides incorporating (partly or entirely) the technical innovation into a product you market, there is another aspect to consider. Can you use the new technology to advantage in your own operation to make it more efficient or effective? Because we are addressing ourselves to new businesses, we are necessarily thinking small. Small companies are most often retail or service enterprises—the kind that would use technical innovation to improve service or cut overhead, or both.

Take the paint roller as an example. Here was a device that an individual could assemble in the basement. The do-it-yourself model could probably compete with the giant manufacturers of paint and painting implements in selling it to retailers. But then consider the painting contractor. By adopting this new device the contractor could finish jobs faster and, therefore, could underbid competitors who were still doing jobs entirely by brush. This is a good example, because painters, like most craftsmen, are traditionalists. They accept change very reluctantly and slowly, if at all. So a person not hindered by such reluctance could reap substantial profit by going with the innovation. The most successful painting contractors today are the ones using such recent breakthroughs as the airless spray gun, which can handle latex paint (that was itself a breakthrough in the 1940s) and requires less masking time than the traditional air gun.

As a concluding observation, we would urge prospective entrepreneurs to monitor the scientific and industrial news for announcements of technical advancements. Analyze each development and decide which kinds of businesses could benefit from it. The obvious beneficiaries may not present the best opportunities for a new business, as they may attract too many competitors. Deeper analysis will often reveal opportunities not apparent to the casual investigator.

9. IS THE BUSINESS INSULATED FROM COMPETITION?

All highly profitable companies have one thing in common: they have some protection from competition. Sometimes they control essential raw material, or they may have a location advantage. At other times, the advantage is simply being the largest in the industry, as this may give a company cost advantages. Technological expertise is also a very important factor in dominating many industries.

The small business will seldom (if ever) have any of the above advantages, but it can still distinguish itself from its competition. It is important to build a reputation for superiority based upon such characteristics as quality, reliability and customer rapport.

By its size, the small business can become much more aware of the customer's needs. It can also be more flexible in supplying them. This opportunity is more available in some businesses than in others. The new entrepreneur should prefer areas that offer some protection from aggressive competition.

10. DOES THE BUSINESS APPEAL TO YOU PERSONALLY?

Regardless of how attractive a business may be from an objective standpoint, a person cannot ignore his or her own personal preferences when it comes to selecting a business to enter. A person works not for money alone, but also for job satisfaction and personal fulfillment. Different jobs have different levels of appeal to different people. Each person must make the choice regarding those businesses that hold the most appeal.

Consider those qualities you possess that will influence your prospects for success in various fields. We usually do best what we like to do most, so the success of your business depends on your personal enjoyment of it. This is just one aspect of business, of course. Success depends on your answers to the other questions in this chapter as well. But this particular question carries as much importance as any of the others.

11. IS THE BUSINESS EASY TO ENTER?

The probability of success or failure in an industry is largely determined by the ease of entry into the field. The easier it is to enter an industry, the more competitive it is likely to be, and the easier it is for you to fail.

The prospective small business entrepreneur has a narrow road to travel. On the one hand, there are businesses that are attractive but too difficult to enter. In these, competition will be stiff. At the same time, there are many businesses that can be entered easily—sometimes too easily. If too many individuals can effortlessly get into a field, they can destroy its profitability. Even if the industry has been profitable, past profitability is no guarantee of future profitability when the field gets crowded.

The following are examples of factors that can restrict the ease of entry into a field.

1. Capital
   - to buy a plant and equipment
   - for working capital
   - for start-up expenses
2. Know-how and expertise
   - technological
   - marketing
   - managerial
3. Legal
   - licenses
   - franchises
   - exclusive contracts
   - copyrights
4. Locational
   - strategic position
5. Marketing
   - brand names

- effective communication
- established consumer base
- distribution

6. Control of essential raw materials
7. Low-cost production facilities

Without one or a combination of the above strategic advantages, a business is doomed to unbridled competition and mediocre profitability. Some of the strategic factors, such as capital requirements, are not appropriate protective devices for the small business owner. Some factors offer exceptional opportunities for controlling your own destiny. Control of a patent, trademark or copyright, for example, permits the owner to limit competition. This "toll-gate" position permits the owner to share in the revenue from the protected article regardless of whether or not he or she actually produces it. The exercises in Figure 8.1 will help you determine whether the business you are considering is an attractive one.

FIGURE 8.1 Evaluation of the Business Worksheet

1. Is the business seasonal?

- Is it dependent on part-time employees?
- Are sales concentrated in one portion of the year?
- Do inventories fluctuate widely during the year?
- Is the business unprofitable in any one quarter?

2. Is the business sensitive to the economic cycle?

- Have unit sales declined in a recent recession year?
- Have sales in dollars declined during recessions?

3. Is the business overregulated?

- List various regulatory agencies that will monitor the business:

  ____

  ____

- List licenses required:

  ____

  ____

- List various taxing bodies that must be paid:

  ____

  ____

4. How certain is supply and price of strategic factors?

- Is the company dependent upon materials which are not readily available from many different sources?
- Are prices of the strategic materials subject to wide variations?
- Are adequate supplies of the strategic raw materials difficult to store?
- Is the company overly dependent on key employees?

5. What are the expansion prospects of the business?

- Is the industry expanding?
- Can the company increase its share of the market?
- Are there potential new markets for the product or service?
- Are there potential new products or services for the market?

FIGURE 8.1 Evaluation of the Business Worksheet (continued)

6. **How profitable is the business?**
   - Does the industry have an above-average return on equity (use 12 percent as average)?
   - Does the company have a higher rate of return than the industry?
   - Can the company increase prices easily if necessary to maintain a profit?
   - Is profitability sufficiently high to finance expansion?

7. **What is the direction of change in the industry?**
   - Will changes in the population trends adversely affect the industry?
   - Are the company's main products approaching saturation of major markets?
   - Have price changes increased or decreased the market potential of the product?

8. **What technological changes will affect the industry?**
   - Are technological changes taking place that will reduce the cost of the product?
   - Are technological changes taking place that could enable the product to displace competitive products?
   - Are there any technological changes that could make your product obsolete?

9. **Is the business isolated from competition?**
   - List the advantages the business has over its competitors:

     ____

     ____
   - List the disadvantages the business has compared to its competitors:

     ____

     ____

10. **Does the business appeal to you personally?**
    - List your non-financial reasons for being attracted to the industry:

      ____

      ____

FIGURE 8.1 Evaluation of the Business Worksheet (continued)

- List any characteristics of the business which you dislike:

____

____

11. How easy will it be to enter the industry?

- List the various factors which will reduce the ability of new companies to enter the industry:

____

____

SELF-TEST QUESTIONS

Multiple Choice

1. A company can reduce seasonal fluctuations in its business by
   a. building inventories in the slow season, if it is a manufacturing concern.
   b. having products or services with different seasonal patterns.
   c. hiring part-time personnel in the busy season.
   d. All of the above

2. A business with a high-risk factor
   a. is seldom a competitive one.
   b. should be heavily regulated.
   c. should have above-average profitability to make up for the higher risk.
   d. should always be avoided.

3. If you are buying a company in a cyclical industry, you should be primarily interested in the company's earnings
   a. this year.
   b. next year.
   c. in an average future year.
   d. in its best year.

4. Probably the least desirable business for one who wants to control his or her own destiny would be
   a. a seasonal business.
   b. a highly regulated business.
   c. a competitive industry.
   d. a cyclical business.

5. The following factor would tend to protect a business somewhat against new competition:
   a. Strategic location is required to enter the business.
   b. High capital investment is necessary for entry.
   c. Specialized business expertise is required to enter the business.
   d. All of the above

6. A growth industry would be characterized by
   a. rising prices of its products.
   b. low degree of technological change.
   c. lack of competition.
   d. None of the above

7. For a person contemplating a part-time business after retirement, the following factor would probably be of above-average importance:
   a. The business is an expanding one.
   b. The business is highly profitable.
   c. The business is personally appealing.
   d. The business is seasonal.

8. Businesses with a high degree of technological change
   a. should always be avoided.
   b. offer both higher opportunity and higher risk.
   c. have lower growth prospects than the average industry.
   d. are particularly attractive for retired businesspeople.

True or False

9. The power to regulate is the power to destroy.
   True ☐ False ☐

10. A cyclical business is seldom an attractive one.
    True ☐ False ☐

11. Dependence on a key employee increases a company's risk.
    True ☐ False ☐

12. A regulated company is guaranteed a satisfactory profit by the government.
    True ☐ False ☐

13. A business that is unattractive to one person would almost always be unattractive to others.
    True ☐ False ☐

14. In the care of retired people, a seasonal business might be desirable.
    True ☐ False ☐

15. A high-priced durable product would tend to be less affected by the economic cycle than low-priced nondurable goods.
    True ☐ False ☐

16. A regulated industry is protected well during inflationary periods.

    True ☐ False ☐

17. A growing business is better able to reduce costs than is a mature industry.

    True ☐ False ☐

18. Sales volume in dollars is the best way to measure a company's success.

    True ☐ False ☐

19. In the early stage of its growth, an industry tends to attract many companies that eventually fail or withdraw.

    True ☐ False ☐

20. A small company can grow rapidly even in a mature industry.

    True ☐ False ☐

Answers

1.d, 2.d, 3.d, 4.b, 5.d, 6.d, 7.c, 8.b, 9.T, 10.F, 11.T, 12.F, 13.F, 14.T, 15.F, 16.F, 17.T, 18.F, 19.T, 20.T

CHAPTER 9

Legal Aspects of Getting Started

Probably the most intimidating part of starting a business is the fear of legal complications and expenses. There is no question that the legal aspects of running a business have been increased by the proliferation of federal, state and local government intervention, regulation and legislation. In certain industries, the cost of complying with governmental requirements has largely eliminated the ability of small firms to compete. In the drug industry, for instance, only large firms can afford the research and testing necessary to bring a new product to the market, and even then the application for introduction of a new drug may be turned down by overzealous regulators. At this point, a company has incurred substantial costs in research and development that can never be recovered.

While the increasing government encroachment upon and interference with our free-enterprise system is disturbing, businesses can still succeed. Skill in avoiding or cutting through red tape must be developed. But it is important to remember that it *can be done*.

Actually, as individual citizens, we operate under a very complex set of laws every day, and all of us undoubtedly violate many laws that we do not even know exist. Yet we survive with very little legal entanglement. Some newspapers used to carry a comic strip titled "This Is the Law," which featured numerous examples of obsolete laws still remaining on the books. In some locales, a person might unwittingly break the law by not going to church on Sunday, by holding hands with his or her spouse in public, and many other similar acts even more ridiculous and trivial.

Not only are many of the laws obsolete, many of them were not even practical when first passed. If a business uses the same price as its competitors, it may be charged with fixing prices and thus violating the law. If one business reduces the price below that of a competitor, it may be charged with unfair competition. In this case, the old saying "Damned if you do and damned if you don't" is especially appropriate.

Legislation that makes absolutely no sense is constantly being passed. In the pollution-control field, business owners may be compelled to install very expensive equipment that will meet standards today but not two years from now. This equipment, which would normally be depreciated over a 30 year period, then has to be scrapped in two years when the laws change, with substantial financial losses for the unfortunate business owners.

To minimize exposure to legal problems, follow these ten rules of thumb:

1. Avoid industries that are highly regulated.
2. Avoid industries in which regulation is undergoing major change.
3. Give preference to service industries first, merchandising businesses second and manufacturing last. The more complex your business, the greater the number of laws that cover it.
4. Stress quality products and services. This greatly reduces violations of consumer protection and fraud laws.
5. Treat customers and employees as you would want to be treated.
6. Give preference to businesses in which you can get to know your customers and develop them as your friends. (This is one reason that a business that serves other businesses has inherent disadvantages.)
7. Avoid businesses in which your product is potentially harmful or dangerous to your customers or employees.
8. Learn all you can about your business, so you can spot legal problems.

9. Find out any exemptions to laws that you, as a small business owner, are entitled to. For example, many federal regulations are not applicable to small companies with fewer than the minimum number of employees.
10. Minimize your exposure to difficult customers. One leading management consultant points out that most of a business's problems can be generated by a relatively few undesirable customers and most of the profits are generated by a small number of highly desirable customers. It is better to get rid of the worst and improve service to the best.

Following the above rules, the intelligent and fair business owner should be able to manage many businesses without serious trouble with the law. There are times, however, when legal opinion may be valuable, particularly when the business is just getting started, and special attention should be devoted to legal considerations.

Then there is the problem of selecting the right lawyer, if you decide that retaining legal counsel is desirable. The small business owner can also learn to economize on the use of a lawyer.

LEGAL COUNSEL—DO YOU NEED IT, AND HOW TO MINIMIZE ITS COST

My first best-selling book was *How To Form Your Own Corporation Without a Lawyer for Under $75*. Before this book was written, incorporating a business was often prohibitively expensive for someone just getting started.

From the title of the book, you might conclude that I am opposed to hiring lawyers, but this is not the case. A business, particularly one just getting started, should make the most out of the dollars it has available to spend. Services of such specialists as lawyers carry a high price tag, which is justified by their expensive education. Yet much of the work the lawyer performs is only routine detail work, and often the lawyer is not as well qualified to handle the routine detail as other people who are earning a much lower hourly wage. You, as the new business owner, would normally earn a considerably lower per-hour rate than the lawyer, so you could economically tackle the job in most cases.

This has the advantage of advancing your education, which is an important sideline benefit. First consider what your own time is worth doing other jobs in the business. Then ascertain what the lawyer's per-hour fee would be. If the lawyer charges triple what your time is worth, it should be a job that he or she can do three times as fast as you can, or one in which legal conclusions or "clout" will be more effective. If neither of these prove to be the case (as is true with much of the routine legal work), then you should not waste money in legal expenses.

Often, the information needed for routine legal work is readily available from low-cost sources, and it is even free in some cases. In the case of legal information, a number of semiprofessionals are valuable sources of guidance, especially paralegals and legal secretaries. The various taxing and regulatory bodies can provide advice on meeting legal requirements in their specialized areas.

For example, many businesspeople would still feel safer having a lawyer check their decisions on legal matters, and I certainly have no quarrel with this. But it would be wise not to waste money having a lawyer do work you should be able to do yourself.

There are two other ways to waste a lawyer's time and run up legal fees. You should not pay a lawyer $50 an hour to teach you elementary legal points that could have been discovered through your own reading. Individuals starting their own businesses should not have to rely on a lawyer to tell them the difference between proprietorship, partnership and corporation. After reading a book on the subject, you may have specific questions to ask. This is making efficient use of the lawyer's time.

A more important reason to enter the lawyer's office with some advance legal knowledge of the subject is that there is less chance of misunderstanding. Specialists tend to forget that the average person may not even have an elementary knowledge of that specialized branch of learning. Consequently, the specialist will often use technical terms that mean nothing (or something different) to the client.

Yet another way to waste time and money occurs when you expect the lawyer to make decisions that are rightfully yours to make. The lawyer often has to drag information out of the client as to what the latter wants done. In many situations, the lawyer's job is simply one of a translator. In the simple case of a will, people should decide ahead of time what they want done with their estate. The lawyer supplies the expertise as to the best ways in which to accomplish these objectives, and then writes the will in acceptable legal language to avoid or minimize the chance of misinterpretation.

Also, if you are going to economize on your legal expenses, you must find the right lawyer. Look for the following characteristics or background:

- Does the lawyer have other small businesses as clients? If so, what do they think of his or her ability?
- Is the lawyer a positive thinker who, after pointing out legal obstacles, goes on to offer suggestions for overcoming such obstacles?
- Is the lawyer willing to treat you as a long-term investment?
- Can you get ideas explained in simple terms, or does the lawyer converse only in "legalese"?
- Will you be regarded as an important client?
- Does he or she resent your trying to economize on legal fees?
- Does the lawyer have broad, generalized knowledge of law?
- Is your legal work performed in an efficient manner so that the cost is kept reasonable?

The lawyer who scores highly on the above questions can be a very valuable long-term business associate and should be treated accordingly. He or she should be consulted at an early stage when a possible legal problem arises. It is easier to head off a problem or negotiate a settlement out of court, avoiding what could be an expensive lawsuit.

BASIC LEGAL CONSIDERATIONS NOT RELATED TO FORMS OF ORGANIZATIONS

Any business will encounter certain legal questions, regardless of whether it is organized as a proprietorship, partnership or corporation. For example, one individual opening a drugstore had to complete five years of training to become a licensed pharmacist. (Because of the ratio of medical to nonmedical sales, a drug store must be under the supervision of a registered pharmacist.) Then he had to obtain the following:

- Sales and occupation license
- Retail tobacco dealer's license
- Wholesale alcohol purchase permit
- Vending machine permit
- Soda fountain permit
- Delivery vehicle permit
- Permit to cover food handling
- Permit to dispense narcotics prescribed by qualified physicians

The pharmacist must comply with various regulations by the Food and Drug Administration concerning the quality of drug products, labeling and dispensation. It was also necessary to comply with various pricing regulations, fair trade laws and laws prohibiting pricing of goods below cost (loss leaders). Other store regulations included hours of sale and sanitary requirements. As an employer, he had to adhere to various labor laws, including the collection of withholding taxes and Social Security deductions.

Although few businesses are as regulated as the drugstore business, many firms are exposed to various licensing requirements. When starting a company in a specific location, check zoning requirements. Many business owners like to point proudly to how their company got its start in the basement or garage, while other individuals have been frustrated by zoning laws prohibiting home enterprises. To find out about various legal requirements, the proper taxing authorities should be contacted. The Small Business Administration, chambers of commerce and trade associations are useful sources of information. Your lawyer is likely to be the best single source of information in regard to meeting the specific legal requirements.

A COMPARISON OF VARIOUS FORMS OF BUSINESS ORGANIZATIONS

The Sole Proprietorship

It is estimated that there are 15–18 million sole proprietorships. Only five million employ more than one person. Due to the much smaller average size of the proprietorships compared to the corporation, the latter is the more important institution in regard to dollar sales and income.

In the case of a sole proprietorship, all net income is taxable as the proprietor's personal income. The owner files only one tax return, so bookkeeping is relatively simple. To start a proprietorship, you need a tax number from your state. If you operate under a name other than your own, you must usually register the firm with the state.

The proprietor form of business offers a maximum of flexibility but has two major drawbacks. The individual may not be able to raise the capital needed for the business, making growth prospects limited. An even more serious problem is the liability incurred by the individual. Should the business be unable to meet its financial obligations, the individual's nonbusiness assets could be lost. Business owners who operate proprietorships should familiarize themselves thoroughly with techniques of debt management and with our country's personal bankruptcy laws.

The Partnership

One of the problems of the proprietorship is inadequate capital, and a common solution to this problem is to bring in additional partners. This type of organization still has relative freedom from government control, and there is no income tax on the partnership itself. The business does file a tax information letter, and there are some additional legal considerations. It is necessary to draw up a partnership agreement that defines the rights and duties of each partner. Also, a partnership is terminated upon the death or withdrawal of one of the principals.

The major drawback of this form of business is the unlimited liability of the major partner. (Limited partners with limited liability can be included in the business, but there must be at least one general partner.) The risk is increased in many respects, since each partner has the capacity to bind the other(s) when acting within the scope of the business. You could be liable for all of your partner's debts and the results of bad business decisions. A partnership has all the disadvantages of a marriage and none of the advantages. A partnership agreement should be worked out carefully by a lawyer and should include provisions for a peaceful method of terminating the partnership if it does not work out to the satisfaction of all parties concerned.

The Corporation

We often think of technological progress in the physical sciences as being the major reason for our past economic growth. Innovation is not restricted to the physical sciences, but also applies to changes in our social institutions.

The development of the corporate form of business is an excellent example of this technological progress. By providing limited liability to investors, corporations were able to attract sources of capital which were unavailable to other forms of business organizations.

A corporation is a legal entity, separate and distinct from its stockholders, officers and employees. In the event the company cannot meet its expenses and its assets are less than its liabilities, bankruptcy may be forced upon the corporation without exposing the stockholders and officers to any personal liability beyond their investment in the stock of the business. The only exception to this rule is the debt owed in unpaid taxes.

Financing does not necessarily become easier when a small proprietorship becomes a small corporation. If debt financing is obtained, such as a loan from a bank, the lender may require a personal guarantee by the owners. If the business owner wants to raise capital by selling part ownership, a corporation is much more attractive to investors who can purchase shares of stock. Owners can transfer their shares of ownership interest without the corporation dissolving. Distribution of ownership among family members is facilitated, and shares of stock can be used for estate planning.

The corporate form of business can also permit considerable tax savings, but the advantage depends upon the relative tax brackets of the corporation and the stockholders. At the present time, the corporate form permits better tax shelters in the form of pensions and profit-sharing plans than do unincorporated businesses.

One of the major drawbacks to the corporate form of business has been the cost of incorporating. Lawyers' fees for incorporating can run from $200 to well over $1,000. It is possible, however, to incorporate without the services of a lawyer, and for a very moderate cost. I would recommend incorporating in the state of Delaware, which has attempted to simplify the process. It is not necessary to live in Delaware or do business there to take advantage of the state's liberal laws covering incorporation. There is no minimum capital requirement, whereas many states require at least $1,000 in funds. One person can also hold the offices of president, treasurer and secretary, and be all of the directors of the corporation. Therefore, there is no need to bring others into a Delaware corporation if the owner does not desire it. Only one person acting as the incorporator is required, whereas many states require three. There is a well established body of laws relevant to corporations that have been tested in Delaware courts over the years, and this reduces legal uncertainties.

Because of the importance of corporations to the state of Delaware, it is extremely efficient in processing applications from new corporations. There is a minimum of red tape, and the procedure is unusually swift.

To form a corporation, you will need a Certificate of Incorporation, which includes such information as the corporation name, corporate address, the nature of the business and the amount of authorized capital, and outlines the powers of the directors. The corporation will also need a set of bylaws that cover such items as the following:

1. Offices
2. Meeting of stockholders
   - When and where the meetings are held
   - Procedure
   - What business is to be transacted
   - Action in lieu of meeting
3. Directors
   - Number and term
   - Resignations and/or removals
   - Compensation
4. Officers

  - Those offices that will exist in the corporation
  - The function of each officer
5. Stock certificates
   - Transfer of shares
   - Rules covering lost certificates
6. Dividends
7. Corporate seal
8. Rules regarding checks
9. Amendments
   - Rules regarding changes in the by-laws

It will also be necessary to keep minutes of meetings held and business transacted during those meetings. For example, where differences of opinion arise between a company and tax agents regarding the intention of a business transaction, the corporate minute books covering its meetings have often been valuable in proving management's intentions. At the time the corporation is formed, a set of organizational minutes should be created, covering such information as issuance of stocks and appointment of corporate officers.

This may sound like a formidable undertaking, but it need not be one. Standardized forms greatly simplify the process. The procedure also has a valuable side effect of making you think of your business as a separate entity from yourself. Many legal situations, especially tax problems, arise because a business owner mixes business financial transactions with personal financial affairs.

SOME FINAL COMMENTS REGARDING LEGAL ASPECTS OF BUSINESS

The subject of law is an extremely complex one, as each general rule has a multitude of exceptions and qualifications. You should learn the general rules that apply to your enterprise and should know, for example, what basic elements make up a business contract and what type of contracts must be in writing. On the other hand, it would be extremely time-consuming to learn all the qualifications and exceptions that affect contracts.

Lawyers and other technical experts may be willing to accept stock options in return for part or all of their services.

This does not necessarily reduce costs, but it does reduce outlays of cash in the early stages of a business when cash is typically in short supply. The entrepreneur is, in effect, shifting part of the risk to business associates.

SELF-TEST QUESTIONS

Multiple Choice

1. Government regulation has had the following effect:
   a. Made it almost impossible for the small business to succeed
   b. Helped small business by penalizing big business
   c. Increased the cost of doing business
   d. None of the above

2. Exposure to legal problems can be minimized best by
   a. consulting a lawyer before doing anything at all.
   b. getting a law degree before entering a business.
   c. stressing quality products and services, and treating your customers and employees as you would like to be treated.
   d. All of the above

3. The following businesses tend to be the most highly regulated:
   a. Businesses that serve other businesses
   b. Service industries
   c. Companies manufacturing consumer products that could be potentially harmful
   d. None of the above

4. A business owner should learn enough about law to accomplish the following:
   a. Know when to consult a lawyer
   b. Understand his or her lawyer when one is consulted
   c. Neither of the above
   d. Both of the above

5. The cost of obtaining legal services can be reduced by
   a. hiring a lawyer just out of school.
   b. consulting a lawyer only after you have definite legal problems.
   c. putting a lawyer on your board of directors to get free legal services.
   d. None of the above

6. Information regarding practical legal problems can be obtained from
   a. regulatory bodies responsible for enforcing specific laws.
   b. nonlawyer specialists who are knowledgeable in legal aspects of their specialty, such as accountants and insurance consultants.
   c. books covering practical business subjects relating to legal considerations.
   d. All of the above

7. In addition to selecting a lawyer for his or her legal expertise, you should consider
   a. how much business the lawyer can bring in from his or her contacts.
   b. what contacts the lawyer has with the regulators and/or judges in case you get in trouble.
   c. whether the lawyer simply points out legal obstacles or advises ways in which to overcome such obstacles.
   d. None of the above

8. You can judge a lawyer's ability to help you by
   a. how well he or she talks in legal terms.
   b. how many important people he or she knows.
   c. whether the lawyer has other small business clients and how satisfied they are with the services provided.
   d. None of the above

True or False

9. To be a good citizen, you should understand all the laws that govern you.

   True ☐ False ☐

10. A business owner who gets to know customers as friends reduces the chance of legal problems from them.

    True ☐ False ☐

11. To avoid legal difficulties, the business owner should expend the most effort in trying to satisfy the most difficult customers.

    True ☐ False ☐

12. The corporate form of business has advantages, but the cost of incorporating is prohibitively expensive for the small business owner.

    True ☐ False ☐

13. The partnership combines the advantages of a proprietorship with the advantages of a corporation.
True ☐ False ☐

14. A business owner with a knowledge of elementary law can economize on legal expenses by making consultation time with lawyers more productive.
True ☐ False ☐

15. There may be occasions when it will be necessary to use a lawyer who specializes in a certain field rather than your own lawyer, who is a generalist.
True ☐ False ☐

16. A major advantage of the corporate form is limited liability.
True ☐ False ☐

17. The corporate form of organization is advantageous only to large businesses.
True ☐ False ☐

18. Laws and regulations are adopted only after thorough consideration is given to all their consequences.
True ☐ False ☐

19. Much work done by legal firms is routine in nature and could be performed just as easily by low-cost semiprofessionals.
True ☐ False ☐

20. Two lawyers may charge the same cost per hour, but one may still provide lower-cost service based on results.
True ☐ False ☐

Answers
1.c, 2.c, 3.c, 4.d, 5.d, 6.d, 7.c, 8.c, 9.F, 10.T, 11.F, 12.F, 13.F, 14.T, 15.T, 16.T, 17.F, 18.F, 19.T, 20.T

CHAPTER 10

Methods of Starting a Business, Including Part-Time, Franchising and Buying Out Existing Businesses

There are several ways of starting a company, but the best method usually depends on the individual involved and the nature of the specific opportunity. For some people starting on a part-time basis is the best way, since its purpose may be to merely supplement family income and/or offer a creative outlet for an enterprising individual. In some cases, the part-time business is meant to be a permanent one, where the person retains his or her full-time occupation but uses the income from the small company to build retirement funds, provide the luxuries or develop a second source of income.

Another variation of the part-time approach is to keep the business as a secondary source of income until such time as the owner is able to enter it on a full-time basis. In this case, planning must be somewhat different from that above. The most difficult aspect of this approach is in deciding when it is time to leave your full-time job and concentrate all your energies on the company you have created. One method that facilitates entry into your own enterprise is the practice of "moonlighting" in the field. This provides a chance to learn the industry while getting paid for it, and also gives you a chance to actually work the field before committing yourself to it totally.

Starting out on a full-time basis involves more risk, but there *are* ways to minimize the unknowns. Franchising is one method of getting started, and the merits of this approach should be considered. Buying out an existing company can reduce the risks in certain respects. But it can also increase the risk in other ways. If you adopt the "buyout" approach, the question of the amount to pay becomes crucial, and this subject will be covered at length.

Beginning your own brand-new enterprise on a full-time basis is the approach with the most risk involved, but, as mentioned previously, there are ways to overcome these risks.

PART-TIME APPROACH—THE PERMANENT PART-TIME BUSINESS

In our economy, it is often necessary to hold more than one job. The second job is usually a low-paying one, being part-time, but it is usually the best most of us can hope for. The after-tax income is even less impressive, since the extra income is taxed at a higher rate than the income from the first job, because it puts you in a higher tax bracket. Because it is "extra," the income also tends to be spent more carelessly than it might otherwise. It is easy to end up on a type of treadmill from which there appears to be no escape.

A part-time business may be the solution to this dilemma, even if you have no intention of ever quitting your current job. There are numerous advantages in spending your extra efforts on building a part-time enterprise rather than simply working extra hours, no matter what the pay rate.

First, the part-time business is a tremendous source of education that can actually help you progress in your primary job. Most people work for large institutions, where they learn only part of the business. Their jobs concern only a minute segment of the total operation, and they have little opportunity to investigate other divisions. A part-time business will broaden your background. It encourages learning about financing, marketing, accounting and a host of other subjects. You learn how all of this specialized knowledge fits together to produce a successful business.

All of this background becomes useful in your primary job, serving to improve communications with specialists in other areas of the company. As you learn the "total picture," there is a better opportunity for advancement up the management ladder, because a broader knowledge of specific fields aids in developing a management attitude. Instead of being content with merely "putting in time," you become output-oriented, learn to use time effectively and become proficient at taking the responsibility for getting a job done. These are qualities that management seeks when considering candidates for promotion.

Choosing a part-time business over a part-time job has a second advantage. You can actually enjoy putting in those extra hours. Many part-time businesses start off as hobbies which eventually become profitable part-time enterprises. Since fatigue is mostly psychological in nature, you tend to get tired at a regular eight-hour-a-day job because it is boring, not because it is physically exhausting. Even though you may be tired at the end of the day, you can transform yourself into a dynamo a few hours later when working in your own part-time business.

A part-time company can also produce more real after-tax income than can a part-time job, even from the very beginning. Over the long-run, the difference in actual cash in your pocket can be tremendous, as your company has no limits to its potential. Working for someone else always has limits, due mainly to limited wage scales and limited hours. Most often, too, the income from a part-time job gets absorbed into the household till and is frittered away. In contrast, the income from your part-time business has much more chance of being reinvested to provide growth in income in future years. This "forced savings" builds wealth over the years, just as much as any savings plan can. To a certain extent, business income is better sheltered from taxes as well.

In the long run, the difference between the part-time job and the part-time business can widen dramatically. When working for someone else, you get paid for the time you put in. In your own company, you also get paid for your expertise, which is a commodity that will expand and grow as you gain more experience. You can leverage your income by use of other people's money, their time, their ideas and their abilities. There is no limit to the amount of money you can earn per hour when you reach this stage.

Should a time come when you want to retire, your part-time business is a valuable asset that you can convert to cash by selling. In contrast, the part-time employee may have nothing to show for the extra hours he or she has worked over the years.

In the case above, the individual's part-time business was intended to supplement a full-time career. Consequently, there was no need to develop it quickly into a complete source of support. Let us consider a completely different situation, where you do not think of your current full-time position as a permanent one. Perhaps you are approaching retirement age, or it may be that your career is intolerable, or at least uncertain, for a number of different reasons. You may feel as if you need a full-time business of your own. Even in these circumstances, it may be better to retain the full-time job temporarily.

As long as you are working for a salary, you will probably find that funds for the new enterprise will grow more rapidly, as income will not be siphoned off to cover family needs. You will also be able to borrow funds for your new company based upon a personal loan or mortgage loan (if you own your own home). Without a predictable source of income, it is unlikely that creditors will lend you very much based on an untried venture.

It is easier to develop your business in an orderly fashion if you have less financial pressure. Most intelligent, long-term business decisions require investment of funds, which will probably be unavailable if your business has to provide daily income needs. Starting on a small scale and having gradual growth also permits you to learn the business properly. And the chances of survival are much greater if a firm has emergency sources of funds to tap when problems arise. The individual who has a steady job in addition to his or her business has much more flexibility.

Even if your financial position is such that you can immediately resign from your job and start a company of your own, it might still be better to start on a part-time basis. The smart investor does not risk everything on one single investment that contains a number of unknowns. He or she invests portions of capital in different ways, increasing the investment in areas that do well and reducing or eliminating investment in areas that are disappointing.

You should not be any different from an investor, except that capital should be defined to include not only money, but also time, energy, education and abilities.

If you want to go into the restaurant business, for example, there are opportunities to test this desire before plunging ahead. A part-time job in the field is one way to learn the business. In this way, the only risk is wasted time if you find you were not as interested in the field as you thought. This experience gives you a chance to learn whether you will like it.

In summary, the part-time approach is especially important if you have limited capital, need time to learn the business or want to reduce the risk involved.

FRANCHISING AS A METHOD OF STARTING YOUR OWN BUSINESS

Franchising is an arrangement whereby the owner of a product or service licenses affiliated dealers, or franchises, to do the distribution. Holiday Inn was born as a result of a disappointing vacation by Mr. C. Kemmons Wilson, who returned home city of Memphis, he built several motels with the intention of building a motel suitable for traveling families. In his home based upon the concept he had developed, and worked out the methods, systems and costs of running such establishments. Once the company had a system that could run smoothly and profitably, it was time to expand.

If a moderate growth rate had been acceptable to the motel founder, the company could have grown by reinvesting earnings and training its own personnel. Management chose a much faster route to success, however. Various builders and businesspeople throughout the country were invited to a seminar at which the economics of the business were presented along with detailed inspection of the original Holiday Inn and its operation. Many were impressed and went back home to set up a Holiday Inn motel in their area. Within a few years, a network of these motels blanketed the country, utilizing the know-how of the founder along with the capital and managerial ability of the individual franchises.

The Holiday Inn franchise has been a very successful one, as it was one that was mutually advantageous to both the franchisor and the franchisee. Unfortunately, many arrangements have been far less successful, although one source has estimated that the failure rate among nonfranchised businesses is eight times greater than that of franchised establishments. Nevertheless, it is important to draw some distinctions between successful and unsuccessful franchise situations.

The first point is that franchising is not a magic method of turning a mediocre product or service into an instant fortune. Holiday Inn filled a definite need at the time it was created, and early franchisees shared in the bonanza along with the company founders. If the product or service had been a dud, they would also have shared in its failure.

A second and related point is that their timing was right. They were the first major national system, so that early franchisees had to compete only against local motels. These locals were often poorly built and inadequately managed. Franchisees of motel chains created at a later date found themselves competing against an already established, well-managed chain of Holiday Inn motels. To make exceptional profits from most franchises, you need to get into an organization with a good product or service fairly early in its growth stage.

Even if the product or service is both desirable and timely, the franchisee has to judge whether the contract between the franchisor and franchisee is a fair one, benefiting both parties. The former may insist that you conduct your business strictly according to its rules or your franchise may be cancelled. These rules may be laid out for a good reason, as one franchisee who conducts the operation in an undesirable manner can adversely affect the prospects of other franchisees of the same chain. A customer who gets badly treated at one Holiday Inn might avoid other Holiday Inns in other areas of the country. As a result, the ethical franchisor carefully screens applicants, while the unethical company is simply interested in selling franchises and is much more likely to use a hard-sell approach on prospects.

To protect themselves against disappointments, people contemplating a franchise can do several things. You should first get acquainted with the product or service of the franchisor as a customer by visiting several of its operations. If the quality varies widely from one site to another, you would be unlikely to get a great amount of customer goodwill from other units. Because goodwill generated by other units is supposed to be a major benefit of joining a franchise operation, the prospective new buyer should be wary. If the quality of service is high and consistent, the prospective buyer should then switch from the role of customer to that of franchise owner. You should talk to various franchise owners to determine the answers to the following:

- Does the franchisor provide the various services that were promised?
- Do any of the restrictive clauses in the contract bother the operator?

- Is the profitability of the operation consistent with what had been estimated?
- Are customers satisfied with services?
- Has the operator experienced any serious problems that were not expected?
- Does competition appear to be increasing with other enterprises in the same business?

It is important to talk to several existing franchise owners in different localities to get a broad point of view. If this investigation gives good results, the next step is to thoroughly investigate the franchise contract with the following points in mind:

- How exclusive is your territory? How protected are you from other franchisees of the same companies?
- Can you open up more than one outlet in your territory?
- What services can you expect from the franchisor (e.g., help with location, raw materials, name, logo, bookkeeping services, supplies, etc.), and are you free to purchase these elsewhere? How do the prices of these services compare to what could be obtained elsewhere?
- Exactly what will the franchise cost be, including initial fee and any extra charges, and what percentage of sales will royalties amount to?
- What happens if you terminate the franchise agreement? Can you sell to an acceptable new party, or do you have to sell back to the franchisor? If the latter is the case, how is the buy-back price determined?
- Does the franchise specify a minimum sales volume?
- Is the contract a long-term one, or renewable at your option?

One risk involved in franchising is that you could add considerable value through your own hard work and not be able to capitalize on it.

BUYING OUT AN EXISTING BUSINESS

In addition to starting a business from scratch, or buying a franchise, the new businessperson can buy an existing business. It is extremely important to know why the current owner wants to sell. Typically the seller has an advantage over the buyer, because the seller knows the details of the business. So the buyer must be able to offset the seller's advantage with one or more of his own. If the buyer has a better knowledge of business in general, he or she may be able to buy a business with a mediocre record and greatly improve results with superior know-how or management capability. A situation where the buyer has an advantage is the business that is up for sale because the current owner is retiring.

A major advantage in buying an existing business is that a start-up period (which is typically unprofitable) is eliminated.

The current owner can also give you the benefit of experience, possibly eliminating many mistakes you might otherwise make. You should also look for a business that is strategically located, adequately equipped and already has a favorable image established. In the case of location and equipment or inventory (in the case of a retailer), you should ask yourself how these compare with what you would prefer if you started from scratch.

The major question in buying a business is knowing what to pay, and this is determined by a number of factors, including

- nature and history of the business;
- general and economic outlook, and industry outlook;
- net value of the company's assets less liabilities;
- earning capacity of the business;
- company goodwill, if any;
- size of the business;
- restrictions on the business; and
- sales price of similar businesses.

VALUATION OF A COMPANY

Numerous factors affect the value of a company, so that valuation is much more of an art than it is a science. The value of a company is not a static figure, and it will vary from changes in the economy, fluctuations in interest rates, changes in the industry and variations in several other conditions. Professionals involved in valuation work have developed rules of thumb as to what price a particular business is worth. Most of these methods had merit at the time they were developed but may have become obsolete.

There are three basic valuation approaches that can be applied to most businesses:

The Market Value Approach. This is based upon the prices for which similar businesses in the same field have sold recently.

The Asset Value Approach. At what price could the various assets be sold if the business was to be liquidated?

The Going Concern Approach. What is the company worth, based on the future earnings it will be able to produce?

The market value approach is based on the assumption that sales take place between a buyer and seller who are both willing and knowledgeable. A seller who had to dispose of a business quickly due to an urgent need of funds might not qualify as a willing seller. Similarly, a buyer who buys without investigating the industry or business might not qualify as a knowledgeable buyer. The biggest drawback to this approach is finding a comparable business that has recently changed hands. Each business has its unique characteristics, and no two situations are identical.

A second approach is to value a business on the basis of what its net assets would be worth on a liquidation basis. This method is especially appropriate when a business has many assets that are underutilized. These assets may not be contributing any profit to the company but may provide considerable funds if sold.

The net asset valuation approach begins with the company's balance sheet, which lists its various assets and liabilities and the difference between the two. The latter is known as book value, stockholder equity or net assets value. Adjustments have to be made to these figures, which are based on cost rather than on current market value. Typical adjustments are as follows in Figure 10.1.

There is one final adjustment that needs to be made. Any business that is being liquidated will incur expenses during the process. Selling expenses will absorb part of the proceeds from the sale. Also, if the time to liquidate is drawn out, net asset value will be reduced by losses incurred during that period. Consequently, net asset value should be reduced by estimated liquidating expenses.

The third approach is the valuation of a company on a going concern basis. It assumes that the buyer intends to keep the company in business and is consequently interested in what the company is worth based upon the future earnings it can produce. Two basic situations are involved in using this approach:

1. How do you estimate future earnings?
2. What price do you pay for each dollar of earnings?

ESTIMATING FUTURE EARNINGS

Forecasting is notoriously unreliable, and the forecasting of future profits is no exception to the rule. Three different approaches are most commonly used.

In the first method, assume that future earnings will approximate past earnings. The analyst using this approach will take the most recent three- to five-year earnings of the company and average them. Greater weight may be given to current earnings if there is a definite trend upward or downward.

In the second method, current-year earnings are used as a base. The analyst then projects future earnings by estimating a future growth rate. More often than not, the future growth rate is largely based on the past growth rate. The most sophisticated analysts adjust past growth rates by segregating nonrecurring factors from recurring ones. A past sales growth of 10 percent may be considered a recurring factor that can be projected into the future. On the other hand, earnings growth due to tax decreases, profit margin increases or earn-

FIGURE 10.1

	Current Assets
Cash	No adjustment
Accounts Receivable	Reduce by the amount of estimated uncollectable items. The longer an amount is overdue, the more likely it is to be uncollectable.
Inventory	Reduce by any amount of obsolete items. If inventory is carried on the LIFO basis (last in/first out), some of the inventory may reflect costs of many years ago. Get an estimate of what these would be worth at current costs and adjust upward.
	Fixed Assets
Land	Land may be worth substantially more than it is carried for on the books, especially if it was purchased many years ago. Adjust accordingly.
Plant or Buildings	If the building has been well-maintained, it will have a replacement value in excess of the depreciated cost at which it is carried on the books. This may be offset by developments that have made the building obsolete or reduced its locational advantages.
	Intangible Assets
Goodwill, Patents, Copyrights, etc.	Some of these, such as patents or copyrights, can be assigned reasonable market values. Much of the goodwill value of a business disappears during liquidation.
	Liabilities
Short-term debts	No adjustment made.
Long-term debts	No adjustment made.
Net Asset Value	Derived from subtracting liabilities from assets, after adjusting value of assets as indicated above.

FIGURE 10.2

	Net Income	*Weight*	*Weighted Estimates*
Year 1 (most recent)	25,000	5	125,000
Year 2	12,000	4	48,000
Year 3	8,000	3	24,000
Year 4	6,000	2	12,000
Year 5	5,000	1	5,000
	56,000	15	214,000
Average Earnings	56,000 =	11,200	
Weighted Average Earnings		$\frac{214,000}{15}$	= 14,267

ings of a windfall nature are eliminated from the growth trend.

The third method estimates future growth by using a rate-of-return approach. If a company earns 10 percent on its investment, its maximum growth rate is estimated at 10 percent. If part of the earnings is paid out in dividends, growth rate is adjusted to reflect this. If the company earning 10 percent pays out half of its earnings in dividends, then its reinvestment rate is 5 percent and the analyst uses this to estimate future growth.

Of the three approaches, the first is the most conservative and also the most commonly used. Where future growth prospects are believed to be above average, an adjustment is then made upward in the valuation factor used to capitalize those earnings. Figure 10.2 illustrates computation of weighted average earnings.

Using average earnings gives a more realistic estimate of what they might be in a normal year. It avoids the common trap that many investors fall into of buying a company based on peak earnings. Most sellers pick a year of peak earnings in which to sell their business. By using a weighted average, more consideration is given to the most recent results.

FIGURE 10.3

Rate of Return Desired	*Each Dollar of Earnings Is Worth*		
4%	1/.04 =	25	times
5%	1/.05 =	20	times
6%	1/.06 =	16.7	times
7%	1/.07 =	14.3	times
8%	1/.08 =	12.5	times
9%	1/.09 =	11.1	times
10%	1/.10 =	10	times
11%	1/.11 =	9.1	times
12%	1/.12 =	8.3	times
13%	1/.13 =	7.7	times
14%	1/.14 =	7.1	times
16%	1/.16 =	6.3	times
20%	1/.20 =	5	times
30%	1/.30 =	3.3	times
40%	1/.40 =	2.5	times

SELECTION OF A VALUATION FACTOR AT WHICH TO CAPITALIZE EARNINGS

The second problem of valuation is deciding how much to pay for each dollar of earnings. This capitalization factor is determined by the rate of return you can reasonably expect to earn on your investment. For a short-term bond, a 9 percent rate of return might be acceptable, whereas an 8 percent rate of return might be appropriate for a bond of a well-established industrial company. On equity-type investments, such as common stocks or ownership of real estate, the rate of return desired should normally be higher than that on high-quality bonds. Note that rate of return should increase as you take higher risk, as higher income is necessary to offset the higher probability of capital loss. On a small company investment, you should expect a rate of return at least one and a half times what you could earn on a long-term government bond. A rate of return twice that of a government bond would not be considered abnormally high.

Figure 10.3 illustrates the capitalization factor that is appropriate for different rates of return, using this formula:

$$\text{Capitalization factor} = \frac{1}{\%\ \text{Rate of return}}$$

As an illustration, assume that long-term government bonds currently yield 7 percent. On an investment in a small company, you could reasonably expect one and a half to two times that rate of return, or between 10 percent and 14 percent. Using the above table, a capitalization factor of 10 times corresponds to 10 percent return, and 7.1 times corresponds to 14 percent. A company earning an average of $100,000 per year would be worth between $710,000 and $1 million.

There may be reasons to buy a business other than the profit earned, and this would affect the price. For example, many people would prefer to work for themselves, and having their own business provides that opportunity. The person is in effect buying a job in addition to the business, and may be willing to pay an additional amount for that opportunity.

ADJUSTING PRICE FOR GROWTH PROSPECTS

In buying a company, you are interested in its future earnings, not just what it is earning now. Most investors are willing to pay more for a company that is growing rapidly than for one that is standing still. There is no formula for calculating how much more should be paid. Some adjustment for the growth factor can be made by substituting estimated future earnings for current earnings. For example, the company earning $100,000 per year now may be growing at a 15 percent rate, and would earn approximately $200,000 per year in five years. A sophisticated investor might be willing to pay twice the capitalization factor that would be paid for the company if its earnings were to remain at $100,000 per year. I would not advise going any further out than five years if estimated future earnings are used, due to the uncertainties of forecasting.

Figure 10.4 is a worksheet to use in evaluating the business you are interested in buying.

FIGURE 10.4 Company Evaluation Worksheet

I. Nature and History of the Business

A. When was the business started?____________________

B. Has the business operated under any other names? ______

C. Has the business address changed?____________________

D. What was the nature of the original business?__________

____

E. What changes in the nature of the business have taken place? What products or services have been added or discontinued?________________________________

____

F. Legal Considerations: __________________________

1. List any restrictions on the nature of the business that can be transacted.

   ____

   ____

2. List any contractual agreements that are unfulfilled.

   ____

   ____

3. List any contingent liabilities not listed in the financial report.

   ____

   ____

4. List any lawsuits pending against the business.

   ____

   ____

5. List all union agreements.

   ____

   ____

6. List patents or licensing agreements including expiration dates.

   ____

   ____

FIGURE 10.4 Company Evaluation Worksheet (continued)

G. **Regulators Involved in the Business:**

1. **What reports must be submitted to regulators?**

2. **What taxes is the business subject to?**

H. **Change in Competitive Factors:**

1. **Has new competition developed and what has been the effect?**

2. **Have technological changes increased or decreased prospects for the company's products?**

II. Economic and Industry Outlook

A. **What are the major economic factors that influence the industry's results?**

B. **What is the outlook for these important economic factors?**

C. **What local economic factors affect the company and how will they effect it?**

FIGURE 10.4 Company Evaluation Worksheet (continued)

III. Evaluation of the Company's Financial Statements

A. Sales

1. What has been the growth rate?

____

____

____

2. What factors have caused any substantial fluctuation in sales?

____

3. What has been the trend in prices of the company's products?

____

4. Has salary growth kept up with growth in fixed assets? What is the ratio of sales to fixed assets?

____

B. Profit Margins: _______________

1. What has been the trend in profit margins?

____

____

2. What factors have influenced trends and fluctuations in profit margins?

____

____

C. Current Asset Position:

1. What has been the trend in the company's cash situation?

____

____

2. What has been the trend in current ratio—current assets to current liabilities?

____

____

FIGURE 10.4 Company Evaluation Worksheet (continued)

3. Have accounts receivable increased faster than sales?
   a. How much of accounts receivable is past due?______

   ____

4. Have inventories increased faster than sales?

   ____

   ____

D. Fixed Assets:

1. What is the value of the land carried on the books and what is its current market value?

   ____

2. What depreciation practices have been used?

   ____

3. What would be the replacement cost of the plant and equipment?

   ____

4. What would be the liquidating value of the equipment if it become necessary to sell? ___________

5. How does the current plant and equipment compare to that of competitors in regard to productivity?______

   ____

6. How does the current plant and equipment compare to the most modern equipment and plants available with regard to both cost and productivity? __________

   ____

   ____

   ____

E. Current Liabilities:

1. What has been the trend in liabilities?

   ____

   ____

   ____

FIGURE 10.4 Company Evaluation Worksheet (continued)

F. Long-Term Liabilities:
1. When do long-term debts come due?

____

____

2. What lease agreements is the company subject to and when do they expire?

____

____

3. List contingent liabilities:

____

____

____

4. What percent of total capital is long-term debt?

____

G. Common Stock:
1. What has been the trend in common stock book value?

____

SELF-TEST QUESTIONS

Multiple Choice

1. Starting a part-time business
   a. is less risky than quitting your job and starting full-time.
   b. is the fastest way to make your business grow.
   c. will reduce your ability to handle your full-time job.
   d. All of the above

2. If you want to enter a business but you lack experience to succeed in the field you could
   a. get a moonlighting job that will provide the needed experience.
   b. buy out an existing business with the provision that the current owner will teach you the business.
   c. get a partner who has that particular expertise.
   d. All of the above

3. If you are considering entering a business through the franchise route, you should
   a. check with other business people with that franchise to see if they are satisfied with the arrangement.
   b. evaluate whether or not customers are satisfied with the business.
   c. Both of the above
   d. None of the above

4. A franchise agreement should
   a. protect you from competition.
   b. guarantee you a high rate of profit on your investment.
   c. reduce your chance of failure.
   d. permit early retirement.

5. In buying out an existing business, the most important factor in determining the price is
   a. what the current owner paid for the business.
   b. the stated book value of the business.
   c. the future stream of earnings from the business.
   d. what the company has earned in recent years.

6. The current earnings of a business may be overstated if
   a. the current owner takes an unrealistically low salary.
   b. certain expenses (such as maintenance and repairs) are being deferred.
   c. assets are being depreciated at a rate below normal.
   d. All of the above

7. A businessperson who bought a certain franchise five years ago can now sell at ten times what he or she paid. You should
   a. expect similar gain if you invest now.
   b. prefer an investment in a franchise that has not gone up in that period.
   c. take his or her advice on what you should invest in.
   d. None of the above

8. An important factor to consider before investing in a franchise is
   a. its tax shelter aspects.
   b. the services to be received from the franchisor and their costs.
   c. Neither of the above
   d. Both of the above

True or False

9. If your part-time business has not expanded into a full-time operation in three years, you should consider it a failure.

   True ☐ False ☐

10. A part-time business is much more educational than a part-time job.

    True ☐ False ☐

11. A part-time job is a better way to accumulate capital than a part-time business.

    True ☐ False ☐

12. A part-time business may improve your prospects for advancement on your full-time job.

    True ☐ False ☐

13. Moonlighting in a business provides an opportunity to see if you really like it.

    True ☐ False ☐

14. In buying a business, it is considered improper to ask why the current owner is selling.

    True ☐ False ☐

15. The seller of a business would normally be expected to have an advantage over the buyer in knowing what the business is worth.

    True ☐ False ☐

16. A seller must voluntarily tell the buyer all the problems of a business or else the sales contract is cancelled.

    True ☐ False ☐

17. Fluctuation in interest rates may affect the price at which a business changes hands.

    True ☐ False ☐

18. In a franchise arrangement, the franchisee should have complete freedom to run his or her operation.

    True ☐ False ☐

19. To be successful, a businessperson should be willing to risk all of his or her capital at one time.

    True ☐ False ☐

20. In a franchise arrangement, it is important to know if you have to sell back to the franchisor when you terminate the business and, if so, how the sale price will be determined.

    True ☐ False ☐

Answers
1.a, 2.d, 3.c, 4.c, 5.c, 6.d, 7.d, 8.b, 9.F, 10.T, 11.F, 12.T, 13.T, 14.F, 15.T, 16.F, 17.T, 18.F, 19.F, 20.T

CHAPTER 11

Financing Your Business

Finance is a key element in any business. Many firms may begin with inadequate financing but cannot survive long. Indeed, lack of financing is often a contributing (if not a major) cause of failure. Even for those firms that do survive, profitability is often lower than it could be if more intelligent financing techniques were employed.

Creative financing helps ensure survival of the firm and enhances its profitability. Minimum financial needs of the business must be provided in its early stages, and additional financial strength can directly improve the rate of return the company experiences. Various types of funding are available, all with differing costs, and they will be thoroughly discussed in this section.

FUNDS NEEDED FOR START-UP AND SURVIVAL

Average people without business backgrounds tend to underestimate the cost of running a business. They see such obvious costs as materials and labor but overlook interest costs, managerial costs, credit losses, legal fees and the like. A good, conservative formula for estimating start-up costs is to estimate all expenses, add up all disasters that are likely to occur, then double the total.

Several basic forecasting errors contribute to the problem of estimating costs. The business owner may underestimate the capital needed for direct investment in plant and equipment, inventory and accounts receivable. It is also easy to overlook certain initial costs, such as decorating and remodeling. Errors in earnings forecasts are common for the early months of the enterprise, as the optimum sales level may take some time to develop. Or various smaller expense items may be overlooked, each of which is small when considered alone but significant when combined with others.

Figure 11.1 illustrates the most common initial capital requirements and methods of minimizing them.

If you conclude from Figure 11.1 that I do not favor tying up capital in fixed assets, you are correct. Expensive facilities could cause you to go broke before you even get started. The cost of fixed assets continues regardless of whether you meet your sales expectations. High fixed costs are an invitation to bankruptcy. The small business owner's main competitive advantage is flexibility, and this will be lost when a high level of fixed costs are incurred. It is no accident that many successful businesses started their operations in the family's basement, spare room or garage, where costs are low.

Other costs should be kept as flexible as possible. Instead of hiring employees, contract for the services that are needed, paying people for what they produce, not for how many hours they put in. Often, very capable people are willing to work on this basis. Using this approach, you do not incur the expense or headaches involved in keeping payroll records or collecting taxes for the government. Also apply this strict cost control to yourself and any family members who might be employed with the firm. Keep your own expenses and salary to a minimum. The start-up period for a business is a time when belt-tightening is appropriate. Plan your business so that you can still survive if sales initially fall well below expectations.

If unnecessary expenses are avoided and most of the rest of your costs are kept flexible, you can accomplish growth even if sales do not meet projections.

FIGURE 11.1 Common Capital Requirements

Asset	*Means of Avoiding Capital Investment*
1. Real estate	Can be avoided by leasing.
2. Decorating and/or remodeling	If leased, the landlord may be persuaded to handle this expense.
3. Fixtures and equipment	Some can be leased, or bought in used condition.
4. Initial inventory	Suppliers are often willing to allow short-term credit in order to sell. Goods may be bought on consignment and not paid for until sold.
5. Accounts receivable	Either sell on a cash-only basis or arrange with finance company to handle your sales.
6. Miscellaneous expenses	Do everything possible to minimize these costs.

HOW STRONG FINANCES CONTRIBUTE INDIRECTLY TO PROFITABILITY

Strong finances contribute to the profitability of an organization in two ways: (1) by increasing the amount of funds available and minimizing their cost to the firm (a concept that will be explored later), and (2) by making it possible to take advantage of opportunities as they arise.

A new labor-saving device may become available to two companies in the same industry. The business that is financially stronger will adopt the new technology, immediately cutting labor costs. The stronger firm may improve sales growth by having a broader line of products to offer or more liberal credit terms, while the weaker may not be able to finance the added inventory or accounts receivable this would require.

Often you are able to obtain lower prices on materials by buying in larger quantities, or by taking advantage of sales or special discounts on needed products. Better-quality employees are attracted to the firm that can offer steady employment. The stronger firm may also buy out weaker competitors in the industry at bargain prices during a period of economic problems.

DIRECT CONTRIBUTION OF FINANCIAL STRENGTH TO A COMPANY'S PROFITABILITY

In one sense, every company is a finance company. It obtains funds from various sources and pays a certain rate of return on those funds. It then invests those funds at a higher rate of return. The difference in the rate at which it obtains funds and the rate at which it invests funds provides the income to pay nonfinancial expenses and provide profit.

The rate of return earned on investment depends on business skills but is also influenced by financial strength, as discussed above. Yet the main contribution that financial management makes to the success of an enterprise is through increasing the funds available to the firm and/or lowering their costs.

The simplest way to illustrate the profitability of skillful financing is to imagine an elementary finance company. An individual has $10,000 to invest and lends it out at 12 percent interest. There is no expense involved in making the loan, so the apparent profit is 12 percent × $10,000, or $1,200 per year. A considerably greater amount than $10,000 could be lent. Certain friends of the lender have funds earning 5 percent in money-market funds, so it is suggested to them that they could also earn 12 percent interest. The friends are debating whether or not to take the extra risk. The 12 percent borrowers are not the best credit risk, and these friends are worried. The original lender, feeling this concern is not justified, is willing to take the risk and offers to pay 10 percent on one friend's $10,000, which is better than he would get at a bank.

This additional $10,000 borrowed at 10 percent is then lent at 12 percent. Total income to the original lender is now $2,400, as computed in Figure 11.2.

On a sum of $10,000, the original lender has increased income from $1,800 to $3,600, return from 18 percent to 36 percent. This example of what can be accomplished with borrowed money is not unusual. A typical bank has more than one dollar of depositors' money for every dollar of capital, and an

FIGURE 11.2 Lender Income on Loans

Available capital	$20,000
Income at 12%	$ 2,400
Paid out to new lenders (10% × 10,000)	$ 1,000
Available for original lender	$ 1,400

Now assume that it is possible to raise $90,000 in new funds by offering 10 percent. The effect on income becomes dramatic, as illustrated below:

Total funds lent out	$100,000
Income at 12%	$ 12,000
Less funds to new lenders (10% × $90,000)	$ 9,000
Available for original lender	$ 3,000

average life insurance stock company has an even higher ratio of policyholders' dollars to each dollar of investor capital.

My first venture was a manufacturing enterprise with assets of almost $100,000, which was financed with $800 in savings, a $5,000 loan from my father-in-law, a mortgage loan of $50,000 and credit from various suppliers. From this, a million dollar nationwide enterprise was built within a few years. This extremely high leveraged approach is not recommended for everyone. The risks were great—perhaps almost too much so. But it is interesting to be aware of such possibilities.

At this point, two opposite questions might occur to you. Why would someone lend money at 10 percent to a middleman when he could lend it directly to the final borrower? The answer is lower risk. The middleman (who is the original lender in the above case) had greater familiarity with the borrower's business and greater expertise than the people who lent the money. Also, the middleman may have more collateral.

People may not be willing to lend money directly to a construction company, because they are unable to evaluate the risks involved. They would prefer to deposit their money in a savings account at a lesser rate of interest and let the banker make the loan to the construction company. The business owner is in a similar position, with expertise that should permit investment in areas that the unsophisticated investor should avoid.

The depositors in a financial institution have a second safety factor operating in their favor. The institution absorbs the first losses, should they occur. In the example, the original lender had $10,000 of his own money at work and $90,000 of funds that were borrowed from friends. A loss of $5,000 occurs as one of the borrowers, a construction company, defaults. The entire loss is borne by the original lender, who has been earning a higher return for taking a higher risk. The rate of return earned from a business should be higher than that available on such safe investments as savings accounts, due to the higher risk factor incurred by businesspeople and the expertise required.

The other question is, should the business owner borrow as much capital as possible? The question is partly answered in the above example. The original lender, who borrowed $90,000 of the $100,000 lent out, had half his equity wiped out by a 50 percent loss of capital. In the long run, maximum financial leverage may be appealing. But there is no long run for those who fail to survive the short term. Another factor limits the value of borrowed funds: the cost goes up as the leverage increases. The business that has substantial equity capital can borrow funds at rates not too different from government bonds, while the financially leveraged company may pay double or even triple that interest rate. A balanced approach is always safer.

TYPES OF CAPITAL

The two major types of capital are equity capital and debt capital. Equity capital represents ownership funds, and is called common stock in the case of corporations. When a business owner sells equity capital in the form of common stock, he is selling part of his ownership. In contrast, raising capital by debt financing involves a creditor to whom funds are owed. The creditor has a legal claim on the assets of the business, which protects his or her interest. When the debt comes due, if the company cannot pay, it defaults. This lender/ creditor can then force the company into liquidation by joining with two or more other creditors. Because he has a prior claim on the assets of the company, the lender must be paid when the assets are sold and before the owner receives anything.

In addition to these two major types of capital, there are sources of funding that lie between these two extremes. Preferred stock is neither equity nor debt. The preferred shareholder usually receives a fixed amount of dividend before the common shareholder receives any. In this respect, a preferred shareholder is similar to a creditor. Unlike the creditor, however, the preferred shareholder does not have the power to force the company into liquidation if the dividend is not paid. Also, a preferred stock does not come due as in the case of debt, so preferred stock represents a more permanent source of capital than does debt, which must be repaid. Preferred stock dividends are not tax-deductible by the company, however, whereas interest payments are deductible. As a result, preferred stock is no longer a common form of financing.

Another type of hybrid capital is the convertible bond or convertible preferred stock. The preferred shareholders or lenders, in the case of the convertible bond, can convert their securities into common stock if things go well for the company. Consequently, the common stock grows in value. On the other hand, if things do not go well, the preferred shareholders or bondholders do not have to convert, but can retain their safer securities.

The term *capital* usually refers to such long-term financing as equity or common stock, preferred stock and bonds. The enterprising company, however, is able to supplement this long-term financing with numerous types and sources of additional funds.

COST OF CAPITAL

The cost of capital varies widely from time to time, depending on supply and demand. Also, different types of loans have different interest rates, and different institutions charge different rates for the same type of loan. In spite of the apparent confusion, interest rates are more logical than they first appear. The factors in Figure 11.3 determine the interest rate on a particular security.

Armed with the above information, the businessperson can reduce interest costs in several ways. Provided the person is a

FIGURE 11.3 How Interest Rate Is Determined

A pure rate of interest	Varies according to demand on any supply of funds
An inflation factor	An estimate of future inflation rate
A risk factor appropriate for each type of security	Varies widely
A factor for costs of processing the loan	Much higher for installment-type loans than one-payment loans

good credit risk, the interest costs can be reduced by borrowing during recessions when interest rates are lower. During depressed periods in the economy estimates of future inflation tend to drop.

The borrower can also reduce costs by being (and giving the impression of being) a low-risk borrower. There are ways of doing this, such as borrowing even if you do not need it and paying the money back promptly. A more direct approach is suggested. If you are starting a business, you should first have your personal finances under control. You should have demonstrated the ability to save some money as a basis for starting your enterprise. It is advisable to have a well-thought-out plan for making your business a success, including contingency funds you may tap if problems arise. My first experience in obtaining a business loan was at the age of 21. After approaching four out of the five major banks in town and being turned down cold, I finally recognized that more complete preparation was necessary. A proposal covering the following points was prepared and presented:

- How much capital I needed
- What form the financing should take
- To what use the capital would be put
- How the debt would be paid back
- What security, if any, could be offered

The loan was granted. Note that the risk to the lender had not changed, but perception of the risk had changed to a great extent. This is an important point to remember and explains

FIGURE 11.4 Obtaining a Bank Loan Worksheet

I. Company Background

A. History of Company: ______

1. Description of operations

______

2. Unique features

______

B. History of Owners and/or Officers, including relevant experience: ______

______

______

______

C. Company's Position in the Industry: ______

1. Nature of industry, including size, number of competitors, growth rate and profitability

______

______

2. Company's competitive position in industry

______

II. Amount of Money Needed and Its Purpose

A. How money will be spent: ______

1. How much for physical plant? ______

2. How much for working capital? ______

3. Do you expect further financing in the next 12 months? If so, how much? ______

______

III. How You Expect to Pay Money Back

A. How much of payment is to be made from future earnings, and when?

______

______

FIGURE 11.4 Obtaining a Bank Loan Worksheet (continued)

B. How much of payment is from sources other than future profits?

1. From future common stock financing ____________
2. From future long-term debt financing ____________
3. From other short-term borrowing ____________
4. From reduction of assets ____________
   a. from sale of physical assets ____________
   b. from reduction of inventories ____________
   c. from reduction of accounts receivable ____________

IV. Financial Summary of Company*

*Attach recent financial statement of company.

Sales	*Profit Margins*	*Net Income*	*Book Value*	*Return on Book Value*
19___				
19___				
19___				
19___				
19___				
19___				
19___				

V. Projections of Company's Sales, Earnings and Cash Position

	Sales	*Net Income*	*Working Capital (Current Assets Less Liabilities)*	*Book Value*	*Cash*
Next year					
Three years from now					

FIGURE 11.4 Obtaining a Bank Loan Worksheet (continued)

VI. What Security Can Be Offered?

____

____

VII. What Other Sources of Financing Are Available to You?

____

____

why many borrowers pay higher interest rates than they need to pay. Figure 11.4 is a worksheet to help you prepare your loan proposal.

For example, an average borrower at a loan company tends to have a lower credit rating than the average borrower at a bank. The person who could be borrowing from a bank but uses a personal finance company is often paying an unnecessarily high interest rate.

The borrower can also reduce the risk to the lender by offering collateral or guarantees, and thus reduce the interest rate accordingly. This is one reason mortgage rates are lower than rates on equivalent maturity unsecured loans. The borrower can also help decrease the paperwork cost to the lender and reduce interest rates by avoiding loans with monthly payments and arranging for a loan with a single payment.

Sources of Funds

1. Your Own Equity
   This is a key source, because other lenders will want to know that you are a good risk. If you have not been able to accumulate any equity, or if you are afraid to risk your own funds, it is unlikely that you will inspire confidence in others.
2. Sweat Equity
   This refers to an individual's equity in an enterprise that has been achieved by working without pay rather than by contributing cash funds. In a do-it-yourself

economy such as the United States, sweat equity is a major source of the average individual's asset value.

3. Family Loans or Investments
   Members of your family will often invest in your enterprise because they respect your ability, not because they understand the business.
4. Loans or Investments by Friends
   As with family loans, friends will often invest in your enterprise because they believe in you.
5. Banks
   These are the "department stores" of finance. They do not provide equity capital. They are most active in short-term loans, but also provide intermediate-term loans and mortgage loans. They are not interested in high-risk ventures unless provided with collateral or guarantees. An individual may be asked to personally guarantee a loan to a small company of which he or she is the major stockholder.
6. Insurance Companies
   One source of an individual's contribution to the financial needs of his or her enterprise could be through a loan against the cash value of personal insurance policies. The life insurance industry is a major source of finance; however, insurance companies tend to specialize in large loans that are long-term in nature, and consequently are not a good source of capital to the beginning enterprise.
7. Finance Companies
   These companies are most valuable, as they make it possible for the enterprise to sell on credit but not have capital tied up in accounts receivable. Some sales finance companies also lend on inventories and lease out equipment.
8. Factors
   This type of business, like a finance company, also makes it possible and often convenient for a business to extend credit without having capital tied up in accounts receivable.
9. Small Business Investment Companies (SBIC)
   These are the most flexible sources of financing, providing equity capital and long-term loans. Companies are eligible if they have assets under $7.5 million, net worth under $2.5 million, and earnings of less than

$250,000 during the past two years. SBIC financing has unique advantages, as it provides not only capital but also business expertise. Its interests coincide exactly with the needs of the small business, improving prospects for compatibility.

10. Credit Unions
    One of the lowest-cost sources of credit is credit unions. Since you have to be a member of an organization, this source is appropriate mainly for individuals holding jobs while operating a part-time business.
11. Equipment Companies
    Instead of buying equipment, the businessperson can often arrange to lease the equipment from the manufacturer. This is equivalent to a source of capital.
12. Leasing Companies
    Even if equipment producers do not offer their product on a lease arrangement, it can often be acquired on that basis through a leasing company.
13. Employees
    These are often overlooked as finance sources. Employees may prefer to invest savings in a field they know and are able to monitor, and they can also contribute to the safety of their investment by performing well for the company.
14. Customers
    If you provide a valuable service, a customer may be willing to help finance its availability. To ensure a reliable supply of steel, a major auto company may provide the bulk of financing for a new steel company. A major retailer might make equity investments in a number of its major suppliers. Manufacturers help finance wholesalers, and the latter help finance retailers.
15. Investment Bankers
    Investment bankers are concerned primarily with supplying the long-term capital requirements of business. The investment banker is the middleman between the business needing funds and the investor with money to supply. In some cases, the investment banker, through a venture capital subsidiary, invests directly in a business.

16. Mutual Funds
    Ordinarily these invest in established companies, but some specialize in smaller, higher-risk situations.
17. Mutual Savings Banks
    A small business owner is more likely to get a mortgage loan on his or her residence than a direct business loan. The funds can then be used for business purposes.
18. Savings and Loan Associations
    The same applies as for Mutual Savings Banks (above).
19. Investment Clubs
    These ordinarily invest in established companies, but some do devote a portion of their funds to new enterprises.
20. Private Individual Investors
    These are often an excellent source of financing, as they have no restrictions except their own. A good source of seed money is a local doctor, dentist or other professional who has a high personal income and an equally high tax bracket. Check your newspaper under the heading "Business Opportunities" for advertisements run by this class of investor.
21. Pension Funds
    These companies are gigantic investors but are primarily interested in established companies.
22. Family Investment Funds
    Unlike broadly held investment funds, which tend to avoid risk, investment funds of wealthy families can be more risk-oriented. They can be a good source of funds if the enterprise has exceptional growth prospects.
23. Foundations
    Wealthy people usually organize foundations to shelter some of their income, or for philanthropic reasons. Many do so not only for charitable purposes, but also because their investments are tax-deductible.
24. Small Business Administration
    This provides several programs to benefit small businesses including the SBIC program mentioned above. The SBA provides funds by direct loans and by guaranteeing loans made by other lenders (such as banks).

The SBA also cooperates with states and localities in business-development efforts.

25. Economic Development Administration
This agency of the U.S. Department of Commerce provides business loans to assist economically deprived areas. Applicants must be able to demonstrate that new jobs will be created by the business.

26. Other Possible Sources
The following may be helpful in either providing funds or helping to acquire them:
    - Colleges and universities
    - Corporate venture capital departments
    - Financial consultants
    - Investment advisers
    - Large corporations
    - Venture capital firms
    - Securities dealers
    - Self-underwriting
    - State and local industries development corporation
    - Trust departments of banks
    - Department of Veterans Affairs

SELF-TEST QUESTIONS

Multiple Choice

1. A financially strong company has
    a. greater flexibility in its operations.
    b. better ability to survive hard times.
    c. ability to take advantage of opportunities that require investment.
    d. All of the above

2. The best time to approach a venture capital firm for financing is
    a. before you start your business.
    b. after you have demonstrated that your company is capable of rapid growth.
    c. when you are ready to sell.
    d. when you are desperate for help.

3. The following is often overlooked as a source of finance:
   a. Customers
   b. Employees
   c. Suppliers
   d. All of the above

4. The following would be the most likely source of equity funds:
   a. Credit unions and banks
   b. Mutual funds and trust departments of banks
   c. SBICs and private individual investors such as physicians
   d. Leasing companies

5. A company can best minimize its need for capital by
   a. leasing plant and equipment rather than buying.
   b. delaying its payments on accounts payable.
   c. staying small.
   d. stressing manufacturing rather than service businesses.

6. Investment in inventories can be minimized by
   a. obtaining goods from suppliers on a consignment basis.
   b. stressing rapid inventory turnover.
   c. Neither of the above
   d. Both of the above

7. The interest rate you pay on funds you borrow will increase if
   a. you decrease your financial leverage.
   b. your profitability increases, so that you are able to pay more.
   c. The rate of inflation increases substantially.
   d. All of the above

8. In evaluating you as a potential borrower, banks use a 4-C formula for determining how good a risk you are. The four Cs would most likely refer to
   a. cash, credit, car and carefulness.
   b. character, capital, capacity and collateral.
   c. contacts, customers, clients and customs.
   d. None of the above

True or False

9. Most new businesspeople overestimate their need for capital in the early years of a business.

   True ☐ False ☐

10. By incorporating your business, you make it easier to obtain a loan from a bank.

    True ☐ False ☐

11. Incorporating your business automatically enables you to raise money by selling stock on the Stock Exchange.

    True ☐ False ☐

12. Inadequate financial strength is often a contributing factor in business failures.

    True ☐ False ☐

13. Preferred stock is the most desirable stock on the exchanges.

    True ☐ False ☐

14. Strong finances can contribute to the profitability of an enterprise in both indirect and direct ways.

    True ☐ False ☐

15. Since interest on borrowed money is a tax-deductible item, you should raise as much money as possible from borrowing rather than from stock sale.

    True ☐ False ☐

16. A highly profitable, stable business can safely use a greater percentage of debt in its capital structure.

    True ☐ False ☐

17. As a company becomes highly leveraged, the interest rate charged by its creditors is likely to increase.

    True ☐ False ☐

18. You can usually reduce your interest rate by lowering the risk that your creditor feels it is taking.

    True ☐ False ☐

19. Cost of capital is usually less for borrowed funds than for equity funds.

    True ☐ False ☐

20. Life insurance companies prefer to make short-term loans, in contrast to banks, which prefer to make long-term loans.

    True ☐ False ☐

Answers

1.d, 2.b, 3.d, 4.c, 5.a, 6.d, 7.c, 8.b, 9.F, 10.F, 11.F, 12.T, 13.F, 14.T, 15.F, 16.T, 17.T, 18.T, 19.T, 20.F

CHAPTER 12

Sources of Information on Business

The business manager must combine a number of ingredients, including labor and capital, into products and services. The most strategic factor in business today is knowledge, and the individual with expertise can attract factors such as labor and capital. The large organization would seem to have a major advantage over the small one, at least when it comes to the control of knowledge. The large corporation has lawyers available, as well as accountants, engineers and, in especially large companies, even more specialized experts in many of the esoteric subject areas. The advantage would seem to be overwhelmingly in favor of the large establishments.

Fortunately for the small businessperson, the situation is not as one-sided as it first appears. As an organization grows larger, it can afford more specialists, but the task of coordinating such specialized knowledge grows commensurately. The value of specialized knowledge in a company is only as good as the ability of the specialists to communicate strategic information upward to the decision makers. And it is only as good as the ability of the decision makers to comprehend the floods of specialized information to which they are exposed.

The situation deteriorates for the large organization if it is bureaucratic in nature. An associate who once worked in a large corporation of this type described how much of the company's experts' time was wasted on irrelevant assignments. In one case, the company president circulated a one-sentence memorandum to eight different executives in the firm, asking their opinion regarding an article in that morning's paper. In the next three weeks, all eight executives assigned the best members of their staffs to answer the memo on a top-priority basis. The average length of the replies to this one-sentence memo was 29 pages, with the winner being a 42-page report. The executive who submitted the longest report was ready to submit a 35-page answer, but, upon hearing that a "competitor" had handed in 40 pages, instructed the staff to add sufficient text to exceed the opponent's report.

In a large bureaucratic organization, upper management often suffers from a similar distortion of the information flow. In ancient times, the bearer of bad news was often put to death, while the bearer of good news was rewarded handsomely. This practice is still continued in large organizations, although usually on a less extreme basis. As a result, top management usually receives a preponderance of good news, which tends to distort their view of reality.

The small business manager does not get this protection from the harsher aspects of reality, and consequently has an advantage over his or her big company counterparts. Finally, it should be noted that the smaller business' major advantage over bigger competitors does not necessarily have to be superior information, but can be the ability to perceive correct information and to react to it faster.

There are many sources of information, each having its own advantages and disadvantages. Some classifications would be

- personal contacts;
- organizations;
- periodicals, magazines and newspapers; and
- books, pamphlets and manuals.

PERSONAL CONTACTS

Personal contact with specialists provides the most current information and has the advantage of being a two-way communication. Any points of misunderstanding can be cleared up with questions and answers. Consequently, a major long-term goal should be to build up a broad circle of business associates who are knowledgeable in various fields.

At first, this goal may seem to be an extremely difficult one to achieve. There are some shortcuts, however, to achieving it. For example, you will be buying insurance, selecting a banker with whom to work, hiring a part-time accountant and communicating with suppliers. Developing these relationships involves important strategic decisions and should not be treated lightly or based on fee schedules alone. It probably costs no more to buy insurance from a knowledgeable professional in the field than it does to buy from a salesperson with a mediocre knowledge of that product.

Each specialist should have the knowledge you need and should be capable and willing (or even eager) to share that knowledge with you. If you are regarded as an unimportant customer because of size, it would be better to find someone else. Look for the specialist who is willing to invest some time in your long-term future. Although small at first, you may be an extremely important customer in the years to come.

The best contacts honestly want to earn their fees or commissions. They genuinely like their profession and enjoy few things better than talking about their specialty. Even when you deal with a specific institution, you often have your choice of people to contact. At a bank, for example, ask for an officer who specializes in loans to small businesses. Once you have a good working relationship with such individuals, start making use of their contacts. You may need some information on investments or employee benefit plans, for instance, and the loan officer may be able to provide it by checking with other specialists at the bank.

It is not necessary to pay expensive fees for such expert advice. Often your contacts will ask only that you recommend their services to acquaintances and friends, or you may be expected to provide free consultation time to their contacts when they need some answers in your area of expertise. Incidentally, it goes without saying that the more of an expert you are in any one subject or subject area, the more sought-after you will become as a business contact.

One prominent economist noted for his above-average forecasting ability was once asked about the secret of his success. He replied that it was the circle of business associates he had built up over the years. Rather than take business statistics published by the government at face value, he would check various industry figures with his knowledgeable contacts in the industry. Not only was their information more current, but they were also able to point out distortions in the figures that could be detected only by an industry specialist. More important, they were usually able to predict changes taking place that could not even be expressed in quantitative terms.

ORGANIZATIONS

While you are building your network of personal contacts, you should not overlook institutions that exist to help you. The Small Business Administration is one example. Listed at the end of this section are some SBA publications that might prove to be helpful.

Another counseling group is Service Corps of Retired Executives (SCORE), which uses retired businesspeople as consultants to small businesses. These consultants work free of charge and are available for advice on such subjects as advertising, marketing, personnel and various operating problems. Your nearest SBA office can put you in touch.

It would be advisable to get acquainted with any trade associations that apply to your industry. They can also be valuable sources of overall industry data and trend information.

If you live in a city that has a library with a good business section, learn to make use of it. Librarians may have a master's degree in library science, but they often find themselves being used as overeducated file clerks. Find ones who are eager to make use of their expertise and ask them questions. Even if they don't have an immediate answer, many are willing to spend some research time to find it.

Another source of information could be a local college or university. Those with business schools often have professors and staff who are knowledgeable in regard to the economics of your area. Sometimes business professors will assign an advanced student to a study project in your field of interest. If the institution offers evening business classes in subjects that interest you, it could be a good investment of your time and money to take one or more. Ask the instructor practical questions that apply directly to your own business. If the responses are helpful, try to turn the professor into one of your business contacts.

Local government agencies can answer specific questions. If you are required to have a license, for example, the agency responsible for the issuance of the license should be a good source of advice on requirements that must be met. Similarly, taxing authorities are an obvious source of information on tax matters.

Business organizations, such as the Chamber of Commerce and the Better Business Bureau, can be of assistance in certain areas. Various clubs consisting largely of businesspeople offer the opportunity for developing close business relationships. Members are usually small company owners who know the area and have already encountered and solved many of the problems confronting the person just starting out. Most are willing to share their knowledge with a newcomer, unless he or she happens to be a direct competitor in the same neighborhood.

PERIODICALS, MAGAZINES AND NEWSPAPERS

Reading is a quick method of expanding one's knowledge, and periodical literature provides many of the advantages of a wide range of personal contacts.

Newspaper and magazine articles are written for broad, general-interest audiences and are likely to be less technical or specialized than academic books. Their content is also likely to be more up-to-date than books, and the length of articles is such that they can be read in a single sitting. They do not provide the opportunity for questions and answers, as do individual contacts, but the number of specialists who offer advice through periodicals is many times the number of business friends you might acquire in a lifetime. Over a period of years, you will find certain writers to be especially helpful in stimulating your thinking and providing insight. At this stage, your reading efficiency takes a giant step forward.

Each person should develop specific sources of information that are helpful. One associate who is a generalist in the investment field lists the following as his reading list for keeping informed on the factors that influence business:

Daily Reading

The Wall Street Journal

A major city newspaper (or one such as *The New York Times* or *Washington Post*)

Weekly Reading

Business Week
Boardroom Reports
U.S. News & World Report
Advertising Age

To keep abreast of current events and trends in marketing:

Monthly Reading

Readers Digest

The Wall Street Journal need not be read in its entirety every day, as it is primarily published for investment professionals with an extremely broad range of interests. Any business manager should find at least several articles of interest in each issue. In addition to *The Wall Street Journal,* a major city newspaper should be read in order to keep informed on social trends and issues, as well as local news that may affect business.

Business Week is read weekly to cover major business and economic trends. *Boardroom Reports* is one of several business-digest publications that present capsule commentaries on a multitude of business subjects such as advertising, investments, consultants, law, management, marketing, personnel, taxes and articles of personal interest. The source from which the digests are prepared is included in the report, so that the reader can get to the source for the complete article, if desired.

Readers Digest is "must" reading for this associate, but he is quick to point out that he may not be typical in this regard. He considers *Readers Digest* to be the voice of middle America, addressing itself to the basic questions asked by the people and presenting a balanced viewpoint.

The above represents a basic, generalized reading list and should be supplemented by a good publication specifically tailored to the needs of your profession. In addition, it would be advisable to select an area of your business in which you would like to become more knowledgeable and subscribe to a publication in that field.

BOOKS, PAMPHLETS AND MANUALS

Individual contacts and reading of periodical literature provide quick elementary knowledge of a subject. When a thorough knowledge is desirable, however, more detailed and inclusive reports are recommended. Consequently, you should become proficient at finding books, pamphlets and manuals in your chosen field.

The librarian or business school contacts mentioned earlier can be most helpful in recommending source books. One word of caution is in order regarding the selection of textbooks, however. Sometimes the academic writer is removed from the business world and will tend to go further into a subject than is necessary for your purposes. Academic texts are usually written as an adjunct to classroom instruction.

In contrast, there are educational books written for the purpose of informing the reader. They start simply, with information that most readers can quickly grasp, and then build gradually upon that base to more difficult aspects of the subject. Strongly advocated are publications that take this step-by-step approach in covering a business topic. In addition, a subject can be learned much more thoroughly if it has immediate practical applications. Practical books on solving business problems can expose the reader to various aspects of accounting, business law, economics, corporate finance and other business subjects that pertain to the problem. The information is not only relevant, but is also organized around a central theme. These characteristics make the information very easy to remember compared to the typical textbook.

Another secret to building a valuable business library is to carefully review the bibliography listed in the books that you particularly like. This is especially helpful when the author not only lists his reference sources, but also comments on those that were particularly helpful and why. The bibliography in this course presents a broad list of good basic sources of general business information with selected commentary.

In addition to a good general business library, you should build up an equally good collection of reference books in your own field of business. Check with successful businesspeople in your area for books they have found helpful. Consult your trade association. Ask the advice of your librarian or business college contact. One very successful business owner who considers a good business library essential for success points out that he has purchased several books for $15 to $30, each of which produced an income return in the thousands of dollars! And, of course, many of these transactions are tax-deductible.

The amount of information available to the entrepreneur is vast, and the secret is to learn how to find what you need. Librarians are experts on this subject. They have at their disposal directories of *Books in Print,* a *Reader's Guide to Periodical Literature,* and numerous directories on sources of specialized information. If you have access to a bookstore with an extensive business section, the dealer may be a good consultant on the subject. A trade association is a helpful source of literature in your chosen field. A guide to various associations is the Gale Research Company *Encyclopedia of American Associations,* which includes trade, business, professional, educational and other organizations. The American Management Association has a good library of business subjects that is available to its members. Information on services offered and membership can be obtained by writing to the American Management Association, 135 West 50th Street, New York, NY, 10020.

To obtain information about business periodicals serving a particular industry, assistance can be obtained by writing to one of the following:

American Society of Business Press Editors
4445 Gilmer Lane
Cleveland, OH 44143

Society of National Association Publications
1735 North Lynn Street, Suite 950
Arlington, VA 22209

MISCELLANEOUS

Some other sources of information that are available to small business owners are described below.

Seminars on business subjects are often available throughout the country. At first the registration fees may seem excessive, but it is important to remember that one useful, workable idea may be worth many times the cost of the seminar itself. *Business book clubs* have been organized in recent years and can be an excellent source of information. To develop a better background in dealing with people and in public speaking, *The Dale Carnegie Institute* and *Toastmasters International* have good records of success and popularity. These courses are particularly useful to individuals who are involved in direct sales on a person-to-person basis.

Correspondence schools offer a practical means of filling in gaps in your educational background. Many basic trades are taught almost exclusively by correspondence rather than through residence schools. Courses are heavy on the practical side and minimize the theoretical side. They are organized to fit into a busy person's schedule, so you can proceed at a rate appropriate for you. Some organizations that offer correspondence courses specialize in that form of education. In addition, most state universities offer correspondence courses on various subjects. Should yours not offer the particular course you want, they can provide you with a directory of correspondence courses offered by other universities throughout the country.

In building a business library, it is strongly recommended that you include a section on inspirational business literature to deepen your individual motivation. Books by Ayn Rand defending individual rights and the free-enterprise system are an important part of my library. Books by Napoleon Hill contain a wealth of case histories on successful business leaders and industrialists, and give valuable insight into those qualities that have made them great. One of the best authors on self-development is Maxwell Maltz, who has written on the subject of visualizing where you want to go as the first step in becoming successful. The writings of Nathaniel Branden in the field of psychology have been especially useful to me.

If at all possible, book learning should always be combined with practical experience. A person minimizes his or her chance of failure in an industry by working in it part-time before jumping in all the way. *Moonlighting* can be an excellent method of advancing your education in areas in which you might be inexperienced, as well as allowing you to learn the fundamentals of the new business. A part-time sales job in a store can give you experience in dealing with customers while permitting you to observe what is essential for success in that field. Such experience, supplemented by reading, is much more effective than experience alone or reading alone.

LITERATURE AVAILABLE FROM GOVERNMENT SOURCES

The government publishes a number of booklets and pamphlets that can be helpful to the small business owner. The Small Business Administration is the best source of aid, providing a number of booklets to small business owners for which it collects a small donation. For information on the SBA's services and the latest publications, call the SBA Small Business Answer Desk at 1-800-827-5722. Below is a list of pamphlets available from the SBA at time of publication.

- Ideas into Dollars
- Avoiding Patent, Trademark and Copyright Problems
- Trademarks and Business Goodwill
- ABCs of Borrowing
- Profit Costing and Pricing for Manufacturers
- Basic Budgets for Profit Planning
- Understanding Cash Flow
- A Venture Capital Primer for Small Business
- Accounting Services for Small Service Firms
- Analyze Your Records To Reduce Costs
- Budgeting in a Small Service Firm
- Sound Cash Management and Borrowing
- Recording Keeping in a Small Business
- Simple Break-Even Analysis for Small Stores
- A Pricing Checklist for Small Retailers
- Pricing Your Products and Services Profitably
- Effective Business Communications
- Locating or Relocating Your Business
- Problems in Managing a Family-Owned Business
- Business Plan for Small Manufacturers
- Business Plan for Small Construction Firms
- Planning and Goal Setting for Small Business
- Should You Lease or Buy Equipment?
- Business Plans for Retailers
- Choosing a Retail Location
- Business Plan for Small Service Firms

- Checklist for Going into Business
- How To Get Started with a Small Business Computer
- The Business Plan for Home-Based Business
- How To Buy or Sell a Business
- Purchasing for Owners of Small Plants
- Buying for Retail Stores
- Small Business Decision Making
- Business Continuation Planning
- Developing a Strategic Business Plan
- Inventory Management
- Techniques for Problem Solving
- Techniques for Productivity Improvement
- Selecting the Legal Structure for Your Business
- Evaluating Franchise Opportunities
- Small Business Risk Management Guide
- Quality Child Care Makes Good Business Sense
- Creative Selling: The Competitive Edge
- Marketing for Small Business: An Overview
- Is the Independent Sales Agent for You?
- Marketing Checklist for Small Retailers
- Researching Your Market
- Selling by Mail Order
- Market Overseas with U.S. Government Help
- Advertising
- Curtailing Crime—Inside and Out
- A Small Business Guide to Computer Security
- Checklist for Developing a Training Program
- Employees: How To Find and Pay Them
- Managing Employee Benefits

SELF-TEST QUESTIONS

Multiple Choice

1. The small company should make use of the knowledge possessed by
   a. its banker.
   b. its insurance company.
   c. the local librarian.
   d. All of the above

2. In selecting business associates, you should consider, among other things,
   a. their expertise in their specialty.
   b. their willingness to share that knowledge with you.
   c. their ability to explain their subject so that it can be understood.
   d. All of the above

3. Getting information from personal contacts has the advantage of
   a. costing you nothing.
   b. not requiring you to study.
   c. developing your ability to ask questions and learn more.
   d. None of the above

4. A low-cost source of consultation on business problems is
   a. a private economic consultant.
   b. SCORE (Service Corps of Retired Executives).
   c. an investment banker.
   d. your stockbroker.

5. Your ability to develop close relationships with a large number of experts will be influenced by
   a. your ability to impress them with your social standing.
   b. your ability to entertain them lavishly.
   c. your ability to impress them with your own value as a source of expertise.
   d. None of the above

6. You should develop enough expertise in each important business subject to do the following:
   a. Evaluate the expertise level of a specialist in the field.
   b. Know what questions to ask and when.
   c. Understand the answers to questions you do ask.
   d. All of the above

7. If you are very busy, you could
   a. eliminate the time you spend reading.
   b. read only articles that specifically address problems you are now facing.
   c. rely on your business associates to keep you up-to-date on important developments.
   d. subscribe to publications that present business articles in digest form.

8. Association with other local businesspeople can be educational in regard to
   a. local business conditions.
   b. competitive developments.
   c. regulation and local laws.
   d. All of the above

True or False

9. Books represent the most current source of information.

   True ☐ False ☐

10. Statistics from the government are helpful, but suffer from time lag and are subject to revision.

    True ☐ False ☐

11. A small business must have better and more numerous sources of information than a large business if it is to compete.

    True ☐ False ☐

12. A small business can usually react faster to information it receives than a big business could.

    True ☐ False ☐

13. Management of a large organization is not able to fully utilize the knowledge of the various experts employed by the company.

    True ☐ False ☐

14. Many academic books are written more for the purpose of classroom instruction than for the needs of small business owners.

    True ☐ False ☐

15. Local librarians may resent your making use of their technical expertise if it interferes with their library clerical work.

    True ☐ False ☐

16. The Small Business Administration is a low-cost source of many publications for businesses.

    True ☐ False ☐

17. You should avoid trade associations, as most of the information they possess is confidential and not likely to be shared with you.

    True ☐ False ☐

18. In building a business library, your main purpose should be to impress your customers with expensive looking volumes.

    True ☐ False ☐

19. Book learning should never be combined with practical experience, as the two approaches are in basic conflict.

    True ☐ False ☐

20. Knowledge of business conditions in a local area may be available from your local college or university.

    True ☐ False ☐

Answers

1.d, 2.d, 3.c, 4.b, 5.c, 6.d, 7.d, 8.d, 9.F, 10.T, 11.F, 12.T, 13.T, 14.T, 15.F, 16.T, 17.F, 18.F, 19.F, 20.T

CHAPTER 13

Records, Bookkeeping and Accounting

There are many reasons to treat the recordkeeping part of your business with respect. Studies indicate that inadequate records are a frequent contributing factor in business failures. It is almost too commonplace to hear a newly-bankrupt business owner bemoan the failure by saying, "I didn't know I was operating at a loss. Sales were doing just fine."

In many cases, the bankrupt business was going reasonably well, measured by sales. But the company suffered failure because of inadequate profitability, bad-debt losses, shortage of cash or a combination of all of these (and other) shortcomings. A sound bookkeeping and accounting system would have pointed out these problems early enough to permit corrective action.

The dislike many businesspeople feel for the accounting function is probably easy to understand when one remembers that much of the recordkeeping is involuntary in nature. Beginning with the birth of income tax in 1913, each business had a silent (though not unobtrusive) partner—the Internal Revenue Service.

Over a period of time, business owners have found that they are not only taxpayers but also involuntary tax collectors. When your business expands beyond a one-person operation and you become an employer, you find yourself involved with records for each employee, for withholding Social Security and income taxes, workmen's and unemployment compensation, accident and health insurance, sales taxes and other items. As government regulation has grown, more and more records have become mandatory.

The government, however, is not the only body imposing recordkeeping chores on you. Before the banker will lend money, the bank will want to review various financial statements. Trade creditors often require the same information, especially when you are just getting started. If you ask investors to contribute capital to the enterprise, they may require detailed historical financial records as well as projections for the future. So it is small wonder that inadequate recordkeeping is associated with business failures.

Without intending to make light of the time and work involved, we nevertheless remark here that bookkeeping—like most problems—appears tougher than you find it to be once you get into it. This is particularly true if you handle it correctly. Furthermore, having complete and neat records is a good feeling. An oversimplified but valid analogy is the uneasy feeling you have when your personal checking account is not balanced. It's a chore, so you put it off; but you find that the mental anguish of not knowing what your balance is can be worse than the tedium of reconciling your tabulation with the bank statement. Still worse is the feeling you get when you discover you have written checks but not recorded them and can't remember what they were for. The feelings are amplified when your business records are incomplete or incorrect. The confidence and sense of being in control, therefore, are worth the diligence and self-discipline required to achieve that mental state. What's more, it's probably a matter of survival.

So before starting your own business, accept the principle that the labor goes with the fruits.

Our purpose in this chapter is to make your accounting and bookkeeping labors more productive and less tedious than they might be without this assistance.

Let us now get into some specifics.

The type of accounting that is basically oriented toward describing what has taken place in the past (sometimes known as custodial accounting) is perhaps rightly regarded as a necessary evil. But accounting can be more future-oriented and, if used correctly, can greatly improve decision making.

Some examples are obvious. A knowledge of what items are selling best permits the store manager to keep such items in stock rather than continually experiencing shortages and losing sales. Being aware of accounts receivable that are past due permits a timely collection. It might, in fact, prevent an uncollectible debt. Even a relatively simple bookkeeping system would aid in these routine decisions.

A more sophisticated accounting system can greatly improve your ability to make informed decisions. The profitability of a business can almost always be improved by more strategic planning, more diligent control, and knowledge of which products and customers provide the most profit. Through accounting, you can learn how to invest your limited capital to get the best return. Shortages of cash can be anticipated before they occur, allowing corrective action to be taken to avoid this situation. Accounting can be transformed from the drudgery of custodial bookkeeping to the valuable tool of management accounting. Now for some basics.

It is extremely important that from the beginning you maintain a business checking account that is separate from your personal account. We emphasize this point because it is a common failing of new entrepreneurs. The reason is simple. When tax time comes and you are paid a visit by your friendly IRS auditor, it will be difficult to prove that the $179.40 you spent for lodging and meals at the Holiday Inn in Los Angeles was for a business trip (not a vacation) if you paid by check from your personal account.

An important point to bear in mind is that virtually everything you spend in order to carry on your business is tax deductible. Maintaining a business checking account simply makes sense. You will have a permanent record of all business expenditures.

Along these same lines, make an attempt to pay all business expenses by check. You may also wish to obtain a "business only" credit card, such as Diners Club or American Express. This will provide you with a permanent record of your expenses where checks are inconvenient or not accepted, and the annual membership fee is tax-deductible. If the expense or purchase is small (for instance, a box of paper clips), always save the receipt and note what it was for.

In the beginning, your bookkeeping records can be very simple. Most entrepreneurs use a common single-entry system, where "income" and "outgo" are recorded on the same sheet of paper. This is much like balancing a checkbook, and you maintain a running balance of the cash available. As your business develops and becomes more complex, you will probably want your accountant to set up a simple system for you, and retain a bookkeeper to handle it. Bookkeepers can be hired as part-time employees of the business or as independent contractors paid an hourly rate or on a contract-fee basis.

If you have a partner, it will be necessary to keep track of how much each of you contributes to the business, as well as how much each of you withdraws. When you hire employees (as opposed to independent contractors or moonlighters, who are paid on a piecemeal basis), you will need a system of recording their earnings and figuring the amount of taxes to withhold, and a method of reporting and paying these payroll taxes. Your bookkeeper should be familiar with these aspects of record-keeping, and it will be well worth your time saved in not having to handle this chore.

When you reach this point, the following are some areas that should be discussed with your bookkeeper and your accountant.

NECESSARY BOOKKEEPING AND ACCOUNTING SERVICES

Installing an Accounting System

The accountant studies the nature of your business, determines the type of transactions that will occur, and plans the necessary forms on which these transactions will be recorded. The accountant should show you how to fill in these forms yourself.

Recordkeeping

This is the actual recording of business transactions on the accounting forms. Generally, this is done by a bookkeeper under the guidance of an accountant, but you may decide to handle it yourself in the beginning.

Preparation of the Financial Statement

At regular intervals, the accountant takes the data collected in the accounting records and summarizes them in statements showing the financial position of the company and its operating results for the period. These documents are used not only for your own information, but may also be required by bankers, investors and others to whom you have applied for credit. Be certain that your accountant thoroughly explains to you the meaning and use of the financial statements.

Auditing

This is a procedure by which accountants examine the records and financial statements to safeguard against error or, in some cases, fraud.

Tax Accounting

This involves preparation of various tax returns that must be filed. Also, the tax accountant can advise the business owners as to the tax implications of certain moves being contemplated.

Cost Accounting

As your business becomes more complex, it becomes essential to keep detailed records of various costs incurred in producing a product or service. Originally developed for manufacturing industries, cost accounting is now becoming more widespread in financial, merchandising and even service industries.

Special Studies

Frequently, accounting is necessary in making certain decisions, such as determining the value of the business, establishing a retirement plan, etc.

Budgeting

This process assists in the preparation of realistic forecasts of income and expenses to determine future profitability, manpower and material needs, and cash flow.

These needs for accounting services may seem to be overwhelming, especially when you have had minimal exposure to accounting "language." Not all such services are required on a continuous basis, though, and there are several methods of reducing their cost.

For example, installation of an accounting system does not have to be a complex undertaking for the small business. Initially, the system can be very simple, provided there is the built-in capability of expansion as the business grows. For a great many standard types of businesses, there are accounting systems already developed and thoroughly tested. With your accountant's help, these can be adapted to your own organization with a minimum of effort. The actual recordkeeping does not have to be performed by an accountant; it can be handled by a bookkeeper, or even a capable clerk.

Again, you may decide to do it all yourself in the beginning. If the system is set up correctly and the bookkeeping is performed in a professional manner, preparation of financial statements becomes a relatively simple matter.

ACQUIRING BOOKKEEPING AND ACCOUNTING SERVICES

Contract for special services whenever possible rather than hiring employees to do the job. There are many accountants who have a part-time accounting business in addition to their regular jobs. Many of these part-timers are experts in the small business area, since large businesses will have full-time accounting employees. Also, the moonlighter is, in effect, running a small business, and is therefore more receptive to your special circumstances.

Expect the accountant to set up the system, to be available on a consulting basis, and to prepare financial statements and routine tax returns. Do not expect your accountant to do the associated bookkeeping work. This type of service is available at a much lower price. Later, when the volume of business warrants it, some form of computer (usually a minicomputer) may become a versatile and time-saving implement.

There are times when the services of major accounting firms should be utilized. Complex tax matters may require consultation with an accounting firm specializing in that field. Likewise, a company contemplating a public sale of securities could be better served by a firm specializing in that field rather than by a general accountant.

In selecting a specific accountant, search for one who understands the problems of a small business, who is able to handle the general duties mentioned earlier and who is willing to take a long-term view of your business relationship.

MAKING THE BEST USE OF YOUR ACCOUNTANT

In making the most efficient use of any specialist, you have to develop a certain minimum level of understanding of that specialized body of knowledge. Accounting is certainly no exception. It has a language of its own and is built upon certain basic assumptions that are sometimes subject to exceptions. It is not necessary that you learn accounting, but you ought to learn the language. The following sections are intended to give you a familiarity with the purposes of an accounting system. Also explained are the basic assumptions upon which the system will be constructed and a review of the major financial documents.

WHAT THE ACCOUNTING SYSTEM SHOULD INCLUDE

The system's complexity depends on the degree of complexity involved in your business. The following outline illustrates this relationship for various types of businesses.

Basic Accounting Requirements for a Business

Classification of Accounts. This should be based on the need for information. For instance, Sales is a major category, as is Expenses. In order to determine where your sales are coming from and what your expenses are, you will need to classify them. In Expenses, you will have several classifications, such as Stationery, Postage, Automobile Insurance and Rent. Under the heading of Sales, you may have Retail, Wholesale, Mail

Order and Discount. Each of these classifications is referred to as an account.

In a small business, 15 to 20 account classifications are usually sufficient. In a large organization, the number of accounts may be subdivided into several hundred different classes. The accounts are summarized periodically in company financial statements.

Accounting Books To Be Maintained. These consist of journals, which are summaries of business transactions in a chronological order, and ledgers, which consolidate the information from the journals by account classification. The journals are books of original entry from which information is transferred (or posted) to the ledgers, which are books of secondary entry.

Business Papers. These are the documents that support the accounting entries. They include invoices, cancelled checks, credit card receipts, etc.

In addition to a basic accounting system, which all businesses have, various enterprises will have other supporting systems applicable to their types of operations, as follows:

A Personal Service Business

A Sales and Collection System. This allows you to keep track of each product you sell. If you are allowing "charge" privileges to qualified customers (your "accounts receivable"), you will also need a method of sending them bills or invoices, monitoring the length of time between sending the invoice and receiving payments, and a system of followup letters when the customers do not pay within a certain amount of time ("dunning").

Timekeeping and Payroll System. When you have employees who are paid by the hour, you will need to keep track of the number of hours they work for you. You will also need to obtain an employer's identification number from the federal government, and the tables necessary to determine withholding taxes.

A Retail or Wholesale Business

A Sales and Collection System
A Timekeeping and Payroll System

A Purchase and Payment System. When you are selling other companies' products in a retail store, for example, you will need a system for keeping track of the goods you have on order, when they are received, and for checking the price on the invoice. This usually involves a purchase order system and a simple filing method whereby you can check the company's invoice to determine whether the goods were actually received, quantity, and if the price on their invoice matches the price you thought you were going to pay (on your purchase order). Those suppliers who allow you to purchase on credit rather than cash are your accounts payable.

An Inventory Control System. Basically, this involves maintaining records on items sold. This is essential to avoid overstocks and shortages of merchandise, because it allows you to monitor how quickly or slowly the products are moving and when you will need to reorder.

A Manufacturing Business

A Sales and Collection System
A Timekeeping and Payroll System
A Purchase and Payment System
An Inventory Control System

A Production and Manufacturing Cost System. This system allows you to determine how your products are being manufactured, how long it takes, how many can be produced in a given time and all the attendant costs involved in production.

It should be emphasized that a small business can operate quite successfully with very simple versions of the systems mentioned. A checkbook can be turned into a highly effective purchase and payment system by the use of proper terminology and coding. Self-contained accounting systems (usually called one-write systems), are definite timesavers for most types of small businesses.

SOME BASIC ASSUMPTIONS ABOUT ACCOUNTING

Part of the confusion between small company owners and accountants is due to certain basic assumptions that underlie the subject of accounting in general. The following are some of the most difficult assumptions for the business owner to accept in the beginning:

- *A business is separate from its owners.*

  This often causes trouble for the small business owner who intermingles personal and business transactions.

- *The business is going to be continued indefinitely rather than liquidated.*

  This involves the necessity of computing the amount various assets would bring if a sale were forced.

- *There is no change in purchasing power of money.*

  This permits most fixed assets to be carried at cost, either original cost or adjusted for depreciation. During periods of high inflation, asset values become greatly distorted.

- *Operations can be stopped in time to end and begin financial periods.*

  This involves the matching of revenues with expenses incurred to produce those revenues. This is accrual accounting, which accounts for things as they are incurred but not yet occurred, in contrast to cash accounting, which is used by most individuals.

Accountants are aware of the problems that some of their assumptions produce, but alternatives also produce problems. Consequently, it is necessary to make allowances for the above when interpreting accounting information.

FINANCIAL STATEMENTS AND THEIR TERMINOLOGY

The two basic financial statements that accountants produce are the Balance Sheet and the Income Statement. The balance sheet is a statement of your financial position at a certain point in time. The income statement is one of operation or activity, and shows profits or losses over a period of time. Neither statement alone gives a clear picture of the progress of the enterprise, and the two must be used as a unit.

An illustrative balance sheet with terminology and explanation is shown in Figure 13.1.

Figure 13.2 is an example of a summarized balance sheet.

Figure 13.3 is a breakdown of the items included in an income statement (also called a Profit and Loss Statement).

Figure 13.4 is an example of an Income Statement.

A number of other items can appear on the financial statement. Among the most important are shown in Figure 13.5.

A third financial tool, Sources and Uses of Funds, is often drawn by larger corporations to aid in managing their cash position. In the case of smaller companies, a cash-flow budget can serve this purpose more advantageously.

MAJOR CHANGES TAKING PLACE IN ACCOUNTING

When selecting an accountant, choose one who is knowledgeable in your field, who is willing to take a long-term view of your relationship and who is able to communicate well. A good accountant should not try to impose a rigid system on you, but should insist on getting your input into the proposed accounting system. It is up to you to determine what information you need and want from the system, although your accountant may make suggestions.

The accountant's primary contribution is to consider your needs and determine how they can best be satisfied at the lowest cost.

A good method of locating a compatible accountant is to obtain references from small business owners who are happy with their accountants and can recommend them.

A major revolution is taking place in the data processing field that is having a great impact on accounting systems and methods. The old pen-and-ink method has become increasingly obsolete as the cost of computers has dropped substantially. Whereas inflation has pushed up the cost of most things, the cost of personal computers is only a small fraction of what it was a few decades ago.

FIGURE 13.1 Financial Statement Terminology

Term	*Explanation*
Balance sheet	"Balance" refers to the fact that assets must equal or balance with the sum of the liabilities (the creditors' equity) plus the capital (the owners' equity).
Assets	
Cash	Includes cash on hand, bank deposits and short-term government securities.
Accounts receivable	Amounts owed to the company by its customers.
Inventories	Raw materials, work-in-progress, merchandise and supplies.
Current assets	The total of cash, accounts receivable and inventories.
Fixed assets	Buildings, furniture, equipment, land and leasehold improvements.
Total assets	The total of Current Assets, Fixed Assets and other assets.
Liabilities	
Current Liabilities	Short-term loans or amounts owed that will become payable in the normal accounting period (usually 12 months or less).
Accounts payable	Those bills that were incurred for materials, supplies, stock, etc.
Long-term debt	Loans that are not due within the next 12 months.
Capital	The owner's equity, which includes the original amount invested in the business by the proprietor, partners or stockholders, plus earnings retained or reinvested since that time.

The accountant you use should be knowledgeable about available hardware and software. It makes sense to use computers for your business, not only for accounting and record-keeping, but also to boost your efficiency in other areas, such as correspondence.

Your accountant should be able to grow with your business and efficiently handle the more complex problems that will be

FIGURE 13.2 Summarized Balance Sheet

Exhibit A
(Company Name) Balance Sheet
December 31, 19

Assets			
Current Assets:			
Cash in banks		$ 5,924	
Accounts receivable	$1,360		
Less allowance for bad debts	41	1,319	
Inventory		32,147	
Loans receivable		5,000	
Prepaid expenses		8,947	
Total Current Assets			$53,337
Fixed Assets:			
Auto	$4,200		
Less accumulated depreciation	2,567	$1,633	
Office furniture and equipment	$761		
Less accumulated depreciation	76	685	
Total Fixed Assets			$2,318
Total Assets			$55,655
Liabilities and Capital			
Current Liabilities:			
Notes payable		$8,512	
Accounts payable		19,217	
Payroll taxes payable		1,856	
State income tax payable		91	
Federal income tax payable		108	
Accrued expenses		17,890	
Total Current Liabilities			47,674
Long-Term Liabilities:			
Notes payable			1,912
Capital:			
Capital stock		$5,000	
Retained earnings—Net income per Exhibit B		$1,069	
Total Capital			6,069
Total Liabilities and Capital			$55,655

FIGURE 13.3 Income Statement Definitions

Term	*Explanation*
Sales	Amount received or receivable from customers.
Costs and Expenses	
Cost of sales	Costs of materials necessary to produce a product; or cost of goods purchased for resale.
Selling expenses	Includes advertising and other expenses incurred in selling the product, including salesperson's salary.
Administrative expenses	Administrative and management expenses, including management and office salaries and all payroll taxes.
Depreciation expense	Deduction from income to allow for the depreciation of plant and all equipment and furnishings used in business.
Operating profit	Sales, less costs and expenses.
Interest expense	Amount required for interest on borrowed funds.
Income taxes*	Federal and state taxes on income of a corporation.
Net income	Final earnings figure.

**These items would not appear on the income statement of a proprietorship or partnership.*

encountered. Ordinarily such a person will command a higher price, but this should be more than offset by greater productivity.

Your accountant should be a generalist and not think in terms of accounting as an end in itself. The best accountant for you is the one who attempts to minimize your bookkeeping and accounting expense while providing all the information you require.

FIGURE 13.4 Sample Income Statement

Exhibit B
Company Name
Income Statement
for the year ended December 31, 19

			Percent**
Net Sales			
Sales	$227,124		
Less sales returns	4,540		
Net Sales		$222,584	100.00
*Cost of Sales**			
Inventory at January 1, 19__	$ 0		
Merchandise	53,812		
Freight in	625		
Total	$ 54,437		
Less inventory at Dec. 31, 19__	8,947		
Cost of Sales		45,490	20.4
GROSS PROFIT		$177,094	79.6
Operating Expenses			
Setting expenses—per Schedule 1	$102,043		45.8
Administrative expenses—per Schedule 1	66,409		29.8
Total Operating Expenses		168,452	75.6
NET INCOME BEFORE INCOME TAXES (OR OPERATING PROFIT)		$ 8,642	3.9
Income Taxes			
State income tax	$ 430		
Federal income tax	1,470		
Total Income Taxes		1,900	.8
Net Income		$ 6,742	3.1

*Cost of Sales for a source business would relate to the *direct* costs of providing the service (salaries, postage, etc.)
**The percent next to figures show each expense as a percentage of Net Sales. This information is very useful for comparing expenses in relation to sales and for future budgeting.

FIGURE 13.4 Sample Income Statement (continued)

Schedule 1
(Company Name) Schedule of Operating Expenses
for the Year Ended December 31, 19

Selling Expenses	*Amount*	*Percent*
Officer's salary	$ 35,000	15.7
Payroll taxes	3,650	1.6
Commissions	23,942	10.7
Auto expenses	796	.6
Travel	5,637	2.5
Entertainment	2,294	1.0
Advertising	20,360	9.1
Packaging materials and supplies	900	.4
Postage	6,897	3.1
Depreciation of auto	2,567	1.1
Total Selling Expenses	$102,043	45.8

Administrative Expenses		
Officer's salary	$ 30,000	13.5
Administrative salaries	14,304	6.4
Payroll taxes	4,630	2.1
Professional fees	9,005	4.0
Office expense	882	.4
Stationery and printing	1,620	.7
Postage	1,724	.8
Telephone	1,362	.6
Professional dues, literature and subscriptions	558	.3
Insurance	1,329	.6
Utilities	132	—
Repairs and maintenance	459	.2
Interest expense	211	.1
Bad debts	41	—
Franchise tax and licenses	76	—
Depreciation	76	—
Total Administrative Expenses	$ 66,409	29.7

FIGURE 13.5 Items on the Financial Statement

Term	*Explanation*
Value of insurance	In partnerships and small corporations, insurance on key personnel is common to guarantee continuation of the business should a key employee or partner die.
Prepaid items	If insurance and other *expenses* have been paid *in advance*, the unexpired portion represents an asset, as it is still owned by you.
Goodwill	An intangible that contributes to the value of the company.
Patents	Another intangible adding value to the company.
Accrued income	This represents such items as unpaid wages and commissions or interest that have been incurred but not yet paid.
Accrued liabilities	This represents income from sales fees and interest that has been incurred but not yet received.
Contingency reserves	Reserves set up for losses that might occur.
Provision for bad debts	A negative figure used to reduce accounts receivable to reflect expectations of bad-debt losses.
Depletion	Similar to depreciation, but applied to natural resources that are being depleted. Timber, coal, oil and other resources are examples of assets subject to depletion.
Dividends	In corporations, a payment to stockholders from company earnings.

SUMMARY

Checklist: So What Do You Do First?

1. Open a business checking account under your company name and address with the earliest financial

transactions. Mark all deposit slips with a notation as to the source of income. Mark all checks as to the nature of the expense.

2. Keep all receipts, paid invoices and company bank statements in one place for easy access and establishment of later accounting systems.
3. Before the business account is one year old, or when you start to have deposits and disbursements (checks) on any kind of regular basis (weekly or daily), interview and hire a public accountant.
4. With the public accountant, decide who will be doing the actual recordkeeping. If you have not decided on a bookkeeper, your accountant may be very useful in helping you choose the best person for the job.
5. After reviewing the details of your business, have your accountant establish the details of maintaining the records and document the reasons for the different procedures. This can be a teaching session with you, if you are to maintain the records, or with the person you hire for the job.
6. With the accountant, decide when you will need the first financial statement. Establish regular intervals for the preparation of these statements.
7. Review financial statements with your accountant. Ask for explanations for whatever is not clear to you. Be sure you understand the significance of the figures. They are crucial to your business, and it is your accountant's job to help make things clear to you. You can keep the information in this chapter as a handy reference for many early clarifications.
8. If you maintain the records yourself, be sure to consult the accountant on any questions or changes that may occur in the business operation and that may affect the account records.
9. At regular intervals, consult your accountant to discuss the business advantages of informal and formal auditing of the company records, the desirability of cost analysis, cash-flow analysis and budgeting.
10. Finally, your records will need to be reviewed to ensure that they provide the data needed for tax return preparation and adjustment for tax savings.

SELF-TEST QUESTIONS

Multiple Choice

1. The ideal accounting system is
   a. a perfect record of what has happened to a company in the past.
   b. one that is sufficient to satisfy the tax collectors.
   c. one that provides the necessary information for intelligent decision making.
   d. None of the above

2. An accounting system for a personal service business would normally include
   a. a sales and cash collecting system.
   b. a timekeeping and payroll system.
   c. Both of the above
   d. Neither of the above

3. Business papers are documents that support accounting entries, and would include
   a. business contracts.
   b. checks and invoices.
   c. minutes of directors' meetings.
   d. correspondence with customers.

4. The following items would commonly appear on a company's balance sheet:
   a. Revenue and costs
   b. Profit or net income
   c. Debits and credits
   d. Assets, liabilities and capital

5. The following organizations would have an interest in your financial statement:
   a. Your banker
   b. The Internal Revenue Service
   c. The stockholders
   d. All of the above

6. Your accountant would normally perform the following function:
   a. Deal with your banker and broker.
   b. Keep records and do the bookkeeping.
   c. Prepare financial statements and tax returns.
   d. None of the above

7. The accounting system for a new business should be developed through
   a. your accountant alone.
   b. you alone.
   c. you and your accountant.
   d. None of the above

8. The reported value of fixed assets in a balance sheet is derived from
   a. original cost minus accumulated depreciation charges.
   b. replacement cost of the assets.
   c. market value of the assets based on a recent appraisal.
   d. None of the above

True or False

9. Bookkeeping and accounting expenses are necessary evils, so your main objective should be to minimize their costs.

   True ☐ False ☐

10. An accounting system for a small business should be designed so it can become more complex as the company grows.

    True ☐ False ☐

11. The term *balance sheet* refers to the fact that assets plus capital must balance with liabilities.

    True ☐ False ☐

12. As long as sales are growing rapidly, a company seldom has a cash-shortage problem.

    True ☐ False ☐

13. Auditing involves examining records and financial statements to safeguard against error and fraud.

    True ☐ False ☐

14. Cost accounting is used only in manufacturing industries.

    True ☐ False ☐

15. A good accounting system would point out excess inventories, overdue accounts receivable and pending cash shortages in time to correct them.

    True ☐ False ☐

16. When selecting an accountant, you should check to see if he or she has other small business customers.

    True ☐ False ☐

17. You should avoid accounting systems that utilize computers because they are too expensive for a small business.

    True ☐ False ☐

18. A cost accounting system should permit you to know which of your products or customers are most profitable and which are the least profitable.

    True ☐ False ☐

19. The best accountant for you is one who will provide all the information you require regardless of how much it costs you.

    True ☐ False ☐

Answers

1.c, 2.c, 3.b, 4.d, 5.d, 6.c, 7.c, 8.a, 9.F, 10.T, 11.T, 12.F, 13.T, 14.F, 15.T, 16.T, 17.F, 18.T, 19.F

CHAPTER 14

Control of Investment in Assets

A company's success is largely determined by how well it makes use of the funds made available to it by the owners and lenders. These funds are invested in various assets that will provide different rates of return. In some cases, it will be possible to measure the rate of return provided by an asset. A new machine, for example, may earn back its cost in five years, giving a compound rate of return of approximately 14 percent. Other assets, such as cash, contribute indirectly to profitability by making it possible to take advantage of discounts and buying opportunities. If the cash is temporarily invested in treasury bills or savings, it will also provide a direct rate of return.

Accounts receivable contribute a rate of return that is somewhat difficult to measure. Yet the company that provides credit, while its competitors do not, may find that its sales will benefit from permitting the extension of credit. If the company also has excess plant capacity, the additional sales may be highly profitable, and part of this profitability must be considered a rate of return on the funds invested in accounts receivable.

The same is true in the case of inventories. The company with a broad selection of goods may capture sales from competitors that have a limited selection of products for sale. Indirectly, profitability can be stimulated, although it is difficult to evaluate the profitability of such assets in a direct way. Consequently, the profitability of many assets is measured by how effectively they are used. A common technique is to divide sales by various assets, such as inventories or accounts receivable, to obtain a measure of how rapidly they are being turned over.

All other things being equal, a faster turnover rate of a given asset indicates that the funds invested in that asset are being used more effectively. It must be emphasized, however, that turnover rates should never be used alone as an indicator. For example, a store owner can greatly stimulate inventory turnover with substantial price reductions, but total profitability could decline drastically. This illustrates a basic principle of financial ratio analysis, which states that no single ratio is significant in and of itself.

Effective asset control contributes to effective control over liabilities and the use of capital. If inventories are excessive, this increases the amount of funds that must be borrowed from lenders or provided by the owners. A reduction in inventories reduces interest costs paid to lenders and/or increases the profitability of the funds provided by the owner.

Another type of financial ratio used for control purposes compares the related balance sheet items to each other to see if they are in line. For example, current assets are divided by current liabilities to develop a liquidity ratio. The business manager who becomes proficient in interpreting profitability, turnover, and liquidity ratios will be in a position to improve the overall results of the enterprise. These three basic types of financial ratios are discussed below.

RETURN ON TOTAL CAPITAL EMPLOYED

The most basic ratio used in management of company funds is rate of return on investment. Successful companies have high rates of return on their capital, which permits them to finance a high rate of growth. Three ratios measuring rate of return are shown in Figure 14.1.

As the size of the denominator in the above fractions declines, the percent of return rises. Total assets include all the resources used by the firm, so it is the largest denominator of the three. Total capital includes both long-term debt and equity capital but is less than total assets, because the latter includes resources financed by short-term debt as well as long-term capital. Equity includes only that portion of assets belonging to stockholders. Note that return on equity uses only net income

FIGURE 14.1 Rate of Return Ratios

1. Rate of return on assets $= \dfrac{\text{Net income + Interest expense}}{\text{Total assets}}$
2. Rate of return on total capital $= \dfrac{\text{Net income + Interest exp.}}{\text{Total equity + Long-term debt}}$
3. Rate of return on equity $= \dfrac{\text{Net income}}{\text{Total equity}}$

Net income:	$100,000
Interest expense:	$ 40,000
Stockholder equity:	$400,000
Long-term debt:	$200,000
Total assets:	$500,000

1. Rate of return on assets $= \dfrac{\$100{,}000 + \$40{,}000}{\$500{,}000} = \dfrac{\$140{,}000}{\$500{,}000} = 28\%$
2. Rate of return on total capital $= \dfrac{\$100{,}000 + \$40{,}000}{\$600{,}000} = \dfrac{\$140{,}000}{\$600{,}000} = 23.3\%$
3. Rate of return on equity $= \dfrac{\$100{,}000}{\$400{,}000} = 25\%$

in the numerator, whereas the other two rates of return include interest as well as net income. Where debt is included in the denominator, interest paid on that debt should be part of the denominator.

Using the financial figures in Figure 14.2, indicate whether company A is improving its profitability.

CONTROLLING INVENTORIES

Inventories have been called the graveyard of business because of their frequent contribution to business failures. The problem is not simply that excessive inventories tie up more funds than necessary. Excessive inventories can also become the serious problem of obsolete goods or products. In the retail field, a poor selection of merchandise results in unsatisfactory sales levels

FIGURE 14.2 Profitability Assessment

Company A

	Current Year	*Last Year*	*Year Before Last*
Income Statement			
Sales	$120,000	$90,000	$80,000
Cost of sales	108,000	81,000	72,000
Operating profit	12,000	9,000	8,000
Interest costs	3,000	0	0
Pretax income	9,000	9,000	8,000
Taxes	2,000	4,500	4,000
Net income	$ 7,000	$ 4,500	$ 4,000
Balance Sheet			
Current assets	35,000	30,000	35,000
Fixed assets	35,000	25,000	10,000
Total assets	70,000	55,000	45,000
Current liability	20,000	20,000	10,000
Long-term debt	15,000	0	0
Stockholder equity	35,000	35,000	35,000
Total capital employed	$ 50,000	$35,000	$35,000

Worksheet

	Current Year	*Last Year*	*Year Before Last*
1. Net income			
2. Interest			
3. Net income plus interest (1. + 2.)			
4. Shareholder equity			
5. Long-term debt			
6. Total capital (4. + 5.)			
7. Total assets			
8. Return on investments (divide 3. by 7.)			
9. Return on capital (divide 3. by 6.)			
10. Return on equity (divide 1. by 4.)			

FIGURE 14.2 Profitability Assessment (continued)

To check your figures, the following is an example of the completed worksheet:

	Current Year	*Last Year*	*Year Before Last*
1. Net income	7,000	4,500	4,000
2. Interest	3,000	0	0
3. Net income plus interest	10,000	4,500	4,000
4. Shareholder equity	35,000	35,000	35,000
5. Long-Term debt	15,000	0	0
6. Total capital (4. + 5.)	50,000	35,000	35,000
7. Total assets	70,000	55,000	45,000
8. Return on assets (divide 3. by 7.)	14.3%	8.2%	8.9%
9. Return on total capital (divide 3. by 6.)	20.0%	12.9%	11.4%
10. Return on equity	20.0%	12.9%	11.4%

Asset Turnover:

Return on investment is a key ratio made up of two other key ratios: profits divided by sales (or profit margins) and asset turnover. The formula is as follows:

$$\text{Rate of return} = \frac{\text{Profit}}{\text{Assets}} = \frac{\text{Profit}}{\text{Sales}} \times \frac{\text{Sales}}{\text{Assets}}$$

Most managers understand that return on investment can be increased by improving profit margins, but a number are apparently unaware that return on investment is improved by increasing asset turnover. For example, a retail grocery chain hired a new top executive from outside the industry. The new executive was appalled at the average profit margin of 2 percent that the company earned, not realizing that this was in keeping with the retail food industry. He emphasized the addition of many nonfood items to the stores' shelves, improving margins but suffering a decline in return on investment as asset turnover plummeted.

To improve total asset turnover, the manager concentrates on improving turnover of accounts receivable, inventories and fixed assets. Each of these is discussed on the following pages.

and above-average obsolescence of the goods. To move the merchandise, substantial price reductions may be necessary. Another cause of excess inventories may be speculation in commodities, and this must be considered risky. Excessive inventory also increases the cost of maintenance. Interest costs are involved in financing, and storage and security costs can be substantial. In many types of inventories, the threat of deterioration is another negative factor. It has been estimated that the cost of carrying inventories is, on the average, about 25 percent per annum.

One ratio for measuring inventory turnover is to divide net sales by average inventory. (Sometimes the cost of goods sold is used as the numerator instead of sales, to eliminate the profit margin factor included in sales). The amount of inventory that is desirable varies with the nature of the business. Dun & Bradstreet, Standard & Poor's, and the Federal Trade Commission have issued studies giving average figures for this and other ratios for various businesses and industries.

The following are key factors to consider when deciding proper inventory levels:

- Sales expectations
- The amount of safety stocks of key materials or parts that would disrupt the business should you run out of them
- The availability of such key materials or parts from nearby sources
- Considerations of economy in purchase. (How much do you save per unit by buying in larger quantities?)
- The operating cost of carrying stock, including interest costs, storage costs and the possibility of theft or deterioration
- The amount of storage space required
- The amount of capital available for investment in inventory

The amount of inventory needed is primarily dependent upon the nature of the business. In the case of wholesaling or retailing, the major investment of the firm is in inventory, as this is the heart of the business. In manufacturing industries, there is a wide variation in inventory costs. One company may produce a product for which material costs are only 25 percent of the total costs. The first will tend to keep more inventory on hand.

The production process is equally important. The company that has a product that can be converted from raw material to finished product in one week will have as much tied up in goods-in-process inventory as would be the case if the production process required a year.

ACCOUNTS RECEIVABLE TURNOVER

There is a danger of being too liberal in granting credit to stimulate sales. This can result in a slowdown in turnover of accounts receivable, tying up capital and increasing interest costs. It also increases the costs of collections and bad debt write-offs. A number of years ago, a super salesperson was made chief executive officer of an agricultural machinery company that had had an uninspiring record of success. He began an aggressive marketing program, courting the company's equipment dealers with lavish sales conventions and greatly liberalizing credit terms and financial incentives for the dealers. Sales skyrocketed, as might be expected. But accounts receivable increased to an even greater proportion, leading to a working capital squeeze. Meanwhile, the dealers were loaded with inventory, which farmers were slow to buy. Company sales slowed down, while accounts receivable remained high. In a financial squeeze, the company was forced to sell out to a large conglomerate.

Bad-debt losses are a major result of slow accounts receivable. The probability of a bad-debt loss increases as accounts receivable ages. Consequently, it is necessary to monitor overdue collections, and this is typically performed by computing average collection periods, as follows:

Compute net credit sales per day:

$$\frac{\text{Net credit sales per year}}{365}$$

Divide:

$$\frac{\text{Accounts receivable}}{\text{Net credit sales per day}}$$

The collection period will be influenced by credit terms of the business. One expert on credit analysis suggests that the average collection period should not be more than one-third greater than the net terms for the business. If accounts are expected to be paid on net terms at the end of 30 days, this would give 40 days as a reasonable average collection period. A discount for payment received within ten days is commonly used to encourage prompt payment. Customers who have records of slow payment should be offered goods on a cash-on delivery (C.O.D.) basis.

CONTROL OF CASH

In many respects, cash is the exact opposite of other assets on the balance sheet. When other assets increase, cash is often reduced to provide the necessary funds. The company that runs short of cash loses its flexibility to adjust to change. The adequacy of cash is sometimes measured by liquidity ratios, as follows:

- Ratio of cash to current liabilities
- Ratio of cash and accounts receivable to current liabilities
- Ratios of current assets to current liabilities

The cash-to-current liabilities is the most stringent of the three ratios, and current assets to current liabilities is least. All three are legitimate measures of cash adequacy, because current assets are, by definition, those assets that will convert into cash during the next 12 months.

Another method of evaluating cash adequacy is to compare the relationship of cash to the other elements of current assets. For example, current assets may have been divided equally between its three main components historically: cash, accounts receivable and inventories. If the latter two increase substantially as a percent of current assets, this would result in a drop in cash as a percentage of current assets.

FIGURE 14.3 Sample Cash Budget

	January	*February*	*March*
Beginning Cash Balance	$ 20,000	$ 27,000	$ 40,000
Additions			
Cash receipts	20,000	35,000	35,000
Receivables collected	80,000	90,000	90,000
Cash sales	100,000	125,000	125,000
Total Cash Available	120,000	152,000	165,000
Subtractions			
Cash payments	15,000	17,000	16,000
Materials purchased	25,000	30,000	32,000
Accounts paid	48,000	60,000	55,000
Expenses paid	5,000	5,000	5,000
Capital additions	93,000	112,000	108,000
Ending Cash Balance	$ 27,000	$ 40,000	$ 57,000

The best way to monitor cash needs is through a cash budget, such as the abbreviated quarterly budget in Figure 14.3.

Figures for additions to cash are estimates and can fall short. Cash from accounts receivable is estimated from the average collection period. Should cash additions fall below expectations, cash outflows will have to be adjusted to prevent a cash deficit. Fortunately, some of the cash payments will be flexible enough to offset part of the shortfall from cash receipts. Also, the cash balance in the budget includes a cushion factor. If that is not sufficient to offset unexpected shortages, most companies have sources of short-term credit on which to fall back. Over a period of time, companies have consistently reduced their need for cash per dollar of sales. This has been accomplished through the use of stand-by credit arrangements, usually with banks.

CONTROL OF FIXED ASSETS

Try to avoid tying up funds, especially in such fixed assets as land, plants and equipment. This is the basic advantage of service companies, where investment in fixed assets can be held to minimum levels. Once an investment is made in fixed assets, the business owner's flexibility is decreased by that amount. Overinvestment in inventories can be corrected by price reduction sales, and overinvestment in accounts receivable can be controlled by more stringent credit screening and collection terms. But incorrect investment or overinvestment in fixed assets may be extremely difficult to correct and can, at best, take several years to overcome.

The reason is that fixed assets are generally bought in sizable unit amounts. A company that has outgrown one plant cannot add a quarter or half of a plant—they do not come in fractions. The same is true to a lesser extent in regard to equipment. The investor in new machinery will often find that the best buy, in terms of productivity, will be a significantly larger unit in terms of output.

Another problem in investing in fixed assets is the long time involved in recovering costs. A plant with a life of 30 years may last that long, but it is likely to become obsolete in 20 years. Due to the ravages of inflation, depreciation costs of the original plant will fall far short of financing a new plant even if it does not become obsolete prematurely. A large investment in fixed assets also requires substantial financing costs, which can be the undoing of a company.

In spite of all these reservations, there are times when an investment in fixed assets can be a strategic move. Consequently, it is important for the business owner to evaluate investment opportunities in fixed assets. The two most important considerations are rate of return and the amount of time needed to recover the investment.

One of the simplest approaches to evaluating investments in fixed assets is use of the payback period, which measures how fast an investment will pay for itself. This, in turn, indicates what rate of return will be earned during the payback period. For example, assume that a machine costing $70,000 will increase estimated earnings by $14,000 a year. The payback period is then five years, arrived at by dividing the investment of $70,000 by annual earnings of $14,000. This also provides a rate of return of 14 percent, since money will double in five years at 14 percent compounded.

The payback period approach to capital investment has some major defects. Two pieces of equipment may have payback periods of five years, but one may fall apart at the end of five years and the other may continue to operate for another ten years. The second is obviously a better investment, even though the payback period is the same. Also, one machine may get most of its return in the first two years of the five-year period, and the other may get most of the return in the latter part of the period.

Where similar distortions occur, it is necessary to use more complex formulas dealing in advanced financial mathematics. Basically, these take the income streams of future years and reduce them to their present value. If interest rates are 15 percent, for example, $1 ten years from now will be worth only $.25 today, since this amount invested at 15 percent would grow to $1 in ten years. Where this more complex approach is justified, your accountant should be able to provide a comparative evaluation.

When equipment purchases are made, it is better to avoid overspecializing in a plant and/or equipment that has no alternative use. Should you make a mistake on your investment, it may be necessary to sell the fixed assets, and the broader the market for them, the less likely it is that loss will be incurred.

With many fixed assets, it will be impossible to calculate a rate of return. For instance, in the case of a parking lot for your employees, the investment seems desirable, but no definite income can be attributed to it. It will still be desirable to know what other effect its cost will have on company income, even though the positive effects are uncertain. This is accomplished by estimating depreciation charges that will result from the investment. The total cost is computed by taking the initial cost and subtracting estimated salvage value at the end of the equipment's or facility's life. This cost, less scrap value, is divided by the number of years the equipment or facility is expected to last. A truck purchased for $20,000, for example, is expected to last ten years and have a scrap value of $500 at the end of that time. Depreciation per year would be $1,950, arrived at by dividing ($20,000–$500) by ten.

A more conservative approach to recovering investment in assets is through accelerated depreciation, which can be accomplished in various ways. Instead of using ten years in the above example, we could have used eight years. (The Internal Revenue Service would frown if the period was unrealistically short, but there is considerable latitude given.) Another method is to increase the amount of depreciation in the first years with a corresponding reduction in latter years. One of these methods, "sum-of-the-digits" method, is compared with straight-line depreciation, using the truck example. The sum-of-the-digits method starts by adding up the digits involved in the number of years of life of the equipment. A ten-year life has digits of 1, 2, 3, 4, 5, 6, 7, 8, 9 and 10, which add up to 55. During the first year, $\frac{10}{55}$ of the cost is depreciated, and $\frac{9}{55}$ in the second year, down to only $\frac{1}{55}$ of the total cost in the last year. The advantage of accelerated depreciation is that it is more realistic in an inflationary economy to recover more costs in the early years. Depreciation is a tax-deductible item, and accelerated depreciation offsets the tendency of taxes to rise unfairly during inflation.

Shrewd business owners can take the problems that others have incurred with fixed assets and turn them into opportunities. It is often possible to obtain low-cost facilities by renting space owned by others. In many industries, it is possible to purchase good secondhand machinery and equipment. Exceptional bargains occur where another business is in financial trouble and must sell off plants and equipment to survive. Other methods of minimizing investment in physical assets are to build your own equipment if you have the mechanical ability, and buy (rather than make) components requiring expensive equipment.

When fixed assets are acquired, the effective rate of return will depend on how intensely the equipment is used. A machine may provide a 25 percent return if utilized 100 percent of the time, but only 10 percent when used 70 percent of the time. In evaluating the need for equipment, you should be realistic when estimating how continuously it will be used.

Proper investment in assets is a major job, and decisions in this area have important effects on the overall profitability of a business. A balanced approach applies to the methods of financing investment in assets.

Historically, banks have considered themselves lenders primarily in the short-term area. They were reluctant to lend money to finance the purchase of land, plants and equipment, although they now make term loans to finance equipment with a fast payback period. A company was expected to provide equity capital, and banks expected to supply only the extra working capital to finance peak seasonal activity. While banks are no longer as rigid in their thinking, they still like to think that the customer can clear up his working capital loans at least once a year.

There is also a strong feeling among financial analysts that long-term assets should be provided by long-term capital, including long-term debt as well as equity capital. The percentage of total capital that should be provided by equity capital is dependent upon the cyclical nature of the business. Extremely stable businesses, such as electric utilities, may use $2 of long-term debt per $1 of equity capital. In contrast, a machine tool company may have no long-term debt in its capital structure because of the wide variation in industry activity.

SELF-TEST QUESTIONS

Multiple Choice

1. A company that minimizes the amount of its inventories does the following:
   a. Reduces cost of storage, deterioration and interest costs associated with inventories
   b. Probably reduces its sales potential
   c. Neither of the above
   d. Both of the above

2. A company anticipates that the major materials it requires will rise 10 percent in price next year. It should
   a. buy all of its next year's requirements immediately in order to save 10 percent.
   b. buy more than its requirements next year.
   c. attempt to contract for next year's requirements at today's prices, but delay delivery until needed.
   d. None of the above

3. If a company has no bad-debt losses on its accounts receivable, its
   a. credit policies may be too strict.
   b. credit policies are excellent.
   c. accounting records are inadequate.
   d. None of the above

4. A company can reduce its need to raise capital or borrow money by
   a. minimizing investment in fixed assets.
   b. selling only for cash.
   c. speeding up inventory turnover.
   d. All of the above

5. An increase in inventory turnover would be unimpressive if accomplished through
   a. clever advertising.
   b. aggressive sales techniques.
   c. better inventory controls.
   d. drastic price reductions to stimulate sales.

6. A company's rate of return on capital can be improved through
   a. improving turnover of capital, provided profit margins are maintained.
   b. borrowing more funds.
   c. reducing prices to stimulate sales.
   d. None of the above

7. A company's cash will increase due to
   a. reinvested profits.
   b. sale of assets.
   c. reduction of inventories and accounts receivable.
   d. All of the above

8. A company buys a machine for $10,000. Its expected life is ten years, and salvage value is expected to be $1,000. Using the sum-of-the-digits method, depreciation during the first year would be approximately
   a. $900.
   b. $1,325.
   c. $1,633.
   d. $1,800.

True or False

9. An asset with a high payback period indicates a good investment.

   True ☐ False ☐

10. Normally, long-term assets should be financed through long-term sources of finance.

    True ☐ False ☐

11. A company with long-term debt would have a rate of return on capital higher than its return on equity.

    True ☐ False ☐

12. A cash budget is unnecessary if a company uses accrual accounting.

    True ☐ False ☐

13. Normally, fixed assets are a good inflation hedge, unless offset by technological change.

    True ☐ False ☐

14. Depreciation tends to be understated during inflationary periods.

    True ☐ False ☐

15. Overspecialized plants and equipment with no alternative uses represent a safe investment.

    True ☐ False ☐

16. A high rate of return on fixed assets will not be achieved if the plant and equipment are used less than expected.

    True ☐ False ☐

17. A company with most of its capital invested in fixed assets has great flexibility to reduce costs during slow economic periods.

    True ☐ False ☐

18. A company without any long-term debt always has excellent liquidity.

    True ☐ False ☐

19. Current assets include inventories and accounts receivable along with cash.

    True ☐ False ☐

20. Used equipment and vacant facilities are often available at very reasonable costs due to overexpansion mistakes of others.

    True ☐ False ☐

Answers

1.d, 2.c, 3.a, 4.d, 5.d, 6.a, 7.d, 8.c, 9.F, 10.T, 11.F, 12.F, 13.T, 14.T, 15.F, 16.T, 17.F, 18.F, 19.T, 20.T

CHAPTER 15

Profit Control

A business receives funds from its owners and creditors, and invests those funds in various assets that will give a return on the investment. Computing the investment return, however, is not simple. The process starts off with sales. All of the expenses involved in producing those sales are deducted, and the difference is either a profit or a loss for the owners and stockholders. Part of the expense, such as salaries and rent, depreciation and real estate tax, will occur whether the company sells anything or not. Other expenses are more directly related to sales, such as materials and wages incurred in selling the product. Whether a profit will be earned depends on the proper combination of these factors.

SALES CONTROL

Sales control is the most basic fundamental of profit control. If company sales fall too far short of estimates, the company will find its cash budget to be in error. An excess of funds may be tied up in more inventories than were needed at the lower sales level. Plant and equipment will be underutilized. To the extent that the company has high fixed costs, it will experience rising unit costs, as overhead has to be spread over a smaller number of units. A shortfall in sales is likely to stimulate an improvement in sales level in order to reduce excess inventories and improve cash position. A substantial shortfall in sales can produce a financial disaster.

It is understandable that considerable effort goes into sales forecasting. Large companies may have research staffs that analyze the overall economy, basic population trends, industry statistics, and such varied internal data as planned sales and advertising as expenditures.

Due to its ability to increase its share of the market, and since there is less dependence on trends in the overall economy, the smaller company can be more of a master of its own fate. New products can be introduced to offset adverse fluctuations in the sales of its older product lines.

In evaluating business opportunities, you ought to choose value-oriented products and services, and avoid those that rely heavily on price competition. This eliminates one of the basic uncertainties in sales forecasting, because it is easier to undersell than to produce a higher-quality product or service.

The beginning of sales control starts with selecting the right business. The other major ingredients are proper pricing of your product and understanding the effects of selling and advertising expenses on sales level.

PRICING STRATEGY

Product pricing can be a complex undertaking, but much can be achieved by simply avoiding the most common pricing mistakes that many businesspeople make.

One very common mistake is in thinking of the price as (cost + mark-up = profit). In mature industries, there is a tendency to offset rising costs by automatically raising prices. This does not necessarily maintain profit, as the amount of product or service sold may decline as a result of the price increase.

The first thing you should know about your product is the effect a price increase will have on the volume sold. A 10 percent increase in price may reduce unit sales by 20 percent so that the effect on dollar sales is negative. If you have chosen the right product, there will be reasonable flexibility to increase prices, if necessary, to offset cost pressures.

The cost-plus approach to pricing can severely limit profits if your product has a high value content as perceived by your customer. While costs represent a floor in determining what a product ought to sell for, the ceiling is represented by the perceived value. It may be possible to manufacture a product at the cost of $1 and turn a good profit by selling it for $2, but many customers may be willing to pay $10. In this example, unit sales are likely to be greater at the higher price, because more funds will be available for advertising.

Another defect of using a cost-plus approach is that cost is not a static figure. If 1,000 units are produced, cost per item may be $5. Cost per item is likely to drop to $1 if 10,000 units are produced.

One of the most basic characteristics of a growth industry is a favorable cycle in which lower prices permit reduced costs, which in turn permit lower prices in a self-reinforcing pattern. Price can be a determinant of cost, rather than vice versa. Estimate at what price your new product must sell to tap a mass market, and then design the product, manufacturing and distribution system so that the cost will be low enough to produce a profit at that price. This is the stroke of genius that made Henry Ford the "father of mass production" in the automobile industry.

The following are some of the restrictions that limit price freedom:

- *Competition* from producers of the same product and substitute products.
- *Technological maturity of the industry*. Price reductions can result in higher profitability if they expand the market sufficiently to introduce better technology. This option is not available in mature industries.
- *Cost of product* restricts price freedom, particularly where material costs and/or labor make up the major cost of the product.
- *Industry capacity* affects prices considerably in high-fixed-cost industries, as companies reduce price in an attempt to keep capacity utilized at a high level.
- *Desired rate of return*. Price is varied in an attempt to reach a certain desired rate of return. At times, price may be deliberately lowered to reduce the rate of return from excessively high levels. This is done to discourage new competition and/or increase a market.

INFLUENCE OF ADVERTISING AND SALES EXPENSES ON A COMPANY'S PRICE

As a company is able to differentiate its products from those of its competition, it obtains greater flexibility in pricing. Consider the case of a very popular product today: blue jeans. Those jeans manufactured and distributed by Levi Strauss (brand name Levi's) can command a higher price than other manufacturers' jeans simply because they have earned the reputation of superior fit, style and durability through advertising. In many cases, the names of "Levi's" and "jeans" are used synonymously. Because advertising and sales expenditures are a method of distinguishing your product, such expenses are a method of increasing price flexibility. Advertising is used to promote a brand-name image, and this improves pricing flexibility. Advertising also influences the overall level and stability of sales, and this, in turn, influences the flexibility of pricing.

CONTROL OF COSTS AND EXPENSES

Profit margins can be increased by raising prices or by reducing costs. The latter is the preferable method, because higher prices can discourage unit sales, as previously mentioned. Consequently, cost control is a major concern of a profit-oriented firm.

As a starting point, it should be stressed that cost and expense control is usually not a simple concept. The story is told of a Soviet plant manager who reported that his efforts at cost control had been successful. His factory had saved thousands of tons of steel and substantial quantities of other materials. When questioned as to the manner in which he accomplished this savings, he replied that his plant did not turn out any product at all. In a variation of this anecdote, the Soviet plant manager is expected to produce 20 tons of metal screws. He finds that the most economical manner of accomplishing this is to produce one giant 20-ton screw.

While these are ridiculous examples of cost reduction, many companies make big mistakes. Advertising expenditures are often considered a percentage of sales, so they are cut when sales drop off. In many cases, the proper economic response would be to *increase* advertising under these circumstances.

Similarly, a company may reduce the material costs per unit of product but greatly reduce the quality and value of the product in so doing. Use of lower-quality materials may result in higher wage costs if the cheaper material is more difficult to work with.

The problem of cutting costs is easily demonstrated in large organizations, many of which take a "meat cleaver" approach. Salaries of nonunion employees are often frozen, an across-the-board reduction in personnel is mandated and any purchase of supplies or equipment must be approved by top management. Such programs are seldom effective, as the best employees may leave when salaries are frozen or their workload is greatly increased. Reduction in purchases of supplies may be merely an imaginary savings, as purchases are actually deferred until a future date.

In spite of the complexity of the cost cutting problem, here are four methods that can produce savings without reducing the value of the product or service.

1. Elimination or reduction of unproductive investment in assets that are greatly underutilized
2. Elimination or reduction of activities that may be common in large companies but that represent an unnecessary luxury to the small business
3. Analysis of major expenditures of the business to determine whether there are better ways to accomplish the same or better results with less costly methods
4. A thorough analysis of the profitability of
   - different products or services,
   - different types of customers and
   - different methods of sales

ELIMINATION OR REDUCTION OF "SHOWY" BUT UNPRODUCTIVE ACTIVITIES

When people who have come from big company backgrounds start their own small businesses, they often fall prey to a very common pitfall. They have the tendency to include certain activities that are unproductive in their businesses. They may be appropriate in large organizations but are luxuries in a small company.

Large companies have many staff functions, while the small business must learn how to use various business associates to fill these vacuums. General and administrative costs should be controlled diligently in the early stages of any new venture. A large company will also take pride in its new buildings and magnificent interior design, but the individual starting a new company may have to be content with sharing an office, or with operating the business from home.

ANALYZING MAJOR EXPENDITURES TO SEE IF THE SAME OR BETTER CAN BE ACCOMPLISHED AT LESS COST

In any activity, certain key costs make up a large percentage of the total costs. These key costs should be continuously surveyed to see if there are better ways of accomplishing the same purpose at lower cost.

Personal selling expenses, for example, can be greatly reduced without affecting sales by using the telephone more and eliminating some of the personal visits. More advertising can be used in this area to presell the customer. It is often better to contract out a part of the production of your product to others who can produce it at less cost than you can.

In many cases, it is possible to save money by simply using the expertise of your suppliers. Let your major vendors know your broad general needs and ask them for their advice as to which materials or equipment they can supply to meet your requirements at the lowest cost. They may be producing a large run of certain material for a big customer, and if you can use it, the cost to you would be considerably less than what you are currently paying. If telephone charges are a major expense, call on the communications experts at the telephone company to determine how you can reduce your costs without endangering your sales efforts. The postal service may help you reduce mailing costs. This type of expertise is usually free for the asking.

A THOROUGH REVIEW OF PROFITABILITY OF VARIOUS PRODUCTS, CUSTOMERS AND METHODS OF DISTRIBUTION

One way of looking at expenses and costs is to treat them as investments in results. If an increase in a certain expense results in an increase in profits, then the added expense is justified. The important thing to measure becomes the ratio between an expense and the results that are produced from it, rather than the expense itself.

Using this basic approach, expense- or cost-reduction projects should concentrate on eliminating unprofitable methods of distribution. This is the basic approach that successful managers take when trying to turn a company around quickly. An almost instant recovery in profits can be achieved simply by discontinuing unprofitable segments of the business and by using freed-up funds to help the profitable part of the company's business along.

In the case of product profitability, the following items should be considered:

- Is there an actual cash loss?
- If this item is dropped, will costs be saved or reallocated to other products?
- Will customers feel the line is adequate without this product?
- Will discontinuance of the product adversely affect the company's image?
- Will liquidation provide losses that will reduce taxes?
- Can unused space, machinery or talent be used on other products?
- What effect will discontinuance have on the prices and sales of other products?
- Is there a profitable use for the capital that will be freed?

This checklist is based upon the concept that a product, while it may not be profitable, may contribute substantially to overhead, advertising, and plant or talent utilization. This does not mean that it should be retained indefinitely. It does suggest, however, that it should be phased out when it can be replaced by more profitable products or services.

Customers also vary considerably in profitability. Affecting customer profitability are such factors as geographical location, size of the order, sales effort required and credit standing. A small order may require as much paperwork as a large one. A credit check is equally expensive for both. It may take as much sales effort to explain a product to a small customer as it does to a large one. This does not necessarily mean that profitability automatically increases with size, as the large customer may demand price concessions and exceptional service. One of my associates who worked in a freight-forwarding terminal claimed that the extra personal attention and paperwork necessary to keep two large client companies happy caused a neglect of the small, less complicated and less demanding clients. This is a dangerous situation that ought to be avoided. Too great a reliance on large clients can bankrupt a business when they are lost. A good mixture of small clients to large is very important.

A relatively small percentage of customers will produce most of a company's profits, while a relatively small percentage of the company's customers produce most of the headaches. A large business may have trouble screening out the difficult customers, but you will have an advantage in this regard since you probably deal with your customers directly. If you have a client who demands such unreasonable service that the account becomes unprofitable, discontinue the relationship. It's not worth it.

There are many other ways to analyze your business to determine the ways in which profitability may be improved. Advertising is the key factor in selling books by mail order, for example. A publishing business should keep very detailed records of the results of advertisements that are placed in various publications to measure their rates of profitability. In other businesses, some geographical areas may be more lucrative than others. Many business managers take a losing product line, customer or method of distribution and try to make it pay. In many cases, it would be better to discontinue these losing relationships and concentrate efforts on the areas of the business that are doing well.

BREAKEVEN CHARTS—A TOOL FOR PROFITABILITY ANALYSIS

As implied above, it is often difficult to determine whether a certain action will improve profitability. A bus company may increase fares 20 percent but suffer a reduction of 30 percent in passengers as a result. This would result in a 16 percent drop in dollar sales (price is 120 percent of previous price level, volume of traffic is only 70 percent, and 120 percent times 70 percent equals 84 percent of previous dollar sales). From the above sales information, it is difficult to determine if the move will increase profits. If it is possible to reduce costs in proportion to the lower volume of passenger traffic, then the calculation would be simple. Dollar sales would be 84 percent as high and costs only 70 percent as high. There would be some improvement in sales, but there might possibly be very little reduction in cost. If the same number of bus runs are maintained, the only reduction in cost would be a small savings in fuel due to lighter passenger loads. It still takes one driver to handle a bus whether it is full or half-full. The price increase in such a case would lower profitability.

In order to cope with situations similar to the one above, the business owner needs to understand which of the costs are fixed and which are variable. Fixed costs are those that do not vary with volume, such as rent, depreciation, interest and salaried personnel. Variable costs are those that are directly related to volume, such as materials. Such other costs as utility bills and insurance premiums are a combination of fixed and variable.

The advantage of operating at a high level of volume is easily illustrated. Assume that a company can produce 100,000 units of a product if it operates at capacity. Also assume that it would be necessary to price this product at $1 to sell this number of units. At present, the cost of your unit is $1, you are pricing it at $1.20, and you are able to sell only 70,000 units. Would it be better to stay at your current level or reduce prices to achieve greater volume and lower cost? These two possibilities plus an intermediate course are evaluated in Figure 15.1.

By reducing the price from $1.20 to $1.10, the total profit was increased from $14,000 to $16,160, as increased volume of 15,000 units and lower unit costs of $.09 per unit were more than sufficient to offset the 10 percent reduction in unit price. Note that a further reduction of the price by $.10 reduced the total profits from $16,150 to $15,000. Unit volume did increase another 15,000 units, but the unit cost reduction this time was

FIGURE 15.1 Price Analysis

	Current Level— 70,000 Units	*85,000 Units*	*Full Capacity— 100,000 Units*
Costs			
Total fixed	$35,000	$35,000	$ 35,000
Fixed per unit	0.50	0.41	0.35
Variable per unit	0.50	0.50	0.50
Total Unit Costs	1.00	0.91	0.85
Price			
Selling price per unit	1.20	1.10	1.00
Unit price/Unit cost	–1.00	–0.91	–0.85
Profit Per Unit	.20	.19	.15
Total Profit	$ .20	0.19	0.15
	×70,000	×85,000	×100,000
	$14,000	$16,150	$ 15,000

only $.05. The decline of $.04 of profit per unit was more than sufficient to offset the increased volume.

The attempt to operate at full capacity can be self-defeating if it can be achieved only by extreme price reductions.

Only three levels of activity were used in order to simplify calculations. Of the three levels, the middle one proved to be the most profitable, given our assumptions. It was not necessarily the most profitable of all possibilities that could be used, however.

One financial tool often used to determine profitability relationships is the breakeven chart illustrated in Figure 15.2.

The breakeven chart quickly gives the profit or loss at various levels of volume, given fixed costs, price per unit and variable cost per unit. By changing the assumptions about sales price and volume, a new estimate of profitability can be quickly obtained. One can also see how a reduction in fixed expenses or variable expenses per unit would affect profitability. In the example above, fixed costs are $40,000 regardless of the company's level of operation. Variable costs, estimated at $.35 per dollar of sales, are added to fixed costs in order to derive a line for total costs.

FIGURE 15.2 Breakeven Chart

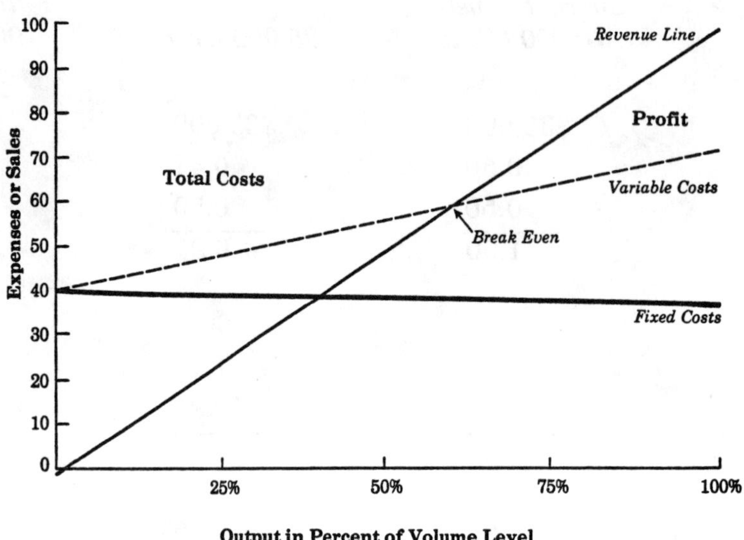

One of the by-products of cost/volume analysis is the marginal income ratio. This is the percentage of the sales dollar available to cover fixed costs and profits after deducting variable costs per unit. In the chart, $.65 of the sales dollar is available to cover fixed costs and profits. When this ratio is known, it is possible to determine what effects an addition or loss of a block of business will have.

Breakeven analysis permits the business owner to do the following:

- Determine profit resulting from any given volume of sales
- Analyze the effect of changes in the selling price
- Know the lowest price at which the business may be expected to utilize facilities and contribute to profit
- Know which products provide the greatest profit
- Determine unit costs at various income levels
- Determine probable effect on investment in new plant and equipment
- Determine most profitable use of scarce resources
- Assist in decisions as to whether to manufacture a given article or have it produced by a subcontractor

- Understand the profit structure of the business

SELF-TEST QUESTIONS

Multiple Choice

1. If a company's sales fall short of expectations, the following will tend to happen:
   a. Inventories will increase above targeted levels.
   b. Cash will fall below expected levels.
   c. Profits will be less than expected.
   d. All of the above

2. A price increase may
   a. increase dollar sales in some cases.
   b. reduce dollar sales in some cases.
   c. have no effect on dollar sales in some cases.
   d. All of the above

3. Price of a product should be
   a. higher than its cost to produce.
   b. lower than the value it provides to customers.
   c. Both of the above
   d. None of the above

4. The following industry factor affects a company's ability to raise prices:
   a. Competition from producers of the same product and/or substitute products
   b. Cost of the product
   c. Excess capacity in the industry
   d. All of the above

5. Good expense control means
   a. reducing expenses as much as possible.
   b. making sure an increase in expense produces an increase in profits.
   c. good recordkeeping of expenses.
   d. All of the above

6. Ideally, a company should know its profitability
   a. by customer.
   b. by product line.
   c. Both of the above
   d. None of the above

7. The following is an example of a fixed cost:
   a. Material costs and direct labor costs
   b. Depreciation and interest charges
   c. Capital expenditure costs
   d. All of the above

8. Without affecting quality of products, the best costs to reduce are those
   a. that are most flexible.
   b. that are the result of overinvestment in fixed assets and excess inventory.
   c. that apply to the most profitable customers.
   d. All of the above

True or False

9. The more unique a product, the better able it is to control its price.

   True ☐ False ☐

10. A company with a high percentage of fixed costs will tend to have a low breakeven point.

    True ☐ False ☐

11. A company with a high breakeven point is under pressure to operate at a high level of capacity even if this means price cutting.

    True ☐ False ☐

12. Suppliers could be a good source of suggestions for reducing material costs.

    True ☐ False ☐

13. An unprofitable product should be immediately discontinued.

    True ☐ False ☐

14. An unprofitable customer may contribute to overhead, advertising and plant utilization.

    True ☐ False ☐

15. Management should concentrate its attention on its unprofitable products and unprofitable customers.

    True ☐ False ☐

16. A growth industry is one in which a company is able to increase prices, resulting in higher profitability.

    True ☐ False ☐

17. Price decreases can greatly increase sales if the new price opens up a much larger market.

    True ☐ False ☐

18. Cost-cutting programs at large companies usually succeed by causing the least-productive employees to leave.

    True ☐ False ☐

19. Many cost savings actually are cost deferrals to subsequent years.

    True ☐ False ☐

20. A major purpose of a breakeven chart is to illustrate how changes in activity level affect profits.

    True ☐ False ☐

Answers
1.d, 2.d, 3.c. 4.d, 5.b, 6.c, 7.b, 8.b, 9.T, 10.F, 11.T, 12.T, 13.F, 14.T, 15.F, 16.F, 17.T, 18.F, 19.T, 20.T

CHAPTER 16

Financial Leverage: Its Uses and Abuses

Financial leverage is the technique of multiplying the power and profitability of your own capital by using capital from other sources. The use of financial leverage is common in most cases of outstanding business successes. Consequently, some entrepreneurs, once they have discovered the principle of the use of OPM (Other People's Money), think they have discovered the secret of success in becoming very rich. They overlook the fact, however, that financial leverage is also a common ingredient in business failure, and there are several business failures for each outstanding success. The purpose of this section is to analyze the differences between successful and unsuccessful uses of financial leverage.

It is advisable to become familiar with the pitfalls involved in the improper use of financial leverage. Learn the basic factors that determine how much financial leverage can be used and when to use it. Finally, you should know how to use "super leverage." There are many examples of this, including control of patents and copyrights and creating your own franchise system. Essentially they all involve control of a key factor in the production or sale of a product. This type of control can be said to put you in a "toll" position and permits the use of super financial leverage without a corresponding increase in personal risk.

THE PITFALLS OF IMPROPER USE OF FINANCIAL LEVERAGE AND HOW TO AVOID THEM

An analysis of individuals who have encountered severe financial problems (including bankruptcy) revealed three common mistakes in debt management:

1. Chronic debtors tended to buy things they didn't really need when they could use credit.
2. Debtors tended to pay higher prices for goods bought on credit than they could have paid if the same items were paid for in cash at the time of purchase. Often part of the interest cost of a product is an extra markup in the price of the item.
3. Debtors tended to use up their debt capacity on low-priority items. When it became necessary to finance an essential item, they either could not do so or had to pay an exceptionally high interest rate.

All of these personal cases of debt mismanagement have their parallels in the business field. There is a tendency for business to overexpand during periods of optimism and easy credit. Sometimes the expansion is in the company's basic business, creating overcapacity. In other cases, the expansion is in other nonrelated businesses, and the results are often disastrous.

The following comment is taken from an investment research report. This is in regard to a leading company in the small-appliance field but is applicable to numerous types of companies.

> . . . years of high profitability and *easy access to cheap money through public financing* [italics ours] contributed to a capital spending spree that has left the company with a large reservoir of unutilized capacity.

In the case of a rapidly growing company, the problem can be solved by restricting its capital expenditures until its sales grow more into line with its plant capacity. In many companies, the problem is not that simple. Expansion programs went into different fields where management was unaware of the major problems. A company that tried to expand overseas found that

50 percent of top management's time was being absorbed by problems of its foreign subsidiary that contributed only 1 percent of sales and *none of its profit*.

Companies having had mediocre records are often acquired by conglomerate empire-builders. Sometimes the only justification for their acquisition is that they are readily available because of the large number of dissatisfied stockholders. In most cases, both the acquirer and the acquired believe they are getting bargains. An inflated price is paid for the acquired company, but the price is usually paid in stock of the acquiring company, and this is also selling at an inflated price. Once the acquisition is over, the end result is often a collection of unrelated, disorganized, low-profitability companies with multitudes of problems. It is quite common for the operating management of the acquired companies to leave after the acquisition, magnifying the problems.

The first principle to remember in the use of financial leverage is: *Never use financial leverage for unnecessary or undesirable uses*. This includes acquiring other businesses, overinvesting in physical assets, carrying excessive inventories, etc.

A second mistake in the use of financial leverage is the failure to understand the full cost of debt. In the use of trade credit, a firm may confine purchases to suppliers who provide liberal amounts of credit. It may result in buying inferior products or paying higher prices for the same quality of product. The financially sophisticated business owner may not take advantage of trade discounts. Typically, trade credit is 2 percent discount if paid within ten days, net in 30 days. In effect, by paying at the end of ten days (or paying 20 days early), you receive a 2 percent discount. While this may not seem to be much, it is equivalent to a 36 percent return on your money over the course of a year. One of the questions that many credit investigators ask when evaluating a company's credit rating is whether the company takes advantage of trade discounts by paying quickly. Failure to take trade discounts is considered a sign of financial weakness.

Another variation of failure to understand financial costs is the risk of using short-term debt to make long-term investments. In the early postwar period, investors could borrow money at 2 percent interest from the banks to buy government bonds yielding 2½ percent. At that time, the Federal Reserve supported the price of government bonds, so there wasn't any immediate risk of their declining in price. Certain investors borrowed heavily to buy such bonds, with 95 percent of the cost being financed by debt (or 19 percent of debt for each dollar of the investor's own money). The effect was as follows:

Bought: $1 million worth of 2½% bonds	
Interest on bonds	$25,000
Borrowed $950,000 at 2%	
Interest on debt	19,000
Available for investor	6,000
Invested by investor	50,000
Rate of return to investor $\frac{6{,}000}{50{,}000} = 12\%$	

Unfortunately, the financial leverage backfired within a few years. To fight inflation, the Federal Reserve stopped supporting the prices of government bonds, which declined rapidly. Meanwhile, the banks that had been willing to lend money at 2 percent found themselves swamped with loan demands and began increasing interest rates. Quickly, the speculators found themselves in a perilous position. They could take a loss on their bond investments, which would more than wipe out their entire investment, or they suffered reverse leverage, as indicated in the following illustration:

Interest on $1 million in bonds	$25,000
Interest on debt (4% of $950,000)	38,000
Interest available for investor	(13,000)
Rate of return to investor $\frac{(13{,}000)}{50{,}000} = 26\%$	

In some cases, investors lost well over $100,000 on their $50,000 investment.

While this illustration goes back a number of years, the problem recurs periodically. In the early 1970s, many banks overinvested in long-term investments by using an excess of short-term funds. By 1973–74, interest rates had risen sharply, so that their long-term investments were selling at substantial losses. (Interest rates and bond prices always move in opposite directions.) Meanwhile, the interest cost on short-term borrowed funds rose above the rates they were receiving on their longer-term investments. If the situation had lasted much longer than it did, many well-known banks would have faced bankruptcy.

Nonbanking companies were caught in the same squeeze. One company borrowed short-term money at 8 percent to acquire a company that should have provided a return of over 12 percent. Within a few years, the cost of its short-term money had risen to 12 percent and the acquired company was only earning a 6 percent rate of return instead of the expected 12 percent. The parent company's real book value almost disappeared within a two-year period.

These examples were not isolated events. Had the period of financial tightness continued, many well-known reputable companies could have been wiped out.

Not only do many people not know what their financial costs actually are, but they also do not know whether they are getting the lowest costs available. By selecting the right loan for the purpose and the right lender for each type of loan, a substantial reduction in financing costs can be achieved. The second rule in the use of financial leverage is: *Know the cost of your financial leverage*. When short-term debt is used to finance long-term investments, be aware that the interest cost may rise substantially when the debt matures and has to be refinanced. Also, know how your financing costs compare to what is available elsewhere.

In the case of personal debtors, many waste their borrowing capacity on low priority items and then find themselves overextended when it becomes necessary to borrow for essential reasons. Likewise, a company may borrow to finance low-rate-of-return investments. When opportunities arise to invest in high-rate-of-return projects, the firm is unable to borrow the necessary funds because it is no longer a top-quality credit risk.

It is tempting to invest in a business yielding 15 percent when the necessary funds can be borrowed at 10 percent, and the after-tax cost is even less, because the interest is a tax-deductible item. However, the rate of return on investment is not guaranteed, while the interest rate must be paid.

As Figure 16.1 illustrates, industries with high financial leverage do not have a high return on investment. The table is based on industry figures for Standard & Poor's stock indexes.

One would expect return on equity to increase for those industries using the greatest amount of leverage. Instead, the least-leveraged industries had higher rates of return.

A study of financial results for 3,400 companies several years ago showed that about 10 percent are operating at a deficit. Whereas the leverage company in the Standard & Poor's industrial stock average had a leverage factor of 2.0, the

FIGURE 16.1 Financial Leverage versus Rate of Return

Financial Leverage Factor	*Rate of Return on Equity*	*Standard & Poor's Industries in Category*
1.5	14.7	8
1.6	13.6	5
1.7	20.0	7
1.8	9.7	4
1.9	13.1	14
2.0	11.6	9
2.1	11.3	8
2.2	11.5	8
2.3	9.5	6
2.4	10.1	5
2.5	14.2	7
2.5 to 3.0	7.2	5
over 3.0	11.6	11

companies suffering losses had a leverage factor of over 3. In several cases, the entire equity of the company was eliminated in one year due to the loss. A review of the most profitable companies in the study showed only average leverage or less. Apparently, companies that are earning below-average profits attempt to compensate by borrowing to meet their needs. This can be accomplished only for brief periods of time if bankruptcy is to be avoided. Principle No. 3 shows us the lesson to be learned is: *Financial leverage is to be used to magnify profitability, not to make up for inadequate profitability.*

HOW MUCH FINANCIAL LEVERAGE CAN BE USED

The amount of financial leverage that can be used in a given business is basically dependent on two factors:

1. The relationship between the profitability of the business versus the cost of using financial leverage

2. The variability of profits in the business

Assume that the after-tax cost of money is 5 percent and there are two business opportunities available, one of which is expected to give a return of 15 percent and one expected to yield 10 percent. In one case, the business owner would have a 3-to-1 safety factor (15 percent divided by 5 percent) and in the other a 2-to-1 safety factor (10 percent divided by 5 percent). The first would appear to be the safer alternative, all other things being equal.

Make a second assumption that the first business is a stable one in which profitability varies between 9 percent and 11 percent, averaging 10 percent. On the other hand, the second business has a return that varies between minus 10 percent and plus 40 percent, averaging 15 percent. In spite of the better average return, this would be a business in which use of financial leverage should be restricted.

An interesting fact becomes apparent as one reviews the financial leverage situation of stable, highly profitable companies. These are the companies that could use a high ratio of financial leverage, but in actual practice seldom do so. With their high, stable profitability, they can finance their growth through reinvested earnings. This contrasts with the tendency of low-profitability companies to use more debt than they should. The stable, high-profit companies can also obtain lower interest rates and better terms should they decide to finance.

The above points should be remembered when reviewing financial leverage ratios of companies in different industries. What is common in one industry is not necessarily what is best.

One further observation should be made about financial leverage. If you can develop what is known as a hedge position, you can increase the use of financial leverage substantially. Whereas a typical industrial company will tend to have a financial leverage ratio in the range of 1.5:3.0, financial institutions such as banks and life insurance companies may have financial leverage ratios in excess of 20:1. This is due in part to the semimonopolistic characteristics of regulated industries. It also reflects, however, the hedge possibilities that are available to the middleman.

A bank borrows money from individuals and pays a certain interest rate. (In the case of checking accounts, the customer gets services instead of cash return.) The bank then lends out the money to borrowers. Should interest rates go up, the bank will pay more to its depositors but should be able to pass along the higher interest costs to the borrowers from the bank. The bank is thus in a hedged position, and is able to use a high degree of financial leverage.

A life insurance company is also a financial institution accepting money from its policyholders, crediting those funds with a certain rate of interest and lending the funds out at a higher rate of interest. The company is hedged as long as the policyholders do not die ahead of schedule. Other variations of hedged businesses are brokers of various types. Brokers arrange deals between buyers and sellers, obtaining a commission for their efforts. The broker is able to operate on very little capital relative to the amount of business he or she transacts, since the broker acts as a middleman only.

USE OF SUPER LEVERAGE

Up to now, financial leverage has been discussed in the conventional sense; so many dollars of other people's capital per dollar of your capital. To understand the concept of super leverage, it is necessary to expand the concept of capital. All examples that follow are a form of borrowing money.

An auto dealer may have very little invested in his or her own facilities. The organization may lease its physical plant, making use of the leasor's capital. Auto inventory may be financed by the local bank, making use of funds supplied by the bank's owners and depositors. The automobiles would not be available if it were not for the auto company's capital. If the concept is carried further, you would have to include all the capital invested by the suppliers to the auto company. Many of these indirect suppliers of capital obtain only modest rates of return on their capital. Entrepreneurs who aspire to be super successes do not invest any of their own capital in low-rate-of-return projects when the same product can be obtained from outside suppliers at reasonable prices.

Instead, your own capital should be invested in areas of the business where exceptionally high rates of return are available. Basically, there are two ways to earn a high rate of return: by taking a high risk, and by taking advantage of technical expertise. The latter is the preferable way and makes it possible to apply super leverage.

Some economists are now using the concept of "human capital." They assert that a company's balance sheet covers only investments in physical assets and ignores substantial investment in personnel, organization and human knowledge. A company investing in a plant may get a 20 percent return for ten years. A successful investment in research may provide a return of over 50 percent for a much longer period of time, and yet the research investment would not usually even appear on the balance sheet. A review of companies earning exceptionally high rates of return on invested capital would reveal that these companies have made substantial investments in nonphysical capital.

There are two basic ways of capitalizing on the above principle. If you have exceptional abilities in business, such as technical knowledge or selling or managerial ability, this can be your method of obtaining super leverage. If your abilities can lead to the development of a unique product, system or process involving patents, copyrights or your own franchise, then you can multiply your capabilities to an even greater extent.

Assume you are an excellent store manager, earning a salary of $20,000 per year. You are convinced that you are worth twice as much or even more, especially if you were not restricted by some of the owner's policies. You are approached by the owners of another store and are offered a better salary. After analyzing the situation, you are now convinced that the store could earn $200,000 under your direction as compared to its present $100,000. In business economics circles, the standard method of evaluating the worth of an asset is to multiply its earning power by a figure ranging from seven to fifteen. Arbitrarily assuming a price/earnings ratio of ten, the $100,000 extra income increases the value of the store by $1 million. If you are correct in your assumptions, your capitalized management ability may be worth $1 million! Of course, it is highly unlikely that you would receive the full benefit of such an increase, but through options or bonus arrangements, it might be possible to obtain a substantial share.

Perhaps your strong point is your sales ability. Ross Perot, the founder of Electronic Data Systems, reputedly made his yearly sales quota at IBM in only three weeks. Even if Mr. Perot had not decided to start his own company, his sales ability alone would have been worth several million dollars to any company having good products but lacking in sales expertise.

Sometimes the key ingredient a company needs is technological ability. In the drug industry, one company had experienced a long losing streak after investing $250 million over several years without coming up with a significant new product. New and improved leadership in the research area substantially improved the value of the company.

There are many abilities that can be turned into opportunities. An outstanding chef can often demand and obtain part ownership in a restaurant that is dependent upon his or her services for its reputation. In an industry in which negotiating large contracts is a key factor in success, a skilled contract lawyer can be worth a veritable fortune. One lawyer who was an expert in shipping and shipbuilding contracts set up a private company that contracted with shipbuilding companies to build ships, financing them 100 percent through government-guaranteed loans. In turn, the ships were leased to the large oil companies, which covered all the expenses of running them. Not only did the lawyer's company earn a differential between leasing income and its interest expense, but it eventually owned a substantial fleet of ships debt-free after the long-term lease income paid off the debt incurred in buying the ships.

Ideally, certain human abilities can be turned into a form that is readily marketable. Technological ability can be converted into patents; creative ability into copyrights; and management ability into franchises.

This country's first patent law was passed in 1790, offering protection to inventors of new and useful processes and devices. Technically, a patent is good for 17 years, but an added period of a few years occurs while the patent is pending. Copyright laws apply to writers, composers, artists, photographers and motion picture producers. A copyright runs for the life of the creator plus fifty years.

Developing your own franchise is also a way to gain super leverage. Many businesses can be expanded through a franchise system. Once an effective method of marketing is developed to sell a unique product or service, a franchising program can be developed. What is vital is a carefully constructed "pilot" operation.

In summary, there are many factors that go into making a product or service. Producers of most of these factors have no strategic position and must accept only an average rate of return. In contrast, knowledge and know-how can earn an exceptionally high rate of return and increase the productivity of the other factors. By controlling the strategic factor, you can command the financial resources of the other factor producers.

Some individuals make the mistake of wanting to control all the factors used in the entire business. It is better to share the earnings of a profitable giant enterprise than to have 100 percent of a marginally profitable small business.

SELF-TEST QUESTIONS

Multiple Choice

1. Companies with very high financial leverage ratios
   a. should theoretically have high rates of return on equity.
   b. do not, on the average, have high rates of return on equity.
   c. Both of the above
   d. Neither of the above

2. Super leverage consists of the following:
   a. Control of a strategic factor in a business
   b. Ability to use other people's money, often on a nonborrowed or low-risk basis
   c. A very high rate of return
   d. All of the above

3. Normally, the highest potential rate of return is available on
   a. investment in current assets.
   b. investment in plant and equipment.
   c. investment in technology and human capital.
   d. None of the above

4. Easy credit often results in
   a. higher checking account balances.
   b. unwise investment.
   c. less financial leverage.
   d. All of the above

5. The following company can use financial leverage with the greatest amount of safety:
   a. A company in a young industry experiencing extremely rapid growth
   b. A cyclical company in a weak economy
   c. A stable company with a high rate of return on capital
   d. A company with heavy lease obligations

6. A company with a 10 percent rate on capital and a 5 percent after-tax interest cost will have the following rate of return on equity:
   a. 15 percent, if it has $1 of debt per $1 of equity
   b. 20 percent, if it has $2 of debt per $1 of equity
   c. 25 percent, if it has $3 of debt per $1 of equity
   d. All of the above

7. The company that will have the highest rate of return on equity, assuming money can be borrowed at an after-tax cost of 5 percent, is
   a. a company with a 20 percent rate of return on capital and no debt.
   b. a company with a 15 percent rate of return on capital and $1 of debt per $1 of equity.
   c. a company with a 10 percent rate of return on capital.
   d. a company with an 8 percent return on capital and $3 of debt per $1 of equity.

8. A company buys goods on terms of 2 percent discount in ten days, net in 30 days. By failing to take the discounts, the company is, in effect, paying the following annual interest rate:
   a. 2 percent
   b. 24 percent
   c. 36 percent
   d. 48 percent

True or False

9. A businessperson who borrows money on a short-term basis to make a long-term investment is hedged in case the interest rates change.

   True ☐ False ☐

10. It is not always necessary to borrow other people's money in order to benefit from its use.

    True ☐ False ☐

11. Many businesspeople make unwise use of their ability to borrow by borrowing for unnecessary or low-rate-of-return projects.

    True ☐ False ☐

12. As a business increases its financial leverage, it will probably be charged higher interest rates by its creditors.

    True ☐ False ☐

13. The financially overextended business often pays higher prices for the materials and equipment it purchases.

    True ☐ False ☐

14. Reverse leverage occurs when a company earns less on the money it borrows than the interest rate it pays on the money.

    True ☐ False ☐

15. Copyrights and patents are good for 50 years.

    True ☐ False ☐

16. Buying a franchise gives you instant super leverage.

    True ☐ False ☐

17. Short-term debt payable within one year does not contribute to leverage.

    True ☐ False ☐

18. Having a patent is somewhat like having a toll position.

    True ☐ False ☐

19. A businessperson should earn a higher return on money that he or she borrows than the rate paid to the creditor, because the risk taken is greater than the creditor's.

    True ☐ False ☐

20. To take advantage of bargains, a company should be able to borrow even during economic downturns or periods of tight money.

    True ☐ False ☐

Answers

1.c, 2.d, 3.c, 4.b, 5.c, 6.d, 7.b, 8.c, 9.F, 10.T, 11.T, 12.T, 13.T, 14.T, 15.F, 16.F, 17.F, 18.T, 19.T, 20.T

CHAPTER 17

Personnel Leverage

Even in its initial stages, a business is seldom the product of one single individual. As versatile as you might be, you may still need the help of an accountant, lawyer, various suppliers and other specialists. As your enterprise grows, its success will depend to a greater extent on your ability to expand your own capabilities by harnessing the energy, intelligence and knowledge of others. When this stage is reached, entrepreneurs sometimes sell out to an established company that already has a broad, well-trained staff, rather than change their one-person approach to running the company.

There isn't any reason, however, that the founder cannot grow personally along with the company. The key requirement is learning to accomplish tasks through the efforts of others rather than trying to do everything alone.

The effectiveness of an organization starts with the ability of the leader, so you might review how other entrepreneurs have improved themselves. Also, it is necessary to learn how to select desirable employees and associates for your team. Finally, it is essential to coordinate your staff into a dynamic successful organization.

DEVELOPING YOUR PERSONAL EFFECTIVENESS

An interesting experiment for executives is to list the various functions they perform and assign a certain amount of time to be spent on each according to its importance. How their time is actually spent should be monitored to determine how close they come to the original estimates. Quite often the two lists will be completely opposite. While long-term planning may be listed as a major function that should receive at least 10 percent of the available time, in actual practice it may not get any attention at all. Much of the day is taken up by minor crises that seem urgent at the time but are relatively unimportant to the success of the business.

One consultant in the field of time management suggests that we divide tasks into five categories in order of importance:

1. Important and urgent
2. Important but not urgent
3. Urgent but not important
4. Busy work
5. Wasted time

It is pointed out that effective individuals will complete the "important but not urgent" tasks where the ineffective one will never quite seem to get around to these responsibilities. Instead, the ineffective executive will be diverted into giving a higher priority to the "urgent but not important" tasks that crop up. In periods between minor crises, many relax by doing busy work, things that have only limited value but are found to be relaxing. Some people judge themselves by the amount of hours put in or by the amount of hustle and bustle, whereas the real measurement is effective output.

To overcome this basic problem, executives have to learn to guard their time jealously. They should learn to say "no" to requests for use of their time for tasks that have low priority. One executive spent an unusually large amount of time attending various public relations functions to which he had been invited out of courtesy. These were found to be totally unnecessary. A certain portion of an executive's time must be protected from interruptions, preferably that time of day when energy level is at a peak. This "prime time" should be used to tackle the tough jobs that require uninterrupted thought and the decision-making process. Often this free time can be achieved by having a secretary take all telephone calls, which is the most common disrupter of concentration. The calls may be returned later at a more convenient time.

Indecision is another common waster of executive time. Some people keep striving for more and more information before making a decision. Effective managers know that all decisions involve uncertainty, and a point is quickly reached where additional information is unlikely to improve the decision sufficiently to justify the extra time. A similar waster of time is encountered when an individual tries to be too much of a perfectionist. The additional time spent is not justified by the improvement the perfectionist achieves.

Probably the most common complaint about ineffective executives is their inability to delegate routine work. There is a tendency to say, "I could do this myself faster than I could tell someone else how to do it." This attitude overlooks the fact that taking the time *once* to explain the procedure can save additional time whenever it comes up again. Not seeing this, the executive spends time filing, delivering mail, photocopying and filling out forms when these jobs could be performed more efficiently by a secretary who costs the company much less per hour.

An important increase in executive productivity can be achieved by better utilization of "waste time." While traveling or waiting for appointments, time can be used productively to attend to simpler, routine tasks.

One of the most difficult problems facing the individual who wants to increase personal productivity is how to avoid those acquaintances who are time-wasters. These people usually call or drop in "just to chat for a while" and destroy productivity in the process. Some careful self-analysis may reveal that such interruptions are unconsciously welcomed and are being encouraged. It is not necessary to be rude, but simply continuing the work at hand when the visitor stops in conveys the message that you are busy. A businesslike approach on the telephone can keep a telephone call from deteriorating into a long, pointless conversation.

As you improve your productivity, it will have beneficial effects on your staff. People are influenced more by the leader's actions and attitudes than by words. If a supervisor always seems ready to relax and socialize, it will signal to others that this is appropriate behavior. Conversely, a production-oriented attitude by the top person tends to spread among associates and employees.

UTILIZING BUSINESS ASSOCIATES

Even when your business is still in its infancy, you should be thinking in terms of your future staff. Get acquainted with a librarian who could be helpful in any research you might do. In selecting a lawyer or accountant, look for those who will consider themselves a part of your organization. They should think of their relationship with you as similar to a long-term investment.

The same comment can be made about numerous business associates with whom you will eventually come into contact. The good insurance salesperson should be an expert in ways of protecting your business. Use this knowledge. Professionals want to have their knowledge challenged; they like to demonstrate their expertise. Avoid those who simply want to collect their fees.

Always be on the lookout for other successful people with whom you might make an alliance. Studies of successful industrialists illustrate the importance of associating with people who can stimulate your personal growth. For instance, Henry Ford's outstanding achievements took place *after* he became personal friends with such outstanding mental giants as Thomas A. Edison, Harvey Firestone and Luther Burbank.

Your staff may not include such famous people as Mr. Ford's acquaintances, but expertise is not limited to the wealthy and famous. One individual who had a number of questions in the general field of banking and finance visited a local banker. The latter was able to answer only two of the ten questions asked, but made eight telephone calls within the space of an hour to various associates who were able to provide answers to six of the remaining eight questions. The banker promised answers to the two remaining questions within a week and lived up to the promise. The interesting point is that all of the telephone calls were made to people who did not work for the bank and had no monetary reason to provide the information requested.

This banker is an exceptionally good business specialist who has built an informal network of information sources over the years. The information is not really "free," because the banker serves as an important source of information to the rest of the network when it comes to finance, banking and investment. Some of the people in the network do not have impressive titles or professional stature. Some are studious clerks, civil service workers, teachers, librarians and secretaries. This banker has an ability to spot hidden talents among the people with whom he comes into contact regularly, and he encourages them to share their knowledge.

DEVELOPING YOUR OWN PERSONNEL ORGANIZATION

During the early stages of a business, it is probably best not to hire full-time employees. It is also better to purchase the services of others on an output basis rather than by employing them by the hour. This eliminates the danger of incurring fixed costs that might not be covered by revenue during a business lowdown. Temporary employees could be hired during peak periods. As the business grows, however, it will eventually become necessary to build your own organization of permanent full-time staff.

This is an extremely important challenge for you. Selection and effective utilization of the right people become the key factors in determining how successful your business will be. One estimate is that 80 percent of the working population are employed in jobs that use only a portion of their abilities. There are also many thousands of unemployed people who are not using their talents at all. If you can effectively match any of these individuals with challenging positions in your organization, you will be making a major contribution to their happiness, to the health of the economy and to the success of your organization. Effective utilization of personnel can mean the difference between low profitability and high, or can even be the determining factors between success and failure. Although there are many people who might be good matches for positions you have available, it is a challenging task to reach, interview and select these prospects in a manner that will not be too costly in terms of both money and time. You can economize on your money and time by following these suggestions:

- Develop clear personnel requirements.
- Communicate your needs clearly to the employment market.
- Select the employee or employees who best meet your requirements.
- Convince your choice of applicants that they should accept employment with your company.

DEVELOPING CLEAR PERSONNEL REQUIREMENTS

Every job has a certain amount of technical requirements, and it is necessary to select people who at least meet these minimums. In reality, this is merely the beginning of the process involved in developing personnel requirements. For every person who fails in a job due to a lack of technical skills, there are several who fail for other reasons. They may be unreliable, difficult to work with, lack initiative, are unable to accept responsibility, are lazy or disinterested in the work, rude to customers, or have any number of other personal traits that can interfere with job performance. Any of these factors can more than offset any technical expertise that might be possessed by the employee. For these reasons, it is advisable to select people more for their general character and personality than for technical ability alone. Highly motivated employees with desirable personal characteristics can improve their technical knowledge far easier than an individual with technical proficiency can correct personality problems.

In developing your organization, look for what some refer to as "overachievers."

Here is a useful list of the characteristics to look for in potential employees:

- Hunger for success
- Intelligence
- Good health (sufficient for stamina)
- Tact (liked by others even when actions cause major changes)

- Persuasiveness
- Humor
- Courage (willingness to take chances)
- Optimism
- Creativity (either in themselves or in the ability to use the talents of others)

The term *overachievers* does not mean a collection of superstars with good track records. There are waitresses and janitors who could be classified as overachievers. These people are interested in being the best at whatever they do, whether it be waiting on tables, mopping floors or managing a company. They have a desire for success and a need to get things done, and they want to be recognized for their contributions.

In looking for overachievers, make an attempt to measure the person's actual accomplishments against what might reasonably be expected. In basketball, a short player is more likely to be an overachiever, whereas a seven-foot-tall player may be on the team simply because of height. A student who comes from a wealthy, highly educated family may get good grades but be less of an overachiever than students with lower grades who are working their way through school.

In looking for these people, it is advisable to avoid a number of "counterfeit" types. These are people who want to rise rapidly to the top but have not demonstrated any mastery of even elementary skills necessary to get there. Such people become rapidly discontented and usually job-hop from one company to another.

Another counterfeit, but one more difficult to recognize, is the person who *does* have obvious abilities and is quite self-confident—perhaps too self-confident. Most overachievers know their strengths but are also aware of their weaknesses. Their strong drive to succeed often originates from some feeling of inadequacy. By being aware of their weaknesses, they can offset and eventually overcome them. This type of person knows that he or she needs the help of others and can become a good staffer. In contrast, the supremely over-confident superstar type is unlikely to give credit to others but wants to claim all the glory. In spite of obvious talents, this individual is likely to be a detriment to your organization.

You may ask yourself, "What can I offer these overachievers that would make them want to work for me?" The answer is "Opportunity!" In a large, bureaucratic organization, overachievers may not advance much faster than the underachiever sitting at the next desk. They may not be able to see how their output contributes to the success of the enterprise. The small company (if it is successful) can grow much faster than a large organization. Consequently, its personnel can grow at a much faster rate. An important psychological benefit of the overachiever is to feel like a key member of the organization, rather than a small cog in a giant machine.

In looking for undiscovered overachievers, attractive hunting grounds for candidates are among groups of people who are occupationally handicapped. For example, there are many outstanding overachievers among women reentering the job market after raising their families, or suddenly finding themselves without a means of support. In addition to special skills they might possess, these women have broad practical managerial experience gained through overseeing the family's affairs.

When looking for either business associates or prospective employees, look for the "free-enterprise spirit." Seek out people who want to be judged on and rewarded for their own merits, who want responsibility, who are output-oriented and who have a strong drive toward self-improvement.

PREPARING A JOB DESCRIPTION FOR A SPECIFIC POSITION

Many misunderstandings that arise between employer and newly hired employee could be avoided by preparing a specific job description to be discussed in the interviewing procedure. It is basic human nature to discuss the more interesting and glamorous aspects of a position and to gloss over the more routine responsibilities. When the new employee discovers that the latter occupy the majority of the day, he or she is likely to be disillusioned. The problem is aggravated by the use of glamorous titles for routine work. The job of a janitor would probably now be termed "custodian" or even "sanitation engineer." Salespeople have recently been relabeled "consultants," with no apparent change in duties.

Another common source of misunderstanding has to do with which person supervises whom. One bank had a rapid turnover in secretarial personnel resulting from

FIGURE 17.1 Sample Job Descriptions

Job Title:	Repair Machinist
Location:	Main Plant
Department:	Maintenance
Primary Function:	1. Set up and operate machine tools. 2. Adjust and repair machine and plant equipment.
Tools and Equipment:	Lathes, drill presses, milling machine, planer, hand tools
Source of Supervision:	Maintenance Foreman
Supervision of Others:	Directs helper or other workers when required.
Physical Requirements:	Frequent lifting of weights up to 30 pounds. Requires working in a cramped position for prolonged periods.
Nonphysical Requirements:	Ability to work under pressure, plan work, solve problems.
Working Procedure:	1. Receives oral instructions from supervisor. Also guided by blueprints and trouble reports. 2. Plans work and selects tools and methods to be used. 3. Overhauls, maintains, repairs and replaces equipment. 4. Sets up and adjusts machine tools. 5. Makes tools and equipment to use for maintenance and operations. 6. Grinds and sharpens cutting tools. 7. Works in plant as required. 8. Keeps equipment and work area clean.

FIGURE 17.1 Sample Job Descriptions (continued)

Position Title: Secretary

General Responsibilities: Involves secretarial, advanced clerical and administrative work. Includes scheduling appointments, receiving visitors, taking dictation and recordkeeping. Requires independent judgment, ability to plan, initiative and ability to meet the public.

Duties Performed:

1. Take and transcribe dictation. Prepare memoranda and notices, including some of a confidential nature.
2. Open, read and sort mail. Prepare answers to routine inquiries and refer other mail to appropriate personnel for answers.
3. Maintain schedule of appointments, meetings and other due dates.
4. Handle telephone calls and meet visitors.
5. Prepare reports, maintain records and handle other administrative work.

Position Title: Clerk

General Responsibilities: Involves general clerical work that follows detailed procedures and is performed under close supervision. Work may require use of a typewriter and other office machines.

Duties Performed:

1. Filing in accordance with system and procedures set up in department. This may include sorting, alphabetizing and inserting materials in proper files.
2. Locate and remove materials from files when requested. Photocopy material if required for permanent removal. Maintain records of papers removed temporarily from files.
3. Type any work necessary for filing system, including index cards, tabs and stickers.
4. Type routine letters, forms, documents, etc.
5. Answer routine telephone or personal inquiries in accordance with departmental procedure.
6. Sort and distribute mail.
7. Operate business machines and perform other clerical functions as directed.

FIGURE 17.1 Sample Job Descriptions (continued)

Position Title: Clerk-Typist

General Responsibilities: Involves moderately complex clerical work that follows established procedures. Typing and use of other office machines are essential functions of the job.

Duties Performed:

1. Type letters, documents, reports, lists, statements and other materials.
2. File correspondence.
3. Act as receptionist, answer routine questions and direct other inquiries to appropriate personnel.
4. Sort and distribute mail.
5. Maintain records and record information by hand or machine.

Position Title: Bookkeeper

General Responsibilities: Requires general knowledge of accounts and bookkeeping procedures and use of bookkeeping machines. Requires care in posting, balancing and reconciling differences. Typing and use of other office machines required.

Duties Performed:

1. Prepare documents and other entries for posting, including sorting, arranging in order and running adding machine tapes.
2. Post entries to assigned account ledger and statements. Balance, post, run trial balances and make reports.
3. Transfer balance to other statement sheets, running trial balances to ensure accuracy.
4. Assist accountant in balancing and other detailed work when necessary.

- failure to explain that a secretary would report to more than one officer;
- using the department head's secretary to make assignments to other secretaries, who resented being "bossed" by someone they considered to be a peer; and
- frequent use of secretarial personnel for clerical work on mass-mailing projects for other departments.

The rapid turnover ceased when new applicants were better informed regarding their total responsibilities and scope of duties.

Figure 17.1 illustrates several examples of the features in a typical job description.

Note that several potential difficulties are anticipated in the job description. For example, the employee in the Repair Machinist position is expected to clean the work area. Since it is so stated in the job description, the person who is hired cannot later complain about being treated like a janitor. The individual is also alerted to the possibility that work in the plant may be expected at times. A job description will often spell out what level of skill is required on certain equipment. If the position is physically demanding, some indication of strength or endurance may be required in the description.

COMMUNICATING YOUR NEEDS TO THE EMPLOYMENT MARKET

Once you have a clear concept of the type of employee you want, it is still necessary to communicate your needs to the people who meet the minimum qualifications. At the same time, your message must be phrased so that it does not attract a multitude of nonqualified applicants, as this only serves to increase the time spent in the selection process. Several avenues of communication are available, including the following:

- Informing friends and business associates of your personnel needs. This method has the disadvantage of limited contact, and could cause ill will if you reject someone recommended to you.
- Private employment agencies can be useful in certain circumstances. A fee is usually involved, however. The employer usually pays the entire fee in highly-paid positions, or, in other cases, sometimes as much as 50 percent.
- College placement bureaus are a potential source of personnel, but unfortunately most of these departments are organized for the convenience of the large employer.

The above is an example of the "shotgun" approach to looking for the right employees. None exposes your job opening to the great number of people who are not actively looking for employment, but who would consider a job change if the right position opened up.

To reach this market, advertising is the best approach. Advertisements are usually placed in newspapers, magazines, trade papers or professional journals. Newspapers and magazines have classified ad sections, but you can also use display ads that include artwork or photographs in other sections of the periodical. An excess of answers may be received, however, and failure to acknowledge the replies could generate ill will. Consequently, some companies resort to "blind" ads, which do not identify the company that is recruiting. One company estimated that it received 20 to 50 resumes for every position that it filled. A well-worded advertisement can cut down responses somewhat, but unfortunately some desperate job applicants reply to many advertised positions for which they are not even remotely qualified.

Some items often covered in help-wanted ads are:

Title of job (the more general the description, the more response you will get)

Salary (often stated as a range and qualified by the words "up to" or "commensurate with experience")

Educational or technical requirements (includes education, experience, skill levels, degrees)

Location (included if out-of-town, but often describes general rather than specific location)

Important attractions of the position (includes such features as fringe benefits, opportunity for advancement, glamorous aspects)

Examples of effective as well as ineffective ads are illustrated in Figure 17.2.

For the advertisement to be most effective, it is necessary to distinguish it from the many others that will appear on the same page. Part of this can be accomplished by a message that is straight to the point and avoids use of trite phrases that are too common in want ads. Additional emphasis can be achieved by utilizing the art of typography. If most ads are written in lower-case letters, consider writing your ad in capitals. A common tendency is to crowd as much text as possible into the space

FIGURE 17.2 Sample Job Ads

Effective Ads, Clearly Stating Requirements

A.

SECRETARY for small business office. Must be capable of working independently, coordinating schedules, ordering supplies and working with the public. Good skills required, including shorthand or speed writing. Salary open, depending on experience. Downtown location, convenient.

B.

CLERK-TYPIST needed for growing business. Excellent opportunity for the right person who has good typing skills, can set up and maintain a filing system, and can deal with clients on the phone. High school grad with some office experience preferred. Salary open.

Vague Ads, Likely To Elicit Unqualified Applicants

A.

UNBELIEVABLE opportunity for the right person. Assist busy executive. Salary open. Glamorous downtown office.

(This is the same job as the "Secretary" position above. It will certainly attract a great many applicants, but it says nothing about duties, qualifications, experience or the type of work to be done.

FIGURE 17.2 Sample Job Ads

B.

Office help, $250 to $350 a week. Experienced.

(It isn't likely that this one will attract many qualified applicants either, because the general classification of "office help" could run the gamut from mailroom clerk/messenger to secretarial positions. This one looks like the ad placer was trying to save money on the ad. Also note that "experienced" doesn't really say very much. Someone who has worked summers at a day camp may consider himself experienced, but it is unlikely that this is what the employer had in mind.)

purchased. By cutting some of the excess words, however, you could leave a border of white space above and below your ad, making it stand out from the rest.

THE APPLICATION FORM

A well-designed application form can be equivalent to a preliminary interview, saving much of your time. The form must not ask for information that could be used to discriminate against the applicant on the basis of race, color, religious creed, national origin, ancestry, sex, or age over 40 years. A statement to this effect should be included on the application form. Because there are always new regulations concerning employment, it makes good sense to have a lawyer review your job application. Figure 17.3 is a well-designed form, broken down into blocked-off sections, with commentary on selected features.

FIGURE 17.3 Job Application

Please Use Ink and PRINT

Name ______________________________

Telephone Number (day) ________________(evening) ________________

Social Security Number ______________________________

Address ______________________________

Length of time at above address ______________________________

List previous addresses within the U.S. for last five years:

____

____

____

____

____

Comments

1. Printing in ink helps legibility and will prevent smudging and fading.
2. Addresses outside of the United States are not required, as this could lead to discrimination charges on the basis of national origin.
3. The number of different addresses and length of time at each can give some indication of the applicant's stability.

Type of work desired ______________________________

Salary requirements ______________________________

How were you referred to the company? ______________________________

Date available for work ______________________________

Are you over 17 years of age and under 65? ______________________________

Are you a citizen of the U.S.? ______________________________

FIGURE 17.3 Job Application (continued)

Comments

1. Type of work desired permits a preliminary matching of the applicant with job openings.
2. Salary requirements helps to screen out applicants in too high a price range. Applicant may avoid answering the question directly by stating "negotiable" or "dependent on opportunity."
3. Referral information is important if an employment agency has been used, as a fee may be involved.
4. Date available for work becomes significant if job opening must be filled immediately.
5. The question of age is not asked directly. However, it is necessary to know if applicant is under 18 years, as special working papers are often required for minors.
6. The citizenship question is necessary, as a work visa may be required. You are not permitted to ask applicant's country of origin.

	Education	*Name and Address*	*Major*	*Date Graduated*
High School				
College				
Graduate Work				
Other				

List scholastic honors, offices held, major activities: ______________________

____

____

Are you planning any further studies? ______________________

If so, when and where? ______________________

Comments

1. The purpose of the above information is to permit a matching of the applicant to any job openings. Educational requirements should not be used to screen out applicants if the educational level has no bearing on the work.

FIGURE 17.3 Job Application (continued)

General Information

Describe the skills, interests and aptitudes you feel could be used in your work with this company: ______________________________

____

____

____

Comments

1. Ideally, the applicant should know his or her strengths and abilities and how these can help a business. If, in addition, the applicant has done some research and knows something about your company and its needs, this would be the place to write it, and it should be favorably noted.

Employment Record

Starting with your most recent position, list all previous employers located in the United States. Include self-employment, summer and part-time positions.

Company______________________________

Address______________________________

Dates Employed: from ______________ to ______________

Position and Duties ______________________________

Salary: Start ______________ End ______________

Reason for leaving ______________________________

If currently employed, why do you wish to leave? ______________________________

____

Comments

1. The period covered is often limited to the last 10-20 years.
2. A number of job changes, especially into different fields, is an indication of instability. Ideally, position and duties should have increased in responsibility during the applicant's career. Salary should have increased at each job, and when job changes occurred. Reasons for leaving may give an indication of stability and ability to get along with others. Though there are undoubtedly some superiors who are impossible to work with, a history of personality conflicts should send up a caution flag.

FIGURE 17.3 Job Application (continued)

Please read before signing: If you have any questions regarding this statement, ask them of the interviewer before signing.

In the event of my employment with this company, I will comply with the rules set forth in the Company Policy Manual.

I certify that all statements made by me on this application are true and complete to the best of my knowledge. I have withheld nothing that would, if disclosed, affect this application unfavorably.

________________ ________________
Signature Date

Comments

1. The above section calls the applicant's attention to important factors that affect employment and discourages fabrications or the withholding of information.

THE JOB INTERVIEW

The application form can serve to screen out many unqualified applicants, but final selection will require an interview. You may want to know about the applicant's ability to converse intelligently or to establish quick rapport. This can best be done through personal contact.

The first few minutes of an interview will establish the tone of the meeting. If the position is a sales job, the interviewer may take the approach that the applicant can prove his or her sales ability by selling his or her own qualities to the interviewer. In effect, the interviewer assumes the role of a skeptical potential customer. Another approach is the stress interview, where the interviewer takes an adversary position to the interviewee. The intention is to test the applicant's ability to think quickly, to handle criticism and to retain emotional control under adverse conditions. Although I do not advocate this approach for the typical interview, either of the above techniques may have some appropriate applications.

A relaxed atmosphere is best for getting a quick understanding of the applicant and his or her potential. You should make it clear that your questions are not meant to be a cross-examination of the applicant's abilities; instead, the two of you are simply trying to determine if the applicant's background and interests coincide with the particular position you have open.

Basically, the interview breaks down into two distinct parts. In the initial stage, you need to determine whether the applicant is a likely candidate for the job. If he or she passes this preliminary test, then you can elaborate more on the specific nature of the position. This second stage can be kept to a minimum if the first stage indicates that the applicant is unlikely to be suitable.

In the first part of the interview, it is necessary to give an overall description of the position, and the job description can be an excellent starting point. After this, the applicant should be encouraged to do most of the talking. Questions should be asked to determine the applicant's attitudes, interests, self-image and opinions. The interviewer's intent is to evaluate the applicant's initiative, self-reliance, motivation and dependability. One method of accomplishing this is to ask people what they liked or disliked about school activities or previous jobs. Ask what the individual accomplished at any previous jobs, both in terms of personal growth and the contributions made to the company's success.

Figure 17.4 is an interview checklist that can be used as a broad, general guide. This can be expanded or condensed, depending upon the requirements of the particular position.

If you are impressed with the applicant who might be your choice, the second phase of the interview becomes a selling job on your part. You can now become more explicit about the position, the challenge and the potential rewards. Encourage questions about the position, the company and its products. A tour of the office or plant might be advisable, along with introductions to other personnel. While you might not want to make a definite offer at this time, the individual can be advised that he or she is a leading candidate for the position.

MAKING THE JOB OFFER

Once you have made a final decision, a definite offer should be made that includes not only salary but also the total compensation package. Fringe benefits have become a substantial portion of compensation and should be spelled out in detail.

FIGURE 17.4 Interview Checklist

Name of Applicant________________________ Date ________________________

Position Desired ____

Characteristics	*Comments*
Appearance	
Cleanliness	
Neatness	
Grooming	
Overall bearing and poise	
Personality	
Friendliness	
Disposition	
Sociability	
Enthusiasm	
Positive attitude	
Ability to get along with others	
Intelligence	
Alertness	
Ability to learn	
Capacity to reason and think	
Willingness to learn	
Communication	
Ability to listen	
Pleasant voice	
Vocabulary	
Ability to express opinions and views	
Maturity	
Realistic	
Knows his/her goals	
Ambition	
Main needs—money, prestige, power, achievement?	
Realistic ambitions	

FIGURE 17.4 Interview Checklist (continued)

Characteristics	*Comments*
Education	
Level	
Subjects liked or disliked	
Self-evaluation or worth of his/her own education	
Scholarships or academic awards	
Extent of education self-financed	
Activities and why chosen	
Office held	
Relationship to education and job	
Work History	
Substantial periods of unemployment	
Progress demonstrated in work history	
Reasons for changing jobs	
Relation of previous jobs to job opening	
Nature of previous work	
Public contact involved in previous work	
Extreme changes in job history	
Likes and dislikes about previous jobs	
Responsibility levels of previous jobs	
Interests and Activities	
Hobbies	
Activities in community	
Reading and other education activities	
Enjoyment of activities with large groups	
Characteristics sought in choosing friends	

After the interview, it is a good idea to summarize your reaction to the applicant. Figure 17.5 is an example of such a summary.

Figure 17.6 points out various benefits, some of which may not apply in all cases, and the amount of extra taxable income that would have to be earned to purchase them.

FIGURE 17.5 Overall Evaluation of Interviewee

Name of Applicant ____________________

Position Desired ____________________

1. Does applicant have realistic understanding of work requirement in the business?
2. Does the applicant communicate clearly?
3. Does he or she listen well?
4. Does the applicant appear to be congenial and friendly?
5. Does he or she establish rapport easily?
6. Is the applicant frank and honest in response to questions?
7. Is the applicant motivated toward learning?
8. Does the applicant appear to be self-confident?
9. Is he or she naturally curious and inquisitive?
10. Is the applicant honest and ethical?
11. Is he or she alert?
12. Does the applicant demonstrate ambitious goals?
13. Does the applicant give the impression of adaptability and flexibility?
14. Does he or she appear to be capable of growth?

Consider hiring for present position ____________________

Not suitable for present position, but consider for future openings ____________________

Date ____________________

MAKING THE ENTERPRISE GO

As the organization grows beyond a one-person operation, some jobs of top management will remain the same but others will be added. Management in small or large companies is responsible for creating the company's objectives and purposes for existence. As a company grows, these goals have to be communicated to new employees.

If your company was founded on the principle of quality and courteous service to customers, a rude employee can undermine your success. Large, successful companies are possible only if

FIGURE 17.6 Fringe Benefits

	Cost to Company	*Value to Employee*
Salary	$20,000	$20,000
Social Security contribution	1,500	1,500
Three weeks annual leave	1,200	1,500
Health insurance	1,200	2,000*
Life insurance	500	1,000*
Pension contribution	500	1,500*
Profit-sharing contribution	500	1,500*
Sick leave (est. 1 week)	400	400
	$25,800	$29,400

*Extra amount of value reflects group purchase and tax savings.

the employees are guided or inspired by a set of basic beliefs. This set of commonly-shared beliefs is the greatest coordinator.

Top management is also responsible for determining and communicating the specific objectives and goals of the company to employees. It is not enough to say "let's increase sales." Such directions must include more specific goals, such as how much sales should be increased, and what methods should be used to accomplish the goal. More important, all managers and employees need to understand their part in achieving that goal.

It is up to top management to determine and put into practice the systems of reward and punishment to guide the behavior of the organization's members. Promotions, for example, are communication devices. If the professional "yes-man" is promoted, it is a signal to employees that the way to get ahead is to always agree with the boss. If the person who takes responsibility for getting the work done is rewarded, it is an announcement that this is the way to succeed. While promotions are an obvious sign of success, there are many other ways that employees know their status in an organization, and top management must make maximum use of all means to signal which employees are doing the right thing.

It is particularly important to encourage initiative and decision-making capabilities. Too often, large organizations have difficulty adjusting to change, because members have been indoctrinated against making decisions on their own.

When the decision is right, there is no reward. When the decision is wrong, punishment is extreme.

Cooperation must be encouraged. In large organizations, one vice president is often competing with the other vice presidents rather than competing with other companies in the field. Everybody is trying to get a better position in the organization, but meanwhile the company may be declining.

Companies have different basic philosophies, and these are primarily determined by their leaders. Some company heads welcome change, because they know that change produces opportunities. Another company sees only the problems that change brings about. One organization goes into a new program with confidence that it will succeed, while another reluctantly moves into a new field only when competition has forced it to do so.

Top management determines the tempo at which the company moves. One of the secrets of Napoleon's success in warfare was the development of a rapid marching pace that enabled him to reach objectives before his enemy was prepared.

Similarly, some businesses possess the ability to seize new and attractive markets before the competition arrives.

Part of the problem in large organizations is the time involved in a chain of command, conflict between department heads and uncertainty as to where responsibility in a certain area lies. Even in a smaller organization, executives can be limited and tend to procrastinate. It is also common to set a goal without a set time limit and planned follow-up. Unless an objective has a deadline assigned to it, it may never get done. Not only should there be a time for the final project to be completed, but there should also be subgoals that state that each portion should be completed by a certain time.

In summary, the successful organization becomes the extension of the successful leader. In a small business that grows beyond your own time constraints, you will need to hire qualified staffers and delegate responsibilities to them. Should these employees be incompatible with your own goals and philosophies, there will be a conflict which could prove detrimental to the success of your organization. So determine your goals now while your business is in its infancy, and as you need to hire assistants you will be in a better position to choose those most qualified and most compatible with your long-term plans.

SELF-TEST QUESTIONS

Multiple Choice

1. The best decision maker is
   a. the fastest decision maker.
   b. one who defers decision making until he or she has all the relevant facts.
   c. one who makes the most popular decision.
   d. None of the above

2. A manager must delegate more decision making
   a. during illness or vacation time.
   b. as employees learn exactly what it is he or she wants done.
   c. as the company grows and expands.
   d. None of the above

3. The best work for an executive to delegate to his or her secretary would be
   a. work that is boring and routine.
   b. work that the secretary can do as well or better than the executive at lower hourly cost.
   c. work that does not require instruction.
   d. work that occurs frequently.

4. Employees base their own behavior on
   a. the boss's behavior.
   b. the behavior of the employees who are getting promotions.
   c. Both of the above
   d. Neither of the above

5. An executive can improve the use of time by
   a. tackling the most challenging jobs during periods of greatest personal effectiveness.
   b. having the most effective time period protected from interruptions.
   c. becoming less of a perfectionist.
   d. All of the above

6. In attempting to build a team of overachievers, you should
   a. look for people with advanced degrees.
   b. look for those who have high incomes compared to their age groups.
   c. look for the people who want to be the best at whatever they do.
   d. look for the supremely confident individual.

7. The small business owner can offer the overachiever the following advantage:
   a. A lifetime of security
   b. The opportunity to be judged and rewarded based on his or her performance
   c. A more peaceful work environment
   d. All of the above

8. To be more successful, business planning should be
   a. more ambitious than your competitors'.
   b. more definite in terms of goals and timetables against which to measure progress.
   c. secretive.
   d. All of the above

True or False

9. "Yes-men" are assets to an organization, as their positive mental attitude inspires others.

   True ☐ False ☐

10. The most effective executives take a management-by-crisis approach to running a company.

    True ☐ False ☐

11. An executive should grow in capability as his or her company grows.

    True ☐ False ☐

12. Capable people tend to develop better when they associate with other capable people.

    True ☐ False ☐

13. Most managers unconsciously allocate their time to various tasks in their proper order of importance.

    True ☐ False ☐

14. Employees should be judged more by the time and effort put into getting the job done, not necessarily the results.

    True ☐ False ☐

15. A right decision deserves no reward, because that is what the employee is getting paid for; but a wrong decision should be punished in some way.

    True ☐ False ☐

16. A manager has succeeded when his or her business associates perform as a team.

    True ☐ False ☐

17. In a successful business, employees are eager to outperform other companies rather than competing with one another for promotions or salary increases.

    True ☐ False ☐

18. Many homemakers returning to the job market after raising their families offer excellent management background at reasonable costs.

    True ☐ False ☐

19. Your management team should include business associates other than your employees.

    True ☐ False ☐

20. Effective leaders increase their employees' confidence by assigning them only jobs at which they will succeed.

    True ☐ False ☐

Answers

1.d, 2.c, 3.b, 4.c, 5.d, 6.d, 7.b, 8.b, 9.F, 10.F, 11.T, 12.T, 13.F, 14.F, 15.F, 16.T, 17.T, 18.T, 19.T, 20.F

CHAPTER 18

Marketing Leverage

Sales are the lifeblood of a business. To make an enterprise a success, it is necessary that either the company head or an associate develop sales abilities. If great success is desired, it is essential to magnify that sales capability to the fullest.

First, you need to review the important elements of successful personal sales performance. You can then devote your attention to the problem of leveraging a personal sales approach by adapting it to such mass communications media as newspapers, magazines, radio and television. Particular attention should be paid to the problem of getting the most results from your advertising and sales promotion dollar.

THE BASIC FACTORS OF SALES SUCCESS

There is always a great demand for effective salespeople. Even in recessionary periods, a review of the advertising section in the newspaper will have a number of attractive ads for sales personnel. Income for salespeople compares very favorably to the income levels of other occupations, many of which have much higher educational requirements.

There are probably many explanations for the number of openings for salespeople. Some may be dead-end positions in which a person can reach an above-average salary quickly but then has little room for future progress. Others require extensive travel and long hours that may not be justified by the income. Some sales positions have a higher degree of income uncertainty than many other jobs, especially when the salesperson is working strictly on a commission basis. Even after allowing for these drawbacks, however, sales must still be ranked as one of the best ways for a hard-working individual to achieve success.

Many people are discouraged from selling because they feel that success in this field is determined primarily by the extent to which they are extroverted. This is not generally true, and there are many examples to prove it. One would be Paul J. Meyer, founder of Success Motivation Institute, who was repeatedly rejected for sales positions because aptitude tests indicated that he was introverted, shy and without sales ability. Yet within a few years he was a millionaire, having succeeded through sales.

There is little question that personality type has an important advantage over competitors in the short run. Over the long run, the successful salespeople are known to be those who:

- make more contacts with customers or potential customers, use time in a more efficient manner or work extra hours, and can offset some or all of the higher success ratios of the "natural" salespeople.
- improve their success ratio over a period of time by obtaining a better understanding of their product and customers than the "natural" salesperson has.
- obtain better repeat business by giving customers better service. They serve as an information/education source for their customers, thereby making themselves indispensable.

The natural salespeople have the ability to make friends quickly, but the friendship is often superficial. Although good talkers, they often need to be better listeners in order to effectively learn the customer's needs. The natural salespeople may be interesting and entertaining, with an impressive collection of jokes and stories, but are more often than not selling themselves rather than the product. An associate tells of the time in a college speech when he thought he had made an excellent presentation but received only an average grade. He complained to the speech professor, pointing out how entertaining and dynamic his delivery had been. Surprisingly, the professor agreed—but pointed out that the entertaining style had completely obscured the message of the speech.

Many salespeople repeat this mistake daily, drawing attention to themselves rather than to the product. If you have selected your product properly, you already have the necessary ingredients for sales success. The various business successes described earlier were market-oriented companies, as opposed to being product-oriented. A market-oriented approach starts with the customer's needs. This is in contrast to a product approach, where a product is developed and then the attempt is made to sell it, regardless of the public's wants or needs.

A product should be created to meet the needs of certain unsatisfied customers. Not only must there be a market for the product, but it must also be an unsatisfied market. While other products meet part of the customer's needs, none are completely satisfactory.

If your product was designed with a market in mind, the nature of your sales approach is already largely determined. You must reach the largest number of possible customers in your specified market and inform them as to the ways in which your product can meet their needs and wants. For the sake of economy, you attempt to present this message at the lowest possible cost to yourself.

The use of mass communication is the method of accomplishing this objective. But before attempting mass selling, try selling your product through person-to-person contact, preferably to people other than your friends or family. When you meet objections to various sales points you make, take such objections seriously.

I know one entrepreneur who was trying to sell a venture capitalist on the idea of using hardwood timber in a complex industrial venture. The hardwood timber was to be floated downriver to the plant facilities. The venture capitalist stopped the entrepreneur with a simple question: "Will hardwood timber float?" Prospective customers can come up with important questions that were not anticipated but can mean the difference between credibility and incredibility.

In some cases, an objection may be sufficiently valid that it requires a modification in your product or service. In other cases, the objection may contain within it a good answer or solution, and this should be incorporated into your sales presentation. In making person-to-person contact, don't overlook positive comments the prospective customer might make. It is especially important to learn ways in which customers might use your product. There may be some uses you hadn't considered important, or ones that you might not have thought of as yet. For example, a nonstick product used to coat the interior surface of cookware was originally conceived as a method through which weight-conscious people could reduce calories by eliminating the necessity of oils, fats or butter in preparing their foods. But a much more gigantic market existed than was originally known. Most people who bought the coated cookware did so in order to reduce the effort involved in cleaning and scouring conventional cookware.

Another example, though lesser-known, involves an entirely different use of a product than that for which it was originally intended. While taking a drawing class in college, an associate was required to purchase a beautifully bound sketchbook, measuring 8½″ × 11″, in a black leather library binding. This book was particularly suited to art students, as it provided the student with a permanent record of his or her progress and developing talent. It had been found that most art students frequently destroy their earliest works, only to regret it at a later date; hence the usefulness of a permanent sketchbook. This was a novel and useful idea, but the student used her book for an entirely different purpose. She was also a writer and an avid journal-keeper. She had been unhappy with the quality of three-ring or spiral binders for her journals, and the sketchbook fit her needs perfectly. Since blank books created expressly for this purpose are now a hot-selling item, you can see where the manufacturer of these bound sketchbooks missed an important marketing opportunity. Had the sketchbook salesperson originally handed that product to an acquaintance and said, "What do you think this would be used for, and who would use it?", the product could have been marketed in a completely different way, to a potentially greater audience.

GOING FROM PERSONAL CONTACT TO MASS COMMUNICATION

Once a successful person-to-person presentation is developed, there is still the formidable task of adapting it to mass communication media. Even in personal contact, misunderstandings arise but can be corrected. When using mass communication media, possible misunderstandings have to be anticipated and avoided. One company, for example, wanted to increase its influence on the Spanish-speaking people of New York City, and presented some of its commercials in Spanish. Unfortunately, the Spanish used was Castilian Spanish, which might have been appropriate for a formal presentation in Spain but was totally inappropriate for the intended audience. It was the equivalent of Americans hearing commercials in Shakespearean English. The Spanish-speaking audience was greatly amused by the commercial but not impressed.

The difficulty is increased as you use the printed word to get a message across. In person-to-person contact, communication includes more than spoken words. Voice tones and inflections vary, and they are accompanied by facial expressions and body gestures that enhance or detract from the meaning of the words. In printed matter, this is lacking, except for such limited devices as underlining, italics or exclamation points.

Another restriction applying to the use of mass communication is cost. Since this is determined by the amount of space used, it becomes especially important to condense the information as much as possible without losing the content or impact of the message.

CREATING THE MESSAGE

To be a good business writer, it is not necessary to be a literary genius. The following are suggestions for developing an effective style:

1. Always start with the customer's point of view. Tell customers what the product or service will do for them. Omit details about the product that are irrelevant to the reason for buying it.
2. Maintain the personal touch. A good public speaker picks out two or three people in the crowd and talks to them. In writing advertisements, imagine that you are writing to a friend about your uniquely great product. This helps produce the sincerity you want (and need) to convey.

3. Let your subconscious meditate on the problem. Read a few pages by an author you particularly like. If possible, think about your task before going to sleep at night. Often you will awaken the next morning with some ideas in mind.
4. When the mood hits you, start writing. Don't be critical of what you're writing as it flows from your mind to the paper. And don't worry about it being too long. Put the draft aside for a while before starting revisions so that it will appear fresh to you.
5. Start revising with the intention of shortening and clarifying the text by
   - substituting small words for big ones when the small one is as good or better.
   - using simple, declarative sentences.
   - examining each word to see if it has the precise meaning you want to convey.
   - striving for short paragraphs and short sentences, while varying the length of both.
   - avoiding jargon, colloquial phrases and technical language as much as possible.
   - using action verbs and nouns that call up images in the reader's mind. Avoid overuse of adjectives and adverbs.
   - putting your main paragraph at the beginning of your text, and beginning each paragraph with a sentence that expresses the main thought of that paragraph.

Remember the message you want to get across to your readers. Do not put in a word that doesn't help convey that message, nor omit one that is necessary. Revise and rewrite until you are satisfied that the advertisement says exactly what you want it to say.

The next problem is to be certain that the customer will read it. You need an attention-getting headline or title. In no more than 20 words, summarize the primary purpose of the product or service. Write a number of headlines on the same subject. Which appeals to you, your friends and your associates most? Go through various publications and pick out ads that catch your attention.

How was this achieved? Keep in mind that the customer you have chosen is unsatisfied with what is available now. Try to picture what would capture attention. If you have really discovered an unsatisfied market, your customer should be looking for your message, at least on a subconscious level. The headlines would be in boldface type and should use provocative words that arouse interest. Overworked adjectives (such as "revolutionary" and "fantastic") should be avoided. Photographs and illustrations can be used to help capture attention.

In spite of all the work involved to this point, you will never know how effective an advertisement is until it is tested. Pick out those you like best and use them as preliminary advertisements to see which one gets the most response. Often one version, with only a word or two changed, will greatly outperform an otherwise identical writeup.

Almost every advertisement follows the basic formula of Attention-Interest-Desire-Action. The headline gets the attention, the various features of the product arouse interest and desire, and the final ingredient must be action. Many sales presentations fall short on this last point. One sales manager who hires many salespeople asks prospective employees what they feel their main job would be. Surprisingly, many applicants answer that their function is to educate the public or act as consultants. The sales manager hires only those who understand that their major function is to make sales, and that instructing and educating is simply a means to an end, not an end in itself. The same applies to the written sales presentation. An easily filled-in coupon with a conspicuously displayed money-back guarantee makes it easy for the customer to respond with action.

SELECTION OF MEDIA

The major media are print, radio and television. Each has its advantages and drawbacks. Television has the largest audience and the closest personal contact, but it is also the most costly. Giant companies with mass markets are able to justify the high cost, as they can spread the cost over a very large number of customers, reducing the cost per customer to a moderate amount. Spot commercials can be made for local markets at a more modest cost, and certain items (such as record albums) are merchandised in this manner. Television is often used to build or maintain a company's image. The cost of television tends to result in companies' attempting to cram as many words as possible into a short time, however, and the message does not come across as sincere and as truthful as a personal presentation would.

Radio lacks the visual aspect of television but has the advantage of being able to command the attention of a listener who is performing routine work. Radio is effective in relaying simple messages and is influential in determining what brand of product the listener will buy. It is less effective in motivating customers to try a new product.

For maximum effect, publications still offer the biggest "multiplier" factor for your dollar. If you wish to reach a large number of people in a local market, the metropolitan newspaper provides the opportunity. If you are interested in reaching a more specialized market, there is a large variety of special-interest publications.

The growth of mail-order sales may be surprising, considering that this type of marketing originally evolved to suit the buying habits of a rural population. At the time Sears Roebuck started in 1887, only one-third of the population lived in cities. The growth of the cities, and the ready availability of the automobile, might have been expected to lead to the death of mail-order merchandising. But mail order still survives, and business has seldom been better. For many, mail-order shopping is more convenient than any other kind.

One successful entrepreneur attributes his own success in mail order to the fact that many customers are dissatisfied with shopping in crowded urban areas, shopping centers and malls. Their major complaints are crowded stores, inadequate parking, and the fact that popular items are often out of stock. Other reasons include the reluctance of retailers to carry slow-moving specialty items that are unprofitable. By specializing in one basic type of merchandise and locating in a low-rent or low--labor-cost area, the mail-order merchant can make profits on items that the shopping district must shun. Often this can be accomplished at a lower cost to the customer.

One of the most crucial considerations in mail-order sales is the correct selection of media in which to advertise. As a starting point, review various magazines to see which ones advertise products or services similar to yours. Then review back copies of those magazines for the same advertisements. Cross-check to see which ads in the older magazines are still running in the recent edition. These are the ads that are consistently profitable, because businesspeople do not continue to run ads that don't pay for themselves.

It is better to place your advertisements in magazines in which similar products or services are being advertised with apparent success. It may seem odd to put your small ad in with a number of others. You might ask yourself if it wouldn't be better to advertise in a magazine with good circulation but limited advertising, particularly competitive advertising. While this argument may appear logical, practical experience has shown that it is better to benefit from the experience of others who have learned which publications are profitable and which are not.

The classified ads in a publication are a good starting place for the beginner with limited cash. By using the classified section, your message is aimed at a potential customer who has indicated an interest in your type of product or service. Otherwise, the ads would not be read. If your product needs extensive explanation, the ad in the classified section can be used to encourage readers to solicit more complete information, such as a pamphlet, brochure or sales letter.

A more expensive approach is to use a display ad. This type of advertisement covers a larger space and may include photography and/or artwork in addition to copy.

Not every section in any given publication has equal drawing power. One mail-order specialist confines his ads to the third, fifth, seventh and ninth pages. The back cover of a magazine has also been found to be a select spot. The upper right-hand portion of the page is most advantageous for capturing attention. Remember that it is important not to have your ad on a page bearing a cut-out coupon on the reverse side, as some (or all) of your advertisement will be lost when someone uses the coupon.

It is essential to test the pulling power of an ad on a continuous basis. The advertiser using several ads in different magazines could be confused as to which replies are in response to which ads, however. To solve this problem, most return coupons include a key code as part of the return address. For example, "Dept. PM-1" may signify that the response was to an ad in the January issue (month "1") of *Popular Mechanics.*) Another method of keying is to vary the return address slightly for ads placed in different publications. You might alternate abbreviating and spelling out street names or the city and state.

There are numerous ways of economizing on advertising. By starting your own advertising agency, you can obtain a discount on space (or time) when you purchase it. You can buy remnant space at bargain prices. (Remnant space is ad space left over in an issue.) It is also possible in many cases to buy space on a P.I. (per inquiry) basis. With this arrangement, the newspaper, magazine, radio or television station runs your advertisement without cost to you. When the orders come in, the medium takes its cut, which is usually a percentage of the retail price. This avoids heavy losses in case of failures, but also reduces the profits of successful ads.

In selecting a publication in which to advertise, you are interested in cost per potential customer. If your product is a general one, total circulation may be the measuring stick. In the case of specialty products, you may reach more potential buyers in a specialty magazine catering to that group.

USE OF DIRECT MAIL

Direct mail merchandising is useful when the product is expensive or unique, or requires a complete explanation. A key to success in direct mail merchandising is the direct mail list. There are lists available that include customers who have purchased your type of product in the past or of specialized groups of people who have some characteristic in common. Because a list becomes obsolete as people change residences, it should have been "cleaned" within the last 12 months.

A mailing list is cleaned by sending out a promotional piece with "Return Requested" printed on the envelopes. All undelivered mail is then returned, and those names are removed from the list.

Over a period of time, you should develop your own list. A starting point would be to consult various directories and yearbooks at your library. The classified section of telephone books is another valuable source. As you receive inquiries and orders for your product, compile a separate list for each. These will be valuable leads in selling other products you have. These lists can also produce added income for you when they reach 5,000 names or so and you can market them to other direct mail marketers.

SELF-TEST QUESTIONS

Multiple Choice

1. The basic formula for advertising is A.I.D.A., which stands for
   a. attention, interest, desire, action.
   b. administer, initiate, define, accuracy.
   c. all ideas demand action.
   d. amuse, inform, develop, advertise.

2. Over the long-term, the successful salesperson will
   a. make more numerous calls.
   b. have above-average success ratio.
   c. derive repeat business.
   d. All of the above

3. A marketing-oriented company
   a. starts with a product and researches for customer groups that could use such a product.
   b. stresses advertising and sales promotion rather than production or finance.
   c. starts with customers with unsatisfied needs, and develops products to meet those needs.
   d. None of the above

4. The announcer often talks at a very rapid pace on television and radio commercials. This is because
   a. rapid talking is more persuasive.
   b. rapid talking gives the impression of sincerity.
   c. the announcer is trying to say as much as possible in a short time.
   d. None of the above

5. Technical language and jargon in an ad serve to
   a. attract the attention of the reader.
   b. show the reader that your company knows what it's doing.
   c. permit complex ideas to be expressed with a minimum of words.
   d. confuse the reader, and should be avoided.

6. An advertisement for a product
   a. should be placed in a publication where there are no advertisements for similar products.
   b. should be placed in specialty magazines only if there is a broad market for the product.
   c. should take into consideration the cost per potential customer when selecting media.
   d. All of the above

7. To minimize the possibility of losing money on an advertisement, you could
   a. buy space on a P.I. basis, where the advertising medium takes a percentage of the income generated by the ad.
   b. advertise only sure things.
   c. not pay for advertising until you see the results.
   d. All of the above

True or False

8. Sales have been called the lifeblood of business.

   True ☐ False ☐

9. Unless a person has a highly extroverted personality, he or she should avoid sales work.

   True ☐ False ☐

10. The most effective way to sell products is through clever and witty advertising.

    True ☐ False ☐

11. Mail order has suffered a steady decline due to the automobile and the concentration of people in the cities.

    True ☐ False ☐

12. Customers are often good sources for suggestions on additional uses of your product.

    True ☐ False ☐

13. An advertisement should include some long, sophisticated words in order to impress the audience.

    True ☐ False ☐

14. Person-to-person communication includes more than words.

    True ☐ False ☐

15. In a main paragraph, the main idea should never be in the first few sentences, as this would encourage readers to skip the rest of the paragraph.

    True ☐ False ☐

16. Remnant space, when available, offers a substantial reduction in advertising cost.

    True ☐ False ☐

17. Most return coupons from an advertisement contain a key code that indicates the publication and issue that contained the ad.

    True ☐ False ☐

18. By starting your own advertising agency, you qualify for a 50 percent discount automatically.

    True ☐ False ☐

19. A mailing list should be cleaned periodically to eliminate names of customers who do not pay their bills.

    True ☐ False ☐

20. Mail order and direct mail are identical.

    True ☐ False ☐

Answers

1.a, 2.d, 3.c, 4.c, 5.d, 6.c, 7.b, 8.T, 9.F, 10.F, 11.F, 12.T, 13.F, 14.T, 15.F, 16.T, 17.T, 18.F, 19.F, 20.F

CHAPTER 19

Tax Guidelines

The impact of taxes upon business is illustrated by the story of a company president who used to begin his shareholders' meeting (held each August) with the comment, "The first six months of the year we worked for Uncle Sam, and in July, we worked for the state. You shareholders will be interested in knowing that for the rest of the year, we'll be working for you."

With taxes taking such a large bite out of income, every legal means should be taken to minimize them. In looking for ways to reduce costs, it always makes sense to scrutinize the largest areas of cost first. Taxes rank at the top.

There are two other advantages to reducing tax costs as compared to cost reduction in other areas. If a corporation is in a 39 percent tax bracket, each dollar saved in most areas improves after-tax income by only 39 cents. A dollar saved in taxes, however, is fully reflected in an improvement of $1 in after-tax income. Another advantage of tax savings over savings of other costs is that cost reductions in other areas are not always pure savings. For example, a savings in material may reduce the quality of a product somewhat. In contrast, a savings in taxes is not likely to reduce the services we receive from the government.

Before commenting on ways to reduce taxes, I should warn you that

- tax regulations and interpretations of existing laws change every year.
- different tax districts interpret tax regulations differently.
- state tax laws must be considered as well as federal (Certain ways of operating a business may be advantageous from a federal viewpoint, but the advantage may be offset by disadvantages in state tax laws.)
- each general tax rule has a multitude of restrictions and exceptions, particularly involving transactions between related parties.

In spite of these drawbacks, each business owner should at least be aware of certain tax regulations that may be advantageous. A tax specialist should be consulted to determine whether or not the tax rule would be useful in any particular situation. One further caution: tax considerations are only one aspect of a business transaction, and should not be allowed to distort your decisions. A bad business decision does not become a good one just because it saves taxes.

While tax management is an extremely complex subject, its basic objectives are fairly simple. You should

- take all deductions to which you are legally entitled.
- reduce taxable income by use of conservative accounting practices.
- minimize the tax bracket at which income is taxed.
- defer taxes to a later date, if possible.
- convert ordinary income to capital gains treatment, whenever possible. In the case of losses, attempt to have them treated as ordinary losses rather than as capital losses.

TAKING ALL LEGAL DEDUCTIONS

Many legal deductions are either overlooked by business taxpayers or disallowed because of inadequate recordkeeping. Records should be kept of any property (such as tables, lamps, chairs, tools, etc.) that is converted to business use. These can be depreciated over their remaining lives, or deducted entirely if they are small in dollar amount. The basis, or amount of expense, is the lesser cost or fair market value at the time you begin using them in the business.

It is advisable to keep a diary for mileage, postage, parking, paper clips and other small expenses for which you will be paying cash. Some small business tax advisers recommend the avoidance of a petty cash fund, which can be too easily abused and consequently turn into a bookkeeper's nightmare. Instead, reimburse yourself every few months for such expenses, supporting the repayment with receipts or the appropriate pages from your diary.

Two areas of expenses that require very careful documentation are travel and transportation expenses and business entertainment expenses. To be deductible, they must be ordinary and necessary expenses for carrying on the business. You may not deduct these expenses to the extent that they are lavish or extravagant, or are incurred for personal or vacation purposes. It is necessary to substantiate

- the amount of the expense,
- the time and place, and
- the business purpose. What business benefit did you derive or do you expect to get from the expenditure?

Records should be maintained in an account book or diary, and must be timely. Credit cards are a great idea for travel and entertainment expenses, because they help to provide documentation that auditors of the Internal Revenue Service appreciate. Diary entries, in addition, help to support credit cards when a record of who, when, where and what was discussed is kept accurately.

In the case of corporations, certain expenditures could be considered dividends that are not tax-deductible. If you use corporate funds to buy a car for the use of your spouse, the fair rental value expenditure could be treated as a constructive dividend and would be taxable to you. Under certain circumstances, interest deductions may not be tax-deductible. This occurs where a security may be called a debt, but has more characteristics of a stock than a bond. A bond that has an indefinite (or a very distinct) maturity, or one that is postponed frequently, becomes similar to a stock. The interest payments on a loan should be clearly spelled out and not be dependent on direct action. If the bondholders bear the main risk of the enterprise, participate in management and/or participate in profit, the IRS is likely to consider them to be shareholders.

Certain portions of salaries of shareholder-employees may be disallowed as tax deductions in a corporation. If the salaries are unreasonably high, tax authorities may consider the excess to be constructive dividends, which are not tax-deductible. Ten factors are important in determining reasonableness:

1. The value of an employee to a particular employer
2. The amount paid to similar employees engaged in similar industries
3. The extent to which the employee's services contribute to the success of the business
4. Contribution of the individual in a capacity other than as employee
5. Testimony as to the value of the employee by expert witnesses, including competitors
6. The portion of the person's time devoted to the business
7. Performance of the company under the employee's direction
8. The control the individual has over setting his or her own salary
9. Whether the salary was set when the profits of the company were known for the year
10. The relationship of the salary to company sales and earnings, to other employees and to the percentage of shares held

A common fault of individual businesses that have been converted to corporations is the tendency to continue to keep records on the business as it had been done previously.

A number of benefits can be obtained through the corporation with tax advantages. One example is the Medical Reimbursement Plan, under which the company pays for your medical charges and those of your dependents. The payments are tax-free to you and are deductible by the company. To take such deductions, a definite plan must be set up in advance and must not discriminate against other employees of the corporation.

REDUCING TAXABLE INCOME THROUGH CONSERVATIVE ACCOUNTING PRACTICES

Basically, the federal income tax is a tax on net income, and expenses of generating that income are normally deductible from gross income. Some expenses are not determinable in a year's time, however, so they must be based on estimates. Expenditures for equipment, for example, will benefit the generation of income for a number of years, and only a portion of the expenditure can be written off in any given year. By using favorable estimates of the life of the equipment, annual depreciation expenses are increased and taxes are reduced accordingly. Reported depreciation expenses are also increased by use of accelerated depreciation. The first-year depreciation for equipment purchased is also affected by the availability of an investment credit on certain property.

The amount of first-year depreciation can also be affected by the use of the ADR (Asset Depreciation Range) method of computing the reasonable depreciation allowance for all eligible property placed into service during the tax year. Originally designed to simplify bookkeeping and reduce disputes between taxpayers and the IRS, the ADR, in some cases, also permits full-year depreciation for assets held for only a portion of a year.

There are also opportunities to use faster depreciation methods when making improvements on property. The cost of building improvements can be added to the cost of a building, which, in effect, depreciates the improvement over the life of the building. Additions or repairs, such as new walls, wiring and plumbing, can be written off over a shorter period of time. In these cases, it would be better to set the improvements up as separate items to take advantage of faster depreciation rates.

In addition to faster depreciation, the company can reduce taxes by conservative accounting assumptions regarding inventory. During inflationary periods, reported earnings are usually minimized by using LIFO (last in/first out) accounting. This method assumes that inventories that are consumed first in the production process are those that were purchased last. Because the most recently purchased inventories are more likely to reflect current price levels than older inventory, this assumption increases reported cost of materials and reduces taxes accordingly. It is also a more realistic approach.

There are other costs that can be either written off in one year (expensed) or written off over a longer period of time (capitalized). It should be emphasized that conservative accounting reduces only reported earnings in the year, not real income.

MINIMIZING THE TAX BRACKET AT WHICH INCOME IS TAXED

Taxes are a major consideration in deciding what form a company should take. If a small business would find it advantageous to incorporate to limit liability but would have to pay higher taxes to do so, it may elect to be treated as an "S" Corporation. If it qualifies, its income will be taxed to the shareholder, much the same as if it were a partnership. If the individuals are in low tax brackets, this would be advisable. As this book went to press, Congress was debating changes to the Tax Code. Be sure to obtain the latest rates when considering "S" Corporation status.

Tax brackets also become an important factor in real corporations when it comes to deciding how much to draw out of the company in the form of salary. Subject to the question of reasonableness discussed earlier, the best salary is determined by

- the stockholder/employee's top tax bracket.
- the corporation's tax rate.
- the prospects for taxes and ordinary or capital gains on the funds left in the corporation. This problem arises because a corporation's earnings are subject to a double tax, once at the corporate level and also at the shareholder level, on dividends that are received.

If dividends are not likely to be paid in the foreseeable future and the company is likely to liquidate, the best salary for the shareholder-employee is that amount beyond which any increase would cost the individual more in taxes than the corporation would save through a larger deduction.

If the individual is in a 39 percent or higher tax bracket, it is probably better to leave the first $50,000 in the corporation to be taxed at the 15 percent tax bracket. Eventually a second tax would have to be paid when dividends are paid from this reinvested income, but the impact becomes less the longer it is deferred. Also, it is possible that the second tax will be of the capital gains type, if the owner gets accumulated earnings out by liquidating or selling the company.

DEFERRING TAXES TO A LATER DATE

Certain employee benefit plans have the advantage of deferring taxes to a later date. A corporation may institute a pension plan or a profit-sharing plan that permits it to make tax-deductible contributions to retirement plans for its employees. The latter do not have to pay taxes on such contributions until they withdraw their funds, and this may be many years later. Corporate benefit plans permit far greater contributions than do unincorporated businesses. A tax-deferred plan (the Keogh H.R. 10) is available if you are the owner of an unincorporated business, a physician, lawyer or other professional person.

Under the Keogh, you may contribute up to $30,000 per year. Benefits may not be paid before you reach the age of 59½, except in the event of your disability or death.

CONVERTING ORDINARY INCOME INTO CAPITAL GAINS AND CAPITAL LOSSES INTO ORDINARY INCOME LOSSES

Because capital gains tax rates are lower than ordinary income tax rates, it is best to convert ordinary income into capital gains income whenever possible. The business owner who reinvests earnings, building up a company's value in so doing, converts this accumulated ordinary income into income taxed at capital gains rates when the firm is sold or liquidated.

An illustration of this would be a carpenter who bought a run-down house, fixed it up and sold it at a profit. If this work had been performed for someone else, taxes would have been paid on wages received. By owning the house, this individual's income consisted of $5,000 profit on the sale, most of which was due to the improvements created by the carpenter's own labor. This profit would be taxable at the capital gains rate, or approximately half the rate that would have been paid on ordinary income. In actual practice, there was no immediate tax, because funds were reinvested in another run-down house in less than a year and the process was repeated. This tax advantage is available only to homeowners who use the dwelling as their main residence.

Over the next ten years, this individual parlayed profits into larger and more expensive homes. Eventually, enough capital was accumulated so that it was possible to own more than one house at a time. The additional houses were rented out at a relatively high rent (compared to his mortgage payments), because the houses were much more valuable after being repaired and remodeled. Except for a modest down payment, no funds were tied up in the rented houses, which paid for themselves through rent.

At the age of 30, this individual had built up a substantial fortune in real estate, having started with practically no capital. This illustration is based on the true case of an individual in a small eastern city but has been duplicated widely throughout the country. A key element of this success was the ability to turn what would have been fully taxed ordinary income into income upon which taxes were deferred and eventually paid at capital gains rates.

In the case of losses, these should be taken as ordinary income rather than as capital losses whenever possible. Readers should be aware that small businesses have an important tax advantage in this regard in the form of Section 1244 stock. A small business corporation that meets certain requirements can issue stock that will receive capital gains tax treatment if a gain is made, but would have losses (up to a certain amount) treated as ordinary income losses. This is a very important advantage in raising both equity capital for new corporations and additional capital for already established corporations. Section 1244 stock must be offered by a small corporation, which means total equity capital of less than $1 million, including current offering; not more than $500,000 of equity. The stock must be issued under a written plan, adopted by the qualified corporation, which indicates the maximum amount to be issued. The plan should state the period—no longer than two years after adopting the plan—during which the stock will be issued. Failure to state the period or the maximum dollar amount to be issued has resulted in the stock being ineligible for Section 1244 treatment, even when the stock was issued immediately.

As complex as Section 1244 may first appear, there are standard forms available from most legal stationers or in my book *How To Form Your Own Corporation Without a Lawyer for under $75*.

There is everything to gain and nothing to lose by issuing stock in your corporation in compliance with Section 1244 rules.

One other note of caution is necessary regarding taking of losses. When a new enterprise is just getting started, and it is difficult to predict whether or not losses will be incurred, it is generally better to start off as an "S" Corporation, where losses can be taken by the individual shareholders to apply against income or gains they would have from other sources. This reduces the cost basis of the stock. Any further losses when the stock is sold or the company liquidates could be taken as ordinary losses under Section 1244 described above.

A number of other potential tax pitfalls threaten the business owner, and an attempt to list all of them would be a lengthy undertaking. Two of the most common involve taxes on accumulated earnings. Retention of corporate earnings cannot be for the sole purpose of avoiding taxes. In the typical corporation, earnings must be retained for the reasonable needs of the business, such as

- expansion of the business or replacement of a plant.
- to acquire a business enterprise.
- to provide for debt retirement.
- to provide working capital.

On the other hand, to retain earnings in order to make loans to shareholders or their friends, or to invest in unrelated assets, would not be considered reasonable accumulation of earnings. The tax is not imposed on any corporation that does not accumulate over $150,000, so it may not be a problem in the early years of a company's existence.

SELF-TEST QUESTIONS

Multiple Choice

1. Tax reduction is an especially desirable means of cost reduction because
   a. it can be accomplished without reducing product quality.
   b. it represents an after-tax savings.
   c. the amount of potential reduction is great, as taxes are a major cost.
   d. All of the above

2. An "S" Corporation
   a. is a corporation in bankruptcy.
   b. exposes business owners to double taxation.
   c. provides limited liability but avoids double taxation.
   d. All of the above

3. A small business that issues Section 1244 stock
   a. assures itself of ordinary income treatment if it makes a profit.
   b. assures its shareholders of the opportunity to apply losses against other ordinary income that they might have.
   c. assures itself of indemnity.
   d. All of the above

4. One of the basic objectives of tax management is
   a. to convert capital gains income to ordinary income.
   b. to defer taxes to a later date.
   c. to avoid tax loopholes.
   d. to increase taxable income by use of conservative accounting.

5. An investment in your own home provides the following tax opportunities:
   a. Convert do-it-yourself labor into increased value.
   b. Defer taxes on capital gains from a sale of a home, provided reinvestment in another home is made within prescribed time limits.
   c. Escape portion of capital gains taxes on home sold after you reach 65 years of age.
   d. All of the above

6. On certain occasions, the tax authorities declare the following to be a dividend, even if the company did not intend it to be:
   a. A portion of interest on bonds, if the company has very little stock in its capitalization
   b. A portion of the stockholder-president's salary if it is unreasonably high
   c. Gifts to family members
   d. All of the above

True or False

7. Each general tax rule has a multitude of exceptions and restrictions.
   True ☐ False ☐

8. A bad business decision does not become a good one just because it saves taxes.
   True ☐ False ☐

9. Use of accelerated depreciation is an example of conservative accounting.
   True ☐ False ☐

10. The president of a small corporation can pay himself or herself any salary chosen without tax implications.
    True ☐ False ☐

11. Transactions between related parties receive close scrutiny from tax authorities.
    True ☐ False ☐

12. Medical reimbursement plans are available to proprietorships and partnerships, but not corporations.
    True ☐ False ☐

13. A company that accumulates earnings and does not pay out dividends must prove that accumulated funds are retained for business purposes, not simply to avoid taxes.
    True ☐ False ☐

14. A Keogh Plan is a tax-sheltered retirement plan available to the owner of an unincorporated business.
    True ☐ False ☐

15. A corporation can avoid taxes on its entire income by contributing all of it to a profit-sharing plan.
    True ☐ False ☐

16. State taxes are deductible against federal taxes, so they can be ignored in tax planning.
    True ☐ False ☐

17. Tax regulations are often interpreted differently in different tax districts.
    True ☐ False ☐

18. The taxpayer has no recourse when treated unfairly by Internal Revenue agents.
    True ☐ False ☐

Answers

1.d, 2.c, 3.b, 4.b, 5.d, 6.d, 7.T, 8.T, 9.T, 10.F, 11.T, 12.F, 13.T, 14.T, 15.F, 16.F, 17.T, 18.F

CHAPTER 20

Profitable Disposal of Your Business

Having built your business into a valuable enterprise, assume you are now considering the best way to cash in on your years of hard work. You may be contemplating retirement or devoting time to some other activity, and you want cash (or a more marketable investment). Or you may be interested in simply seeing that the enterprise stays in the family after your death, and you want to be sure that estate taxes can be paid and that the firm can continue to prosper without your leadership.

It is at this stage that many otherwise prudent businesspeople make some serious mistakes. One business owner may expect a son or daughter to follow in his or her footsteps, ignoring the fact that said child is more interested in a career in another field. Or the business owner may leave the firm to the surviving spouse, who would have to hire someone to run it.

Family disputes often arise when part of the family needs dividends to be paid to them, while other members would prefer to plow earnings back into the business. This often happens when one child takes over the business and receives a salary from it, while the other children end up with stock that does not provide them with income.

Somewhat different problems arise if the attempt is made to sell the business. Many small company owners sold their businesses to rapidly growing conglomerates, receiving stock in the merged company in exchange. Unfortunately, the stock price of the acquiring company often fell precipitously after the exchange, wiping out most of the owner's lifetime accumulation of capital in the process.

In view of these problems, it is wise to devote some attention to profitably disposing of the company. One set of problems is encountered in selling during your lifetime, and another set must be considered if the intention is to transfer the company to younger members of your family to carry on the business.

SELLING THE BUSINESS

Advanced planning is essential if your business is to be sold at maximum profitability. A sophisticated prospective buyer will want to review your financial records covering recent years. The buyer will be interested not only in the present value of your company's assets and most recent earnings, but also in the trends in the last several years. Profit margins and the rate of return on investment, as well as trends in these key items, will be of particular interest.

It will be to your advantage to make these figures look as good as possible at the time the sale of the firm is contemplated. This is not to suggest any dishonesty in accounting and management practices that have tended to understate your earnings and the net asset value of your business. It may have been advantageous, for example, for you to take as much salary as possible out of an incorporated business. If the sale of the business is planned, however, this practice may no longer be advisable.

If you have been growing at a rapid pace, a slowdown in the expansion rate will often produce an acceleration of earnings. Many new products are good investments over the long run but lose money in their initial stages. These start-up expenses, which tend to depress current earnings, are not restricted to capital expenditures alone. Hiring new personnel or initiating a big advertising campaign will cause higher expenses in that year, whereas they may actually benefit future years' performance.

If you have been using accelerated depreciation, a slowdown in capital spending will tend to reduce the average rate of

FIGURE 20.1 Earnings Trends

	Earnings	*Weight*	*Weighted Earnings*
Year 3	$3.00	3	$ 9.00
Year 2	2.00	2	4.00
Year 1	1.00	1	1.00
		6	$14.00

$$\text{Weighted earnings } \frac{\$14.00}{6} = \$2.33$$

Value (assumes a price-earnings ratio of 10) = $23.30

Year 3	$1.00	3	$ 3.00
Year 2	2.00	2	4.00
Year 1	3.00	1	3.00
		6	$10.00

$$\text{Weighted earnings } \frac{\$10.00}{6} = \$1.67$$

Value (assumes a price-earnings ratio of 10) = $16.70

depreciation expense. Ideally the business should be sold in a favorable economic period, when earnings will tend to be higher. In an optimistic investment climate, the purchaser is likely to project a higher rate of future earnings than might be the case in more pessimistic times.

A period of good earnings will also improve the look of your balance sheet. Higher earnings will increase the net asset value or book value of the stock. A slowdown period in capital expenditures will tend to improve the cash position of the company.

By preparing ahead of time, you can produce a financial record that enhances the value of the company. Figure 20.1 illustrates the importance of earnings trends in determining a company's value. A business's earnings average $2 per share annually in the last three years, but in one case the earnings trend is up, and in the other case it is down. A common valuation technique is to give the most recent years greater weight than earlier years. The approach in Figure 20.1 increases the value of the company 40 percent by reversing the trends, even though total earnings in each case are the same in the three-year period.

Actually, it is possible to increase average earnings by making the management and accounting changes discussed earlier. Each dollar of added average earnings increases the value of the business, not by one dollar, but by whatever price-earnings multiple is applicable at the time.

It is important to dispose of your business when the demand is great for stocks of companies in your field or in your size. There have been years when the Dow Jones Industrial Average rose insignificantly, but the average low-priced stock rose 100 percent as measured by Standard & Poor's low-price stock index. Under such optimum stock market conditions, stocks of companies with glamorous product lines and rapid earnings growth increased several hundred percent in price within a brief period of time.

In the case of most companies, investors usually base their prices on current earnings. However, if your company appears to have great future growth prospects, and the investment climate is right, the price is likely to be based largely on what earnings may be achieved at some indefinite date in the future. This is the secret of stock market fortunes such as that achieved by Ross Perot when he sold part of his Electronic Data Systems to the public at 100 times current earnings! (In effect, it would take 100 of that year's earnings to equal the price at which the stock was sold. This was at a time when nongrowth companies were selling at less than ten times their earnings. Investors were willing to pay much more for Electronic Data Systems stock, because they expected earnings to grow rapidly.)

For help in acquiring a purchaser, talk to your attorney, accountant or banker. They may have to put you in contact with a business broker or a large bank in a financial center. It is unlikely that your business can be sold at the first meeting with a prospective buyer, however, as studies have to be made and questions have to be answered. An informative brochure about your company should shorten this period of getting acquainted. Leave yourself some room in negotiating by asking a modestly higher price than you are willing to accept as rock bottom.

Be aware of the tax consequences of any agreement. If you receive stock in exchange for your company, it may or may not be a taxable transaction, depending on the method of acquisition. There are other tax considerations in selling a business. It is desirable to spell out the details of the purchase price—what amount is for various assets, what amount is for land and, particularly, what amount is for goodwill, which would be treated as capital gain income. It is also advantageous to the seller if land is given a relatively high value. In contrast, the buyer should want a relatively small portion allocated to goodwill and land, because these items are not depreciable. The allocation of purchase price thus becomes subject to negotiation.

When selling your company, be wary of exchanging for stock in what I will call a "wheeler-dealer" organization that owes its growth rate largely to mergers. These companies may offer a price for your business that is double what you could get in cash. However, the stock they offer in exchange may be selling at a price several times its intrinsic value.

There will be times when it will be advantageous to sell your stock in a public secondary offering. Selection of an investment banker then becomes a key decision. Not all investment bankers are interested in handling a small company, and others have questionable reputations. For a small company, the cost of legal, auditing and SEC registration can absorb a significant amount of the proceeds that are also reduced by the investment banker's commission. In spite of these drawbacks, public financing is an alternative that should be considered.

PASSING THE BUSINESS TO THE FAMILY

Many business owners are not interested in selling during their lifetimes, but they should still plan their affairs so that at the time of their deaths, their closely held businesses are assets for their families rather than liabilities.

A basic problem is that the closely held business is not a liquid asset. Sometimes there are not funds with which to pay estate taxes and other costs of estate administration. The problem is complicated by the fact that the IRS may consider the closely held company to be of considerably higher value than the owner's estimate, so that estate taxes could be much higher than expected.

Where there are other major stockholders or partners in the business, the problem is often solved by a carefully constructed buy-and-sell or stock-redemption agreement with the funds to be provided by life insurance on each of the major stockholders or partners. A properly drawn-up agreement will generally establish the value of the stock for estate tax purposes, and the insurance proceeds provide the funds to buy stock from the family of the decedent shareholder/partner.

The situation becomes more complex when most of the stock is held by one individual. A typical scenario is a father who would like to turn the business over to his child, who is now helping to run it. The company has invested earnings into the expansion of the business and has not paid any dividends. The current owner also has two other children who do not participate in the business. They wish to receive dividends on the stock willed to them, while the first child (who will get a substantial salary from the company) prefers to pay minimum dividends.

In an actual situation similar to this one, the following estate plan was developed. The bulk of the company's common stock was exchanged for nonvoting preferred stock, which was to pay dividends after the owner's death. The remaining common stock was given to the son to assure his management control. The corporation also took out life insurance on the owner, so that the corporation could buy sufficient stock from the estate to pay estate taxes. Where a closely held business is the bulk of an estate, the corporation (under Section 303 of the Tax Code) can redeem a certain amount of stock from an estate without the proceeds being considered dividends subject to tax. Under certain circumstances, estate taxes can be paid in installments.

Estate planning has always been important to individuals with wealth, and this has been particularly true where a closely held company was a substantial part of the estate. This is an area in which your lawyer, a certified life underwriter in the insurance field and the trust department of your bank can be helpful. You should be aware that recent changes in tax legislation will have an important effect on the valuation of closely held companies. If the value of a privately held company declines in the years following the owner's death, his or her heirs may have to pay higher taxes when they eventually sell than they would have to pay if they sold immediately after death. These and other pitfalls can be explained by a knowledgeable estate planner.

SELF-TEST QUESTIONS

Multiple Choice

1. When you dispose of your company,
   a. you automatically incur a capital gain.
   b. you may not have to pay a capital gains tax, depending on the method of disposal.
   c. you incur a tax based on the amount of earnings the company has retained.
   d. All of the above

2. When offered stock of another company for stock in your own company, you should
   a. accept exchange if the market value of the stock received is greater than what your own stock is worth.
   b. consider the exchange attractive if market value of the acquiring company has been rising rapidly.
   c. refuse the offer if you and your family are not guaranteed continued employment.
   d. ask yourself if you would invest all your life savings in the stock of the acquiring company.

3. When approaching the time when you will want to dispose of your business, you should maximize company earnings through
   a. using less conservative accounting procedures.
   b. paying yourself a more modest salary.
   c. reducing expenses that do not benefit current-year earnings.
   d. All of the above

4. If you are leaving your business to your family, you should
   a. make sure your successor gets all the training necessary to run the company.
   b. consider recapitalizing the company if some of your family will need income while others want growth.
   c. consider the need to pay estate taxes.
   d. All of the above

5. You can probably get a higher price for your company if
   a. earnings have remained the same on a year-to-year basis.
   b. earnings have shown a sharply rising trend.
   c. you appear eager to sell it.
   d. All of the above

6. The following could be helpful in selling your company:
   a. Advising its availability on the national stock exchange
   b. Advising your lawyer, banker and accountant of your decision to dispose of the company in case they hear of potential buyers
   c. Attempting to sell your stock directly by sending form letters to trust departments of banks and mutual funds
   d. All of the above

7. If you sell your stocks through an investment firm, the cost to you
   a. will be zero, because buyers pay the commissions.
   b. will be approximately 1 percent.
   c. may be a substantial portion of the sale proceeds if the offering is small.
   d. All of the above

8. A buy-and-sell agreement
   a. establishes the value of the stock in your company for estate purposes.
   b. is unnecessary if the business is to stay in the family.
   c. becomes null and void when the owner dies.
   d. All of the above

True or False

9. Life insurance on each of the major shareholders or partners is one method of guaranteeing sufficient liquidity for estate purposes.

   True ☐ False ☐

10. A trust officer at a bank can be helpful in estate planning.

    True ☐ False ☐

11. When one part of the family needs income from the business and it doesn't pay dividends, a good solution to the problem would be to add these family members to the payroll even if they don't do any work for the company.

    True ☐ False ☐

12. A closely held company is usually classified as a liquid asset.

    True ☐ False ☐

13. The IRS will generally use a company's book value as an indicator of its value.

    True ☐ False ☐

14. Under certain circumstances, an amount of stock in a closely held company can be redeemed to pay estate taxes.

    True ☐ False ☐

15. You would not be expected to reveal your financial statements to a prospective buyer, as this is confidential information.

    True ☐ False ☐

16. A brochure about your company could be helpful in acquainting prospective buyers with your firm.

    True ☐ False ☐

17. Always withdraw as much cash as possible from your company before offering the business for sale.

    True ☐ False ☐

18. The value of your business will be influenced by the state of the overall economy.

    True ☐ False ☐

19. When offering your business for sale, make it clear that your price is nonnegotiable.

    True ☐ False ☐

20. The details of sales agreements may affect the amount of taxes you will have to pay.

    True ☐ False ☐

Answers

1.b, 2.d, 3.d, 4.d, 5.b, 6.b, 7.c, 8.a, 9.T, 10.T, 11.F, 12.F, 13.F, 14.T, 15.F, 16.T, 17.F, 18.T, 19.F, 20.T

CHAPTER 21

Attitudes and Abilities

To achieve success in any field, specialized knowledge is essential. Business is certainly no exception. Even more fundamental than specific knowledge, however, are broader factors: attitudes, ways of thinking, values, organizational abilities and personal growth.

FREE-ENTERPRISE ATTITUDE

Don't take your freedom for granted. Throughout recorded history, individual freedom has been the exception, not the rule. At one time, your future vocation would have been determined at birth. You would have been expected to follow in the footsteps of your ancestors, regardless of your abilities. Even the geographical area in which you could have earned a living might have been restricted. You might have been regarded as nothing more than personal property, especially if you were a female or a member of a minority group.

In the United States, there is considerable grumbling about the gradual loss of freedom caused by government regulation and increasing intervention. But the potential for free enterprise in this country is still tremendous, and is not being fully utilized by the business sector of the economy. Large companies that become bureaucracies cannot triumph over imagination, initiative and ingenuity. This emphasizes the need for younger companies that are full of the free-enterprise spirit to provide flexibility and added growth to the economy.

To increase your appreciation of the private-enterprise system, develop an awareness of other rapidly growing younger companies. Magazines such as *Forbes, Fortune* and *Inc.* carry stories on such enterprises, as does *The Wall Street Journal.* Many investment firms publish recommendations on small companies that stress factors contributing to their growth. You can gain many insights and ideas from such success stories, and they can serve as important sources of motivation.

Free enterprise is more than simply an economic system. It has a built-in value system that is necessary for its operation. Fairness is a central theme, because customers do not have to buy from anyone unless they find it in their best interests to do so. If consumers are cheated by one company, they are not likely to patronize it again. Employees do not have to work for you if it isn't advantageous for them. This is the meaning of the phrase, "It's a free country."

VALUE OF CONTRARY THINKING

One example of contrary opinion is that of the enterprising individual who looks at a problem but sees an opportunity instead. Similarly, some people rise above setbacks by seeing them as learning experiences or sources of motivation. When others are carried away by optimism during times of prosperity, the contrary-thinking business manager becomes cautious, cuts unnecessary expenses, strengthens the financial position and otherwise prepares for trouble. Conversely, during periods of doom-and-gloom pessimism, the contrary thinker looks for opportunities that are being overlooked.

This does not mean that you should automatically adopt an opposing viewpoint to that held by the majority; the majority is often correct. Instead, you should look at widely held conventional opinions or forecasts with healthy skepticism, trying to judge which of those consensus views could possibly be erroneous. If your forecast of some area of economics or business is better than that of the majority, this could lead to a major business opportunity.

At first it may appear egotistical to expect your judgment to be better than that of the majority. In your own areas of business, however, you will probably be the better judge. You can observe developing trends firsthand, which may not be noticed by others until considerable time has elapsed. Also, your information network, once it is developed, will provide better information on which to base your own forecasts well ahead of the masses.

Cultivate the acquaintance of other people who take pride in thinking for themselves. Search out books and articles that disagree with the viewpoints of the majority. Often you will find elements of truth in the contrary opinion expressed, even though the overall conclusion of the article appears wrong to you.

LEARNING THE VIEWPOINT OF OTHERS

If you can learn to accept the points of view of others, you can avoid many of the problems and misunderstandings that might otherwise occur. First, learn to play the role of the customer. Your product or service should be created for your customer's needs, not your own. Advertising should be written from the viewpoint of customers, emphasizing what your product can do for them. Employees should be trained with the customer in mind.

One banking department, which was responsible for sending income checks to customers, was often late in getting the payments in the mail. One payday, the department head called the group together and told them their payroll checks were delayed due to a computer error and would not be available until the following week. Instant pandemonium resulted. How could they buy their food and pay their bills?

After letting the impact of the announcement sink in, the department head apologized for misleading them. Their checks were available, and they would be paid on time. He pointed out that the deception was intended to let them know how their customers felt when their checks were late.

The supervisor must learn to play the role of the employee and vice versa. Many organizations are successful when small, due to the abilities of the founder. The company may fail to grow beyond a certain point, however, due to the founder's inability to develop a working staff. Inability to understand the views of employees is often the cause.

In addition to understanding the viewpoints of customers and employees, the successful businessperson should learn the roles of suppliers, competitors and government regulators. Legal problems, cutthroat price competition and poor public relations can be minimized or avoided altogether by understanding the other person's viewpoint.

LONG-RANGE PERSPECTIVE

One major purpose of a business plan is to provide a long-range viewpoint. Of necessity, much time is wasted dealing with the day-to-day problems you encounter. A long term perspective is necessary to keep you moving ahead toward the firm's goals and objectives. Often there are several equally good ways to handle a short-term problem; one may be best from a long-range viewpoint, while another would be detrimental to progress.

A long-range point of view is also necessary for measurement purposes. It is possible to be very active while running around in circles, so being busy is not a good measurement of progress. A set of goals and subgoals can serve as benchmarks against which to measure progress. With long range perspective, day-to-day problems do not become exaggerated into unmanageable crises. Progress toward your goals will act as motivation for further effort and build your self-confidence.

CHAPTER 22

Planning Your Company's Goals and Images

Some people achieve a great deal in life, while others (with apparently equal ability) achieve very little. The difference is often a simple one: the successful people know what they want to achieve and concentrate their efforts and energies accordingly. The less successful people tend to dissipate their energies trying to run in several different directions at one time.

The same problem confronts companies, but the establishment of goals and objectives becomes even more difficult as a company grows beyond a one-person organization. The entrepreneur must know what the company is to become before it is born. This image is the underlying force that permits the coordination of various persons of diverse backgrounds into one unit.

The company that lacks a personality tends to be a confused and confusing organization. It is difficult to know even what field the business is in, as it seems to be continually chasing after the latest fad. Trying to be all things to all people, the company fails to truly excel in anything. Not being an innovator, its profitability is consistently low. Such an organization suffers from internal stress, as employees follow their own personal goals rather than the company's vague and ill-defined objectives. The firm is likely to disintegrate when the founder leaves, if not before.

In contrast, the successful company seems to maintain an identity of its own, regardless of the many changes that inevitably take place. A former student returning to school many years after graduation may feel a remarkable familiarity, even though the students and teachers have changed and the buildings may be new. The school still has the same traditions, the same academic reputation, and the same attitude among students, teachers and administrators. There is clearly a personality about the school that outlasts buildings and people. The same is true of many companies.

A business organization starts off with an "act of faith," espousing a certain course of activity and set of objectives. Over a period of time, an identity emerges that makes the organization unique. Once a corporate personality is established, it is difficult to change. Because your patrons expect consistency from you and your products or services, any significant change may drive them away.

Suppliers have a certain impression of your company and will come to you with new products and services that would fit into your sales mix. The employees who stay with you through the years do so because they like the pay and working conditions you have created. They also feel comfortable with your company's personality. This identity determines what type of new personnel will apply.

To a person contemplating his or her own business, it may seem presumptuous to worry about such vague concepts as "company image" or "identity." Even the smallest business, however, quickly develops a reputation for such things as quality, reliability, friendliness and speed. It is better to consciously plan for a desirable image than to unintentionally develop a boring or even an unattractive personality.

A good starting point in developing your business image is to review the approaches taken by other successful organizations. Often this basic company philosophy is revealed in the companies' annual reports. For example, the most successful venture capital firm of all time, American Research and Development, states that the company was created in 1946 for the following purposes:

> To give worthwhile, imaginative, constructive ideas an opportunity to blossom out into useful and profitable enterprise. To give forward-looking, courageous and hard-working men and women an opportunity to create and lead

a team that will transform an idea, a service, a product, a new concept into a successful enterprise.

Specifically, American Research and Development concluded that

- it did not want control or management of the companies it helped.
- it would not be a supplier of capital only, but would be ready to supply any kind of help that was required.
- it would seek equity common stock options or the equivalent in all ventures.
- it would invest only in situations and companies in which able management by people of competence and integrity seemed assured.

American Research has assisted in the growth of numerous organizations. Few other venture capital firms have even remotely approached its success. Many venture capital firms that have been failures owe their lack of success to violation of some of the policies adopted by American Research from its inception.

One of the most spectacular successes that American Research has sponsored is Digital Equipment Corporation, a company in which a few hundred dollars invested in the beginning would now be worth millions. From its beginning, Digital Equipment had a plan for its future, as indicated in the following statement from its founder:

> Digital Equipment Corporation is a company built on the idea that computers can be simple, and that anyone and everyone can learn to use them. When Digital first began making computers in 1960, computers were looked on as mysterious creations far beyond the comprehension of ordinary people. Digital never sold mystique, just functional tools to get the job done, tools that could be brought to the problems. We believe that computers belong on a factory floor and in the laboratory and the classroom—the office, printing plant, hospital and railroad yard.

Starting from a completely different viewpoint from that of International Business Machines, Digital became highly profitable. In contrast, the companies that attempted to compete directly with IBM number their losses in the billions. By developing a unique approach, Digital Equipment did not share this fate.

One company that clearly states its objectives in its annual reports is Chemed, a specialty chemical company. Chemed management begins by stating that it is interested in businesses that

- are recession-resistant.
- are above-average in profitability.
- should generate capital on balance.
- should not be labor-intensive.
- produce a rising stream of earnings and dividends for its shareholders, inevitably reflected in higher stock values.
- maintain a strong balance sheet.
- maintain a high quality of earnings.

In developing a corporate personality or image, some precautions should be taken. An image should be an honest representation of the company, not a public relations gimmick. One of the most successful image creations in recent decades was the advertising campaign that established Avis as the company that "tried harder." Yet Robert Townsend, president of Avis at the time, has this negative comment to make about image:

> It seems to me that image is one of the most dangerous concepts in modern organizations. One of the great advantages that a small, new company has over a big, mature one is that the small, new company knows the difference between form and substance, between appearance and reality. Image is not a goal. It's a by-product. A good image has to be earned by performance.

Another mistake to avoid in setting a company's objectives and goals is defining your business too narrowly. Possibly the most widely read article on the subject of marketing is "Marketing Myopia," by Theodore Levitt. Mr. Levitt points out how major industries have approached extinction from a lack of understanding of which business they were actually in.

Levitt's thesis is that the railroad industry should have defined itself as being in the business of transportation instead of railroading. Motion picture companies, if they had defined themselves as entertainment companies, would have welcomed the development to television as a new area in which they could grow. Instead, Hollywood considered television an enemy. Likewise, oil companies should consider themselves to be operating in the energy industry. The customer's needs for transportation, entertainment and energy will always exist, while individual industries serving those needs will mature and eventually decline.

DEVELOPING A BUSINESS PLAN

Once you have developed the long-term objectives and images of your business enterprise, you have, in effect, selected your destination. The next step is to develop a road map for getting there. This is commonly known as a business plan. Donald Dible, a noted business writer, makes the following comment:

> A properly researched business plan will represent a 'dry run' of the early years following the formation of the business and should expose the founders to every major problem they can reasonably expect to encounter. Obviously, not all problems can be foreseen. But by anticipating and preparing for some problems, more of the founder's time will be available for solving hidden difficulties.

A well-prepared business plan can be an important tool in acquiring finances, source of supply and customers. Some points you should consider in making your business plan are as follows:

- Do you have the special technical skills needed in your business? If you do not have them, do you have business associates who have the background you lack?
- Have you had business experience?
- What are business conditions likely to be in the next few years?
- What are business conditions in your specific locality and industry?
- What sales volume do you expect by what time?
- How much capital will you need to launch your enterprise?

- How long will it take for your business to reach the break-even point where revenue equals expenses?
- What should net profits be when the business has passed the start-up stage?
- How does the rate of return on capital compare to alternative investments?
- Do you have other money to invest in your business if the need arises?
- Do you have sources of additional financing should the need arise?
- What records will you maintain?
- What laws affect you?
- Has your plan been reviewed by specialists in business fields?

As a prospective entrepreneur, you may not be able to answer all of the above questions in an optimistic manner, but you will greatly improve your chances of success if you know wherein your strengths and weaknesses lie and have plans for correcting the latter. One stunt pilot who survived a great number of near-disasters was asked the secret of his survival capabilities. His answer was that he spent much of his waking hours imagining all of the things that could go wrong in his stunt-flying activity, and then analyzing what the best reaction would be. When troubles did occur while he was in the air, he reacted instantly without panic. A company with clearly stated objectives and a well-thought-out business plan, like the stunt pilot, has a much greater survival capability than does the company starting with little or no preparation.

While the intrinsic nature of the company is determined by its policies and objectives, customers and prospects are also influenced by name and appearance. People tend to be at least partially judged by their names. "John" is considered to be trustworthy; "Michael," masculine, "Wendy," active. "Ann" is considered to be passive, and "Agnes" is perceived as old. Teachers tend to give higher grades to papers bearing popular names like "Lisa" and "Karen," and lower grades to those bearing so-called undesirable names like "Hubert," "Elmer," and "Bertha."

A similar situation exists for company names. After the success of Xerox, it became popular to have an *x* in the company name. It is found to be more popular to have *electronics* in the name rather than *electric,* and *calculator* loses out to *computer.*

Usually, the intention in modifying the name is to give an image of being progressive and growth-oriented.

The names of individual products also affect their sales potential, as illustrated by the ability of brand-name products to command a premium price over equivalent products with unknown reputations. Following the success of nylon, most new synthetic fibers and plastics were given names ending with *-on*. The name of Gillette is symbolic of quality in shaving, enabling the company to introduce new shaving related products more readily than would be the case with other companies. A brand name by itself becomes a valuable asset of a company.

Even more basic than the name of the company and its products' brand names is the company's symbol. Historically, signs have played an important role in influencing people. The cross has been a source of strength and inspiration to the Christian, and various flags have inspired heroic deeds by the patriot. On a lesser scale, the corporate symbol provides identity to both employees and customers.

An illustration of the use of symbols was provided by the Great Atlantic & Pacific Tea Company, which attempted to reverse a long-term decline. New advertisements were built around two imaginary A&P managers, "Mr. Price" and "Mr. Pride." The company also introduced a new logo, the first change in the familiar A&P sign since 1888. The new logo, a red oval with white A&P letters, is followed by arcs of orange and red which is meant to imply forward movement.

The use of symbols may not seem to some people to have much relevance to a small business. It is important, however, to give an appearance of permanence, uniqueness and stability, and symbols help to achieve this goal.

When customers visit the enterprise, as in the case of retail stores, physical appearance of the premises will greatly influence their judgment about the company. With their massive columns and thick exterior walls, bank buildings were originally intended to denote financial strength and solidarity to their depositors. The original discount stores were located in low-cost areas and were sparsely decorated, giving symbolic support to their claim of being economical through low overhead. The interior color scheme of a commercial aircraft may be selected to have a calming effect on the passengers; horizontal stripes on the exterior suggest flight stability. In certain establishments, such as restaurants and cafeterias, the appearance of absolute cleanliness is vital to success. A retail store with cluttered aisles will repel many customers by giving the impression of bad management.

A successful securities dealer who has to take many clients out to lunch or dinner became so interested in restaurants that he started one of his own on a part-time basis. When he finds a new restaurant that he likes during his travels, he tries to analyze what has influenced him. While the food is important, more often than not it is some feature, custom or special service of the establishment that impresses him and creates the special ambience necessary for successful restaurants. Over the years, he has greatly enhanced the reputation of his own restaurant by adopting ideas of other successful enterprises.

The following are some questions to ask yourself about your business, your industry and your locality that will be useful to you in developing your business plan.

FIGURE 22.1 Industry Background

1. **What do you know about the industry in which you plan to do business? List all the characteristics with which you are familiar regarding total sales, the amount of capital invested in the industry, the growth pattern of the industry, its stability, the amount of regulation to which it is subject and its profitability,* where relevant and applicable.**
   ******Much of this information may be obtained with the help of your librarian.***

Your Position in the Industry

1. **In this question, it is necessary to envision your place in the total picture. List, where relevant and applicable, your geographical market area, your specific market sector, your share of the total market and your market-share goals in the coming years.**

2. **List your competitive strengths and weaknesses in regard to patents held, technical knowledge, strategic contracts held, managerial expertise, customer base, production costs, location and exclusivity.**

3. **How might you go about correcting your possible weaknesses or disadvantages?**

FIGURE 22.1 Industry Background (continued)

Your Sales Outlook

1. Give a brief description of the economic outlook in your particular area; the sales outlook for the industry in which you will compete; your own sales expectations for the coming years; and the amount by which you expect prices (of both materials and products) to increase or decrease, where relevant and applicable.

____

____

____

____

Cost Expectations

Costs will have a direct influence on most businesses in the coming years. It is important for you to be aware of what trends there might be in the future, and how you expect them to affect your business.

1. Describe the ways in which your labor costs will change from their current figures, in relation to adding employees to your organization and raising salaries of current personnel.

____

____

____

____

2. How will price changes in your materials affect the profitability of your business?

____

____

____

____

3. How will changes in the cost of sales affect your profitability?

____

____

____

____

FIGURE 22.1 Industry Background (continued)

4. Determine your total costs per product unit you manufacture, or per assignment (if you provide a service). Using the information you have supplied in questions 1, 2, and 3, determine what your cost per product unit (or assignment) will be under minimum, maximum and most probable sales conditions.*

____

____

____

____

**As an example, let's assume you are a freelance writer. You do not have any labor costs (employees), and your only material costs are typing paper, office supplies and postage. Your sales costs are minimal (perhaps a letter or phone call once a week). The effects of increases in postage, telephone rates and paper will have some effect on your profitability, but not really enough to worry about. It would be safe to assume, then, that cost increases are not crucial to the performance and profitability of your business. If you are a manufacturer of a product, however, cost increases are a factor that must be projected and monitored carefully.*

Profit Expectations

1. Using the information you supplied under Cost Expectations, determine your profitability per product unit or assignment. Describe your profit expectations under minimum, maximum and most probable conditions.

____

____

____

____

Assets Necessary To Meet Sales Goals

1. Describe those fixed assets and materials you will need to meet your sales expectations. Remember that assets can take the form of physical facilities, equipment, strategic holdings and material supplies.

____

____

____

____

FIGURE 22.1 Industry Background (continued)

Managerial Capability Needed

1. Describe your own managerial background, with particular reference to the ways in which it applies to your current business. Include relevant positions held in the past, degrees held or special education pursued.

2. If you have other persons helping to manage your organization, provide the same information on them. If yours is a one-person business, describe those characteristics you would look for in a potential associate, including job title.

Available Capital Sources

1. How much has been invested in the business already in terms of equity, preferred stock, long-term debt, etc.? Give the amount, nature and source.

2. List the amount, nature and source of capital that is (or may be) available to you for expansion.

FIGURE 22.1 Industry Background (continued)

Contingency Planning

1. What arrangements have been made for insurance, materials, expansion of customer base, replacement of key personnel and major changes in competitive factors?

Further Considerations

1. Describe the length of time you believe is needed to break even or to reach optimum profitability.

2. Describe what you will be withdrawing from the business in terms of salary, benefits and dividends.

3. Describe the managerial and accounting controls you will put to use in your business.

FIGURE 22.1 Industry Background (continued)

4. Describe the sales channels you use or will use, including the method of compensation of your salespeople.

5. Describe the areas in which you can expand your product or service line.

6. Describe the possible methods of cost reduction.

7. Describe any other business interests or talents you or your key personnel might have.

You have just completed an exercise designed to help you realize where you are now, and where your business is going. While all the factors may not apply to some businesses (as in the example of the freelance writer), it is important for you to orchestrate a well-formulated business plan that reflects your own goals. Bankers and investors will frequently request a written business plan before considering your business as an investment.

SELF-TEST QUESTIONS

Multiple Choice

1. The most successful company is usually one that
   a. enters a business in which other companies are experiencing a high rate of profitability.
   b. has definite goals it wants to achieve.
   c. does not worry about having an image.
   d. All of the above

2. A company's image is determined by its relations with
   a. its customers.
   b. its employees.
   c. its community.
   d. All of the above

3. A restaurant's reputation is determined by
   a. the quality of food it serves.
   b. the appearance of the facilities.
   c. the speed and courtesy of service.
   d. All of the above

4. A business plan should
   a. be a road map for reaching the company's planned destination.
   b. be an important tool in acquiring finances.
   c. help the company to anticipate many future problems.
   d. All of the above

5. A business plan should
   a. provide for all the possible things that could go wrong.
   b. establish the various procedures to be used in the business.
   c. be an inflexible guideline for employees to adhere to.
   d. None of the above

6. A business plan should consider
   a. what skills will be needed in the business.
   b. business conditions in the industry, the overall economy and the locality.
   c. how much capital will be needed and where it is coming from.
   d. All of the above

7. A company with a well-established image can
   a. sell a low-quality product at a high price.
   b. avoid advertising expenses.
   c. ignore public relations expenditures.
   d. None of the above

8. A company with a quality image for its present products
   a. risks its reputation by introducing low-quality products.
   b. has an advantage in introducing new products similar to its current line.
   c. Both of the above
   d. None of the above

True or False

9. An organization's image is greatly affected by the personality of its founder.

   True ☐ False ☐

10. It is easy to change your image if you have the right advertising agency.

    Truc ☐ False ☐

11. A company with a number of strong, independent leaders may have an image problem.

    True ☐ False ☐

12. A company's image will change each time its leader changes.

    True ☐ False ☐

13. A trademark permits a company's products to be more readily recognizable.

    True ☐ False ☐

14. A company's reputation is the responsibility of its public relations department.

    True ☐ False ☐

15. A good image has to be earned by performance.

    True ☐ False ☐

16. Many companies have made the mistake of defining their business too narrowly.

    True ☐ False ☐

17. Brand-name products tend to sell at a premium compared to their competition.

    True ☐ False ☐

18. A discount store can be plain and located in a low-rent area without hurting its image.

    True ☐ False ☐

19. A company's image helps unify people of different backgrounds into one force.

    True ☐ False ☐

20. It is not a good idea for an organization to try to be unique.

    True ☐ False ☐

Answers

1.b, 2.d, 3.d, 4.d, 5.d, 6.d, 7.d, 8.c, 9.T, 10.F, 11.T, 12.F, 13.T, 14.F, 15.T, 16.T, 17.T, 18.T, 19.T, 20.F

SUGGESTED READINGS

Business Opportunities

The Complete Franchise Book, by Dennis Foster. Rocklin, Calif.: Prima Publishing. How to realistically evaluate a franchise opportunity before investing is covered in the book.

The Complete Guide to Consulting Success, by Howard Shenson and Ted Nicholas. Chicago: Enterprise•Dearborn. Being an expert in your field is only the first step in becoming a consultant. How to set pricing, sell yourself, find your niche and other necessary skills are covered.

The Complete Guide to Nonprofit Corporations, by Ted Nicholas. Chicago: Enterprise•Dearborn. Readers can start their own nonprofit corporation for under $85 with this useful, hands-on guide from Ted Nicholas. Extremely readable, this book has the information, forms and instructions to answer any question about nonprofits.

The Complete Guide to "S" Corporations, by Ted Nicholas. Chicago: Enterprise•Dearborn. Ted Nicholas, a national expert in "do-it-yourself" incorporation, demonstrates that almost any business, even a one-person operation, can take advantage of the "S" Corporation laws.

The Home-Based Entrepreneur, by Linda Pinson and Jerry Jinnett. Dover, N.H.: Upstart Publishing. Every aspect of starting a home-based business is covered in an organized fashion—from legal and tax aspects to marketing, pricing and recordkeeping.

How To Buy a Business: Entrepreneurship Through Acquisition, by Richard Joseph, Anna Nekoranec and Carl Steffens. Chicago: Enterprise•Dearborn. This book tells exactly how to purchase a business at the right time and for the right price. It shows how things work in the active small business marketplace, and covers in detail such subjects as finding and evaluating candidates for acquisition; financing, negotiating and structuring the deal; handling post-acquisition management issues; and determining the current and future value.

How To Form Your Own Corporation Without a Lawyer for $75, by Ted Nicholas. Chicago: Enterprise•Dearborn. Gives complete information on how to gain the legal and tax advantages of incorporation without having to pay attorneys' fees.

Successful Retailing, by Paula Wardell. Dover, N.H.: Upstart Publishing. Consultant Wardell helps retailers deal with the issues confronting them, such as inventory management, analyzing consumer demand and financial controls.

Management

Anatomy of a Business Plan, by Linda Pinson and Jerry Jinnet. Chicago: Enterprise•Dearborn. Everything you need to design, research and write your own business plan is found in this book, including organizational issues, marketing and financing your business. You will be creating a powerful, winning business plan when you follow the step-by-step process laid out by these authors.

Beyond Entrepreneurship, by James Collins and William Lazier. Englewood Cliffs, N.J.: Prentice-Hall. By looking at companies that have become household names, this book attempts to spot elements that ensure the long-term health of a new business.

The Business Planning Guide, by David Bangs. Dover, N.H: Upstart Publishing. Leads you through the most important steps in founding or monitoring a business—putting together a complete and effective business plan and financial proposal. This book helps you test ideas on paper before implementing them, allowing you to spot opportunities you may have overlooked and develop super-fortified niches for your products and services.

The Complete Book of Corporate Forms, by Ted Nicholas. Chicago: Enterprise•Dearborn. Contains virtually all the forms needed to keep a corporation's minutes and resolutions to satisfy banks, the IRS, and other government agencies. Instructions and samples of completed forms are included.

The Complete Guide to Business Agreements, by Ted Nicholas. Chicago: Enterprise•Dearborn. Lawsuits are common in business today, and protecting yourself is necessary. Business owners can use the legal agreements found here to cover almost any business situation.

The Complete Small Business Legal Guide, by Robert Friedman. Chicago: Enterprise•Dearborn. Packed with checklists, cross-references and more than 60 ready-to-use forms, this all-new edition provides you with the hands-on help you need to start a business, maintain all necessary records, properly hire and fire employees, and deal with the many changes a business goes through.

Getting to Yes, by Roger Fisher and William Ury. New York: Penguin Books. Techniques are provided for reaching agreements without giving in.

Government Giveaways for Entrepreneurs, by Matthew Lesko. Chevy Chase, Md.: Information USA. Free sources of information and money are provided in this guide.

Growing a Business, by Paul Hawken. New York: Fireside Books. Unorthodox methods for making a business work at different stages in its life cycle are presented without any "get rich quick" hype.

Secrets of Entrepreneurial Leadership, by Ted Nicholas. Chicago: Enterprise•Dearborn. Find out how to develop a sense of mission in your associates, get them to set their own goals and stimulate them to make improvements in your company.

Selling Your Business, by Paul Sperry and Beatrice Mitchell. Chicago: Enterprise•Dearborn. This book explores how to avoid making expensive mistakes when it's time to cash in on the business you've built. You're taken from making the decision to sell to negotiating final terms.

The Small Business Computer Book, by Robert Moskowitz. Dover, N.H.: Upstart Publishing. Computers can make your business operate more efficiently. Moskowitz shows how to choose the right system for your business after looking at the options available.

The Start-Up Guide, by David Bangs. Dover, N.H.: Upstart Publishing. A one-year guide to establishing a business that shows what to do each month. Forms and worksheets are included to serve as road maps to success.

Thriving on Chaos, by Tom Peters. New York: Alfred A. Knopf. New tools are introduced to help managers cope with change.

Marketing

The Golden Mailbox, by Ted Nicholas. Chicago: Enterprise•Dearborn. After decades of successful direct selling through ads and letters, an industry leader gives his secrets.

The Marketing Planning Guide, by David Bangs. Dover, N.H.: Upstart Publishing. This is a step-by-step guide to help you prepare a complete marketing plan. Examples, forms and worksheets take the mystery out of planning your marketing approach.

The Complete Selling System: Sales Management Techniques That Can Help Any One Succeed, by Peter Frye. Dover, N.H.: Upstart Publishing. Peter Frye's selling system will help you achieve the structure and discipline you need to succeed in your selling efforts. Selling is the bottom line in every business, and this comprehensive hands-on guide will give you the tools you need to radically improve sales.

Positioning, by Al Ries and Jack Trout. New York: Warner Books. A basic guide to finding ways to appeal to your customers that will differentiate your company from its competition.

Talking with Your Customers, by Michael J. Wing. Chicago: Enterprise•Dearborn. A hands-on guide to understanding and serving your customers better. The book shows business owners how to survey their customers and use the results strategically.

Winning with the Power of Persuasion: Mancuso's Secrets for Small Business Success, by Joe Mancuso. Chicago: Enterprise•Dearborn. Long-time entrepreneur Joe Mancuso shares the secrets he has gleaned from over three decades of interacting with the best and the brightest, the most committed entrepreneurs in the nation, via his nonprofit Center for Entrepreneurial Management (CEM). He provides easy-to-use methods to help you master the art of getting what you want from other people and learning how to negotiate every situation into a win-win success.

Accounting and Finance

Accounting for Non-Accountants, by John N. Meyer. New York: Hawthorn Books, Inc. Explains the accountant's function in clear, easy-to-understand language—from income statements to balance sheets, depreciation to net income. Comes with a companion workbook.

Borrowing for Your Business, by George Dawson. Dover, N.H.: Upstart Publishing. A former banker tells how to work with banks to secure finance when you need it.

Keeping the Books, by Linda Pinson and Jerry Jinnett. Dover, N.H.: Upstart Publishing. Comprehensive yet user-friendly, this book offers a model of simplicity to set up exactly the records you need to maintain a smoothly running business. Includes forms to create budgets and update projections, maintain iron-clad travel and entertainment records, analyze cash flow to avoid crises and keep the right records for every kind of tax—income tax, estimated tax, FICA, unemployment tax, partnerships and "S" Corporations.

Economics

Economic History of Europe, by Herbert Heaton. New York: Harper Brothers. Provides a valuable perspective on the development of modern business industry. Numerous examples of economic fluctuations, inflation, the rise and fall of economics, taxes and wasteful government spending in ancient and medieval history.

The Economic Problem, by Robert L. Heilbroner. Englewood Cliffs, N.J.: Prentice-Hall. This book traces the emergence of modern economic society. Economics is not considered in a vacuum, but is related to the social environment and placed in historical perspective.

Economics of American Industry, by E. B. Alderfer and H. E. Michl. New York: McGraw-Hill Book Co. Provides a framework for analyzing an industry in terms of its history, technology, nature of the product and competitive factors. Includes history of mass production and major manufacturing industries.

The Ecumene, Story of Humanity, by William H. McNeil. New York: Harper and Row. This balanced history book includes the many contributions that business and industry have made to the advancement of civilization.

Small Is Beautiful, by E. F. Schumacher. New York: Harper and Row. This classic book correctly predicted the increasing importance of small businesses to the U.S. economy.

General Readings

Think and Grow Rich, by Napoleon Hill. Los Angeles: Wilshire Book Co. Hill has devoted his life to the science of personal achievement. Drawing upon the lives of many famous and successful people, he provides valuable insight into the factors that determine success.

Atlas Shrugged, by Ayn Rand. New York: Random House. An outstanding defense of human liberties, particularly of individuals who are making contributions to the progress of our civilization.

Capitalism, the Unknown Ideal, by Ayn Rand. New York: Signal Books. Provides numerous examples of how capitalism has contributed not only to the material progress of humanity but also to our freedom and human progress.

Made in America, by Sam Walton. New York: Doubleday. The story of Wal-Mart Stores' success.

100 Predictions for the Baby Boom, by Cheryl Russell. New York: Plenum Press. A look at how the baby-boom generation will continue to affect our economy and lives as they age.

INDEX

U

V

W–X